On Becoming Neighbors

On Becoming Neighbors

THE COMMUNICATION ETHICS OF
FRED ROGERS

ALEXANDRA C. KLARÉN

UNIVERSITY OF PITTSBURGH PRESS

Published by the University of Pittsburgh Press, Pittsburgh, Pa., 15260

Manufactured in the United States of America

Printed on acid-free paper

10 9 8 7 6 5 4 3 2 1

Cataloging-in-Publication data is available from the Library of Congress

ISBN 13: 978-0-8229-4590-1

ISBN 10: 0-8229-4590-8

Cover photograph: Fred Rogers courtesy of the Fred Rogers Company

Cover design: Alex Wolfe

To my beloved parents,
Sara and Peter

Contents

Acknowledgments

THIS BOOK PROJECT HAS TAKEN the support of many people. First, I am most appreciative of the team at the Fred Rogers Center for welcoming me at the archives and for providing a neighborly environment for me to study Fred Rogers's work. Former *Neighborhood* producer Hedda Sharapan was extremely generous in providing me interview time and primary source content. Her contribution deeply enriched my understanding of Fred Rogers and his project in a most authentic and sophisticated way. To her I am deeply grateful. I want to thank Emily Uhrin, the Fred Rogers Center archivist, who went above and beyond her call of duty to provide me with research assistance. Furthermore, she graciously transferred much of her vast knowledge of all things Mister Rogers to me in conversation, demonstrating her expertise on the program's creator and history. I thank Rick Fernandes, former Fred Rogers Center executive director, who offered emphatic support and belief in my work. I am grateful, also, to Rita Catalano, former executive director at the center, to the Academy of Television Arts and Sciences, and to the Grable Foundation for the Fred Rogers Memorial Scholarship I was awarded in 2012 for this research project. This scholarship provided me with the necessary support to begin the project in the kind of thorough and in-depth fashion it called for.

My deepest thanks to my colleagues at the Johns Hopkins Carey Business School, especially Lindsay J. Thompson, Jaana Myllyluoma, Kevin Frick, Brandon Chicotsky, and Steven D. Cohen, for their enthusiastic and generous support of this book project. I am indebted to Nora Lambrecht for her deeply intelligent and invaluable assistance in editing the final version of this book manuscript.

I also wish to thank Ronald J. Zboray, director of the doctoral dissertation that gave birth to this book, and Mary Saracino Zboray for their intelligent and helpful feedback. I thank Brenton J. Malin for our many conversations on media theory and history, in which he generously shared his knowledge of the field, and for his dedicated support. I also want to thank Tyler Bickford for his insightful contributions to my thinking and for his most helpful feedback on this piece of research.

Many thanks to communication ethics scholars Amanda McK-endree, John H. Prellwitz, and Craig T. Maier for their insightful commentaries that provided stimulus for the completion of this book project. Receiving the Best Paper Award in the Communication Ethics Division of the 2017 National Communication Association Convention for a paper based on the fourth chapter of this book has bolstered my confidence to continue my line of research in the subfield of communication ethics.

Thank you to the anonymous readers of this book, whose insightful feedback helped this project gain further focus and clarity. I am grateful, also, to Josh Shanholtzer, senior acquisitions editor at the University of Pittsburgh Press, for his interest in *On Becoming Neighbors* and for his shepherding of the project to its final completion. Many thanks as well to Amy Sherman for her meticulous care in editing this book.

Finally, I thank most profusely, my parents, Peter Klarén and Sara Castro-Klarén, for inspiring me throughout my life to think critically about the world, to believe in myself, and to call upon my grandfather, José A. Castro's sense of mote when life's challenges present themselves. Thank you for to your unceasing love, strength, care, and support.

On Becoming Neighbors

Introduction

IN HIS 1997 COMMENCEMENT SPEECH to the Memphis Theological Seminary, titled "Invisible to the Eye," Fred Rogers, at the age of sixty-nine, reflects back on defining moments in his life. He recounts the experience of being bullied when he was an overweight and timid young boy. Afraid to go to school each day, he was, in his own words, "a perfect target for ridicule." One day, after being released from school early, he decided to walk home. Soon after leaving the school grounds, he noticed that he was being followed by a group of boys who quickly gained on him while taunting him verbally. "Freddy, hey, fat Freddy," they shouted, "we're going to get you, Freddy." Rogers recalls breaking into a sprint, hoping that he would run fast enough to make it to the house of a widowed neighbor. He remembers praying that she would be home so that he would be taken in and sheltered from the ensuing threat. She was indeed home, and Rogers found "refuge."[1]

As one might imagine, the painful feelings of shame that resulted from the social abuse and ostracism of bullying affected Rogers deeply. He recounts how, when he told the adult caretakers in his life about the bullying, the resounding message he received in response was to "just let on that you don't care; then nobody will bother you." But, Rogers recalls, he did care. He resented the treatment and cried to himself whenever he was alone. "I cried through my fingers as I made up songs on the piano." He sought out stories about people who were "poor in spirit" and derived identification and meaning from those narratives. "I started to look behind the things that people said and did; and, little by little, concluded that Saint-Exupéry was absolutely right: 'What is essential is invisible to the eye.' So after a lot of sadness, I began a lifelong search for what is essential; what it is about my neighbor that doesn't meet the eye."[2] Rogers, who transferred from Dartmouth to Rollins College in order to study music composition, planned to become a minister. But an experience viewing the new technology of television during a break from college triggered his painful childhood experiences and prompted him, he recounts, to get involved in the novel mass medium. "I got into television because I saw people throw pies at each other's faces . . . [a]nd if there's anything that bothers me, it's one person demeaning another."[3]

In this book I explore Rogers's search for "the essential," that which is "invisible to the eye," through a detailed and dynamic look into his groundbreaking, long-running public television program, *Mister Rogers' Neighborhood*—his life's work. Integrating his advanced studies in both child development and Christian theology into the foundational rhetorics of his program, Rogers offered viewers a space of refuge, safety, and affirmation where dialogical connection, learning, and experience could take place at the parasocial level of television.[4] Rogers's identification of the ways he responded to the hurt of bullying, both by finding emotional articulation and release in playing and composing music and by encountering God's compassionate presence during his own periods of suffering, encapsulates well the overarching directive and ethos of *Neighborhood* and speaks to the ways Rogers conceived of the program as his "television ministry."

My overarching goal is to examine and analyze the vision, production, and reception of *Neighborhood* from the perspectives of communication, media and culture, rhetoric, and communication ethics. One cannot gain a thorough understanding of the breadth and dynamism of Rogers's communication project and the cultural phenomenon of *Neighborhood* through a consideration of the program alone; likewise, an inquiry solely into viewer mail lacks the critical other half of the communication puzzle that prompted its writing—the rhetorical offerings of the program. My study thus echoes the stages that Rogers's television creation went through from conception to production, reflection to refinement, utterance to reception and answerability. What follows covers an arc from imagining the program to implementing it and then moves on to an examination of how it was received through an analysis of viewer mail from the 1970s and 1980s. By analyzing Rogers's comments on the program, as well as episodes, scripts, other *Mister Rogers' Neighborhood* regalia, and viewer mail, this work elucidates how Rogers conceived of his project, employed communication strategies that set the program apart from other children's programming of the time, reached viewers, and sustained interest for more than thirty years.

With *Neighborhood*, Rogers conceived of and implemented a dialogical rhetorical foundation that masterfully exploits the parasocial elements of the televisual medium. Rogers's project evolved through layer upon layer of dialogical practice—creating music to express human emotion, interactive learning with children at the Arsenal Family and Children's Center, using dyadic address, constructing and deconstructing everyday objects on the program, and corresponding with viewers via letter writing—and thus follows a structural format of dialectical unfolding. *On Becoming Neighbors* establishes *Neighborhood* as a media and cultural event of indispensable importance in the creation of a specific social and emotional sensibility that millions of Americans identified with and embraced as their own.

In this regard, I have structured the study in the following sequential and dynamic communication staging: First, I situate Rogers's project in the sociocultural milieu of the period, paying special attention to the discourses on television, technology, and culture in order to show the ways Rogers is dialoguing with the culture at large. Next, I examine Rogers's own statements on the program, television, education, psychology, theology, and culture across his lifelong work on *Neighborhood*. From there I move toward a detailed analysis of the program itself and offer a dynamic reading of the child development theory that guides his rhetorical choices—in particular, his focus on secure attachment and object relations. Finally, I turn toward reception of the program and of Rogers's dialogical communication efforts through an examination and analysis of viewer mail.

In "Discourse in the Novel," Mikhail Bakhtin writes that "the listener and his response are regularly taken into account when it comes to everyday dialogue and rhetoric."[5] For Bakhtin, a text is always an intertext: a space for the dialogic interaction of multiple voices and modes of discourse, all of which are not just verbal but constitute in fact a sociohistorical phenomenon. It does not express a readymade and immanent autonomous individuality. Instead, the prose-text emerges in the course of the relationship between speaker and anticipated audience and in dialogue between different sociolanguages. Moreover, for Bakhtin, "the word in living conversation is directly, blatantly, oriented to a future answer-word: it provokes an answer, anticipates it and structures itself in the answer's direction."

Leah Vande Berg extends Bakhtin's concept of the dialogic to the televisual text, asserting that a text is ambiguous because its meaning relies in large part on who is creating it and constructing the meanings.[6] The people who "read" texts tend to remake and reweave what they have read in terms of their own personal experiences and perceptions.[7] In turn, John Fiske argues that "texts are the sites of conflict" between their sources of production and modes of reception.[8] Further, different viewers may "see" remarkably different shows.[9] In this regard, the intentions of a television producer and a the perceptions of a viewer can significantly diverge or can achieve high degrees of convergence—as in the case, as we will see, of *Mister Rogers' Neighborhood.*

On Becoming Neighbors thus focuses on vision, production, and reception. A dialogic approach that necessarily includes reception keeps us from falling into the trap of looking at the film text alone, which would be like listening to the sound of one hand clapping. These three aspects of investigation have never been studied in their inherent and essential dynamic play of interaction on *Mister Rogers' Neighborhood.* Textual studies, semiotic studies and rhetorical studies, and reception studies make up the core of critical approaches to television today. My study makes a refreshing contribution to rhetorical studies with special regard to questions of communication ethics, persuasion, and the challenge of multiculturalism in the fabric of an assumed, but perhaps not fully justified, American *sensus communis* of the time. By engaging in a critical dialogic reading of Rogers's envisioning texts, episodes of the first year of *Neighborhood*, and viewer mail, my findings show the effects of the permeating power of the dialogic on the program and illustrate the ways that Rogers was able to create a heightened parasocial dynamic between himself and his viewer as a result of his keen understanding of embodied communication (e.g., speech tone, sustained eye contact, and relaxed but controlled body movement), opportunities for which television uniquely affords.

My discussion of Rogers's pedagogical communication project is grounded in several compatible interdisciplinary theoretical perspectives on communication ethics and pedagogy that speak to the fundamental rhetorical frameworks of the program as designed by Rogers and his primary consultant, University of Pittsburgh professor of child development and Arsenal Family and Children's Center cofounder Dr. Margaret McFarland. At the core of Rogers's approach is a highly developed empathic, invitational, and dialogic ethos that creates a heightened parasocial dynamic between him and his viewer. By beginning each "television visit"—his term for an episode of his program—with an ethical orientation that seeks to establish a relationship of trust and care, Rogers, over the course of thirty minutes each weekday, creates the conditions for a dialogue in which participants explore possibilities and questions within the social dynamic of friendship and the larger imaginary social world of a neighborhood.

During the musical introduction to the opening song, "Won't You Be My Neighbor," a camera pans aerially through a miniature view of the neighborhood where Rogers apparently lives. The model neighborhood includes tree-lined streets alongside quaint houses and parked cars, like those of a typical middle-class, suburban neighborhood from the postwar period. We eventually arrive inside the home of Mister Rogers, who enters the scene looking straight into the camera and singing, "It's a beautiful day in the neighborhood, a beautiful day in the neighborhood. Would you be mine? Could you be mine?" He continues,

> I have always wanted to have a neighbor just like you!
> I've always wanted to live in a neighborhood with you
> So, let's make the most of this beautiful day
> Since we're together we might as well say,
> Would you be mine?
> Could you be mine? Won't you be my neighbor?

Won't you please,
Won't you please?
Please won't you be my neighbor?[10]

In his short song of welcome, in the performance of which he immediately establishes direct eye gaze with the television viewer, Rogers creates a dyadic relationship with the individual viewer, whom he asks, in the most intimate of phrasings, "Would you be mine?" Indeed, the first few lines of the song, which serves as the ritualized introduction to every episode, sets the relational ground from which the program unfolds as dialogical and intimate at the very start. Rogers first greets the day in an adoring and positive fashion, calling it "beautiful." His orientation is open and embracing of the world, the day, and his interlocutor, the viewer. He exudes confidence, pleasure, and reassurance in his nonverbal approach as well, by smiling, standing tall, and moving into the home with purpose and good speed. After acknowledging the day, he asks the viewer to step into this space with him—"Won't you be my neighbor?" he asks. Notice, if you will, that his invitation here is not a statement but a question that requires a response. He does not simply state, "Welcome to the show." In this seemingly simple choice of asking the viewer to join him on the program as his beloved neighbor, Rogers places the viewer in an active subject position in which she is called to accept or decline his invitation. Accepting the invitation swiftly and simply brings the two into relationship as host and viewer and establishes the relational and communicative ground from which dialogue and exploration of the world ensues.

I deploy the Belgian ethicist, philosopher, and theologian Roger Burggraeve's concept of "ethical emotionality" as an illuminating theoretical matrix for examining and analyzing Rogers's various points of departure in creating and recreating the social and moral world of *Neighborhood*, as illustrated above. Burggraeve reflects on the dynamic between education and values that he argues accounts for the construction of a holistic and moral religious education. Burggraeve establishes as first principle for the project of such an education the orientation and practice of an "ethical emotionality" that gives way to an "experience of belongingness in security and participation whereby both the confrontation with what is 'reasonable' and ethically responsible as well as the integration in a sustaining perspective of meaning is embedded and made possible."[11]

In explaining the concept of "ethical emotionality," Burggraeve lays out the fundamental conditions for a "holistic moral and religious education according to a "triptych of emotionality, rationality, and meaning." In this triptych, "emotionality" is posed as the "primary foundation for holistic education" due to its experiential nature, constituted by a sense of belongingness in security and participation, "whereby both the confrontation with what is 'reasonable' and ethically responsible, as well as the integration in a sustaining perspective of meaning is embedded and made possible."[12] Burggraeve's theorizing on the essentiality of "ethical emotionality" in education is rooted in a Christian theological framework that posits a "relational and emotionally involved God" who "comes near" and "binds himself" with his human children in a forgiving, reconciliatory, and loving way.[13] For this reason I will use Burggraeve's concept of "ethical emotionality" as a framework for understanding Rogers's communication ethos and affect.

Burggraeve's emphasis on the body in regards to the conveyance of such ethical emotionality is keenly important to Rogers's communication project, as television's nature of secondary orality affords—through its embodied execution, location in the intimate space of the domestic, and episodic nature—a penetrating parasocial interactional sensory dynamic. Burggraeve's discussion of a relational and emotionally involved God places emotionality and dyadic relationship at both the start and the center of the educational process and in this regard helps to clarify and better explain Rogers's ritual practice of relational affirmation throughout the enactment of *Mister Rogers' Neighborhood*.

Burggraeve draws from child development theorist Donald Woods Winnicott's insights into the ways "emotional embedment" creates the necessary "potential space" for education to further elaborate the importance of ethical emotionality as first principle in education. Winnicottian psychological understandings of the emotional life of the child clarify Rogers's rhetorical frameworks and discursive thematics. Rogers's consistent movement from dialogical engagement and the embodied creation of an invitational ethos and atmosphere to the investigation and manipulation of an object speaks to a Winnicottian understanding of the necessary acts for the development of healthy personhood, which begins with the process of forming a secure attachment to one's mother and continues toward the growth of a more independent self who is able to detach from his or her mother and engage in culture (i.e., the constructive engagement with the wider material and social world).

Rogers saw the production of his children's television show as a space infused by the Holy Spirit in which he, as a servant of God, strives to minister to the *deepest* and most *essential* needs of children—to be loved and accepted just as they are.[14] Rogers appears to understand the relationship between God and human beings as a dialogical process of communication in which both sender and receiver are engaged in a mutual dynamic of discovery. In Martin Buber's "I-Thou" framework, "all real living is meeting" and "no system of ideas, no foreknowledge, and no fancy intervene between *I* and *Thou*."[15] That is to say that in Buber's conception of being, the "I-Though" dynamic replaces the indivdual, solitary "I" of Descartes. Existence is predicated, thus, on the notion of mutuality. Rogers, too, is keenly interested in this meeting and posits it as primary for his "television visit." "I'm not that interested in 'mass communications,'" Rogers wrote. "I am much more interested in what happens between this person and the one watching. The space between the television set and that person who's watching is very holy ground."[16] In such a dynamic, God is neither dictator nor judge.[17] Rogers thus envisioned his program as a possible space for giving birth to what he calls "a holy ground of communication"—that space between any two people in which each is accepted "exactly as you are."[18] This is the space that is essential and yet "invisible to the eye," Rogers asserts, quoting Antoine de Saint-Exupéry's *The Little Prince*.[19]

The invocation of such a space between the television persona and the viewer suggests a lengthy consideration of communication ethics from the perspective of dialogue. In my discussion of Rogers's dialogical approach, I further draw upon key concepts in communication ethics articulated by Robert C. Arnett. In *Communication Ethics Literacy: Dialogue and Difference*, Arnett and his coauthors posit that in the increasingly fragmented society of postmodern America, the application of various ethical goods is "negotiated and enacted through discourse."[20] Considering Rogers's practice of ministering through narrative and dialogue, Arnett's understanding of narrative and dialogic communication ethics proves helpful in analyzing and interpreting Rogers's approach.

Rogers's dialogic understanding of television is clarified when he later asserts that, contrary to those who believe that television presupposes a passive audience and has little influence on people, the medium is in fact quite powerful not only because it can persuade but because of its invitation to response. "Why would advertisers pay so much money to put their messages on a medium that doesn't affect us all that much?" he asks. "I do feel that what we see and hear on the screen is a part of who we become."[21] It would seem here that Rogers's vision entails an understanding of the viewer as an active participant in what television critics of the time had characterized as a monologic communication process.[22] Moreover, his understanding of television's communication process points to an even deeper layer of consciousness that is constitutive of who we are—his statement borders on an ontological claim.

Television changed the definition and understanding of home entertainment by bringing the oral culture and dramas portrayed on screens once exclusive to the movie theater into domestic life.[23] With the introduction of television, we see a blending and overlapping of the times and spaces of entertainment. Television erased the boundaries between private and public time/space, and entertainment and family life. With the installation of television in domestic space, "the primary site of exhibition for spectator amusements was transferred from the public space of the movie theater to the private space of the home."[24]

If we differentiate space into distinct zones of nonverbal communication, depending on how far the speaker stands in relation to his/her audience, as Edward T. Hall does in *The Hidden Dimension*, we find that Rogers tends to occupy alternatively both personal and social space. Rogers does not cross into the sphere of intimate space and stays shy of public space. Hall identifies spatial zones in relation to the ways that physical environment, space, and territory become forms of nonverbal communication. He identifies four spatial zones—intimate space, the most personal communication, in which people are 0 to 1.5 feet apart; personal space, where most conversation between family and friends occurs and in which people are 1.5 to 4 feet apart; social space, where the majority of group interactions take place, in which people are separated by 4 to 12 feet; and public space, where, for example, a speaker is at least 12 feet away from his audience. As an object that belongs within the category of home furniture, the television is imbued with symbolic meaning tied to the social space of kinship and domesticity.[25] Rogers is keenly aware of this symbolic space that television, as a system of communication, has come to play in the midst of the family, where before, outsiders were not embodied participants.

In regards to understanding these spatial dimensions between the viewer and the television's representation of social life and sociability, it is useful to keep in mind psychologists Donald Horton and R. Richard Wohl's thesis regarding the development of a new space of communication called the parasocial.[26] Writing in 1956, Horton and Wohl argue that the characteristics of new media create the illusion of a personal relationship for the viewer between himself and the performer. They add that images presented on television create specific sociobiological responses in viewers. "In television, especially," they argue, "the image which is presented makes available nuances of appearance and gesture to which ordinary social perception is attentive and to which interaction is cued." Especially when an actor is playing himself, as Rogers does on *Neighborhood*, audience members respond "with something more than running observation." That "something" is *active* participation. This "simulacrum of conversational give and take," the authors write, "may be called parasocial interaction."[27] Though the authors refer to the family only once in their article, I contend that given this unanticipated dimension of the capacity of the television set to communicate within the family milieu, a revolution has taken place in the socioaffective space of the family. And this transformation is acknowledged and capitalized on with the creation of the character of "Mister Rogers." In retrospect, it would seem that *Neighborhood* is predicated on this phenomenon of the parasocial and the harnessing of developmental psychologist Erik Erikson's understanding of the interpersonal and familial foundations of the human psyche.

Prior to this unanticipated but momentous discovery of the parasocial effects of television on its viewers, childrearing experts attempted to intervene in the educational dimensions of the family by providing advice to mothers. From reading Erikson, Rogers and his collaborator, McFarland, understand that the primary scene where the child develops is the family. Within that family milieu, the primary object of social concern is the figure of the mother as the chief educator in the family.

Mister Rogers' Neighborhood was created for broadcasting on the National Education Television network, later renamed the Public Broadcasting Service. As such, it was designed to provide educational programming to very young children and their families. Identifying early on that because of the television's physical location within the family domain television discourses would likely become part of the family communication culture, Rogers eventually named his production company Family Communications Inc. Further exploring the educational elements of *Neighborhood* and the ways Rogers exploited its unique parasocial nature, I draw critical connections between the dialogic educational theory of Paulo Freire, Walter Ong's understanding of secondary orality and the ways embodied communication functions at primal biological levels, and Horton and Wohl's conceptualization of parasocial interaction that relates the critical episodic and domestic nature of television.[28]

In chapter 1, "Situating Rogers's Vision: A Sociocultural Framing," I contextualize Rogers's understanding of his project relative to the historical moment and to the dominant, residual, and emergent cultures of the American postwar era. I argue that Rogers, who was highly critical of the vaudevillian and slapstick performances dominant in early television, set out to employ television to restore the anthropocentric and community values of a residual, yet once dominant, mainline Protestant ethos through the integration of romantic agrarianism, an arts and crafts aesthetic, a gospel-inspired perspective on personhood and pastoral care, and the new and groundbreaking findings of the changing and increasingly influential field of child development. I further situate Rogers's prescient articulations on television, its communicative power, and its parasocial possibilities within broader historical discussions of communication technologies and their cultural implications. Rogers set out to employ television to communicate through dialogical pedagogy a set of anthropocentric behavioral, ethical, and cultural values that he hoped would contribute to the formation of postwar subjectivities in a rapidly changing and culturally contested period. In this way, he performs a pedagogical intervention in the public sphere by privileging a televisual interpersonal communication ethic, with an emphasis on mutuality, the management of feelings, and the maintenance of ethical social relationships, in order to counter the increasing privileging of commercial, slapstick forms.

Chapter 2, "Creating the Dialogic: Christianity, Child Development, and the Parasocial," analyzes the ways Rogers incorporated psychological and ethical insights derived from his experience working with children as a student of child development at Pittsburgh's Arsenal Family and Children's Center and as an MDiv student of pastoral care at the Pittsburgh Theological Seminary. I argue that he developed a dialogical, I-Thou communication ethic and practice centered on social emotional learning and the creation of meaning, which he honed and developed for the television medium. McFarland, who consulted with Rogers on every script that he wrote, profoundly influenced and assisted Rogers's understanding of how children might read each rhetorical choice; Rogers's theological formulations and the debates ensuing at the seminary while he was a student show how he incorporated this critical element of understanding into his communication project.

In chapter 3, "Inside *Mister Rogers' Neighborhood*: Objects, Play, and the Cultural Dialectic," a detailed look at a selection of programs that ran during the first year reveals that a consistent and ritualized emphasis on investigating the uses of everyday

material objects, their social meanings, and their creative potentiality is central to the show's construction. The object thus
becomes the starting point for the creative, enacted, and embodied unfolding of a culture and a people who constitute and occupy
the small, manageable world of the neighborhood. The program, I
argue, constitutes the representation of a culture's materiality that
is organized by social principles that promote values of discovery,
transformation, and growth at the levels of the material world, the
social world that gives meaning to the material world, and the
emotional and moral world of *Neighborhood.*

In the fourth chapter, "'Won't You Be My Neighbor?': Intergenerational Dialogics in *Mister Rogers' Neighborhood* Viewer Mail,"
I examine correspondence between viewers and Rogers—correspondence that reveals the success of Rogers's dialogic ethos
in prompting discursive responses among viewers. Viewer letters affirm Rogers's sense of dialoguing with his audience; he
responded to each one. That he retained all the correspondence
over thirty-three years testifies to the unusual importance it holds
for his communication project. As in previous chapters, I draw on
Burggraeve's conceptualization of ethical emotionality as a theoretical framework for analyzing the letters. These letters reveal
a remarkable consistency in their collective thematic quality and
constitute a field of study about the dialogical relationship between
"Mister Rogers," the historical Fred Rogers, and *Neighborhood*'s
audience. Most viewers write to express an emotional and affective identification with Rogers, illustrating well the success of his
dialogical ethos, the social-emotional developmental emphasis of
the program, and Rogers's ability to create emotional safety that
breaks through the parasocial dimension and into the realm of
individual communication exchange.

When I embarked on this project, I did not expect that the
questions I asked would be answered with such overwhelmingly
complex, dialogical interplay between the fields of developmental

psychology, communication ethics, television studies, and American and religious studies. While I knew that what many people see as a dull, slow, and simple children's program was likely to be revealed as more complex and dynamic beneath the surface, I did not expect to find such complexity of thought, integration of knowledge, practical engagement, and contemplative idea creation displayed both behind the scenes and in front of the camera. This book reveals the hardworking dedication, intellectual and emotional struggles, and intensive consideration of a television artist striving to create a dialogical production that placed valued ideas and practices from a residual American culture (an agrarian and mainline Protestant ethos) in conversation with an emergent and influential discipline of study (postwar child development psychology) to create a cultural product that spoke to the perceived needs of transitional subjectivities searching for new meanings and ways of coping and being in a new mass-mediated age.

Rogers displayed prominently in his WQED office the quotation from *The Little Prince*, "And now here is my secret, a very simple secret. It is only with the heart that one can see rightly. What is essential is invisible to the eye." It served as a contant reminder to himself and to those involved in the production of *Neighborhood* that the program envisions the affective life as the defining faculty of being human. Rogers's mass communication project was thus constituted by the dialogical communication acts of seeing and being seen. For Fred Rogers, one can only truly see through the heart—the symbol of the socioemotional psyche. In Mister Rogers's neighborhood, the heart, the symbolic home for affect and emotion. is the organ of vision and the dialogic is the place where we begin.

Situating Rogers's Vision

A SOCIOCULTURAL FRAMING

IN THE OCTOBER 1969 VOLUME of the *Pittsburgh Area Pre-school Association Publication*, Fred Rogers coauthored a piece with Linda J. Philbrick, former head teacher of Oakland Nursery School, titled "Television and the Viewing Child." In it, Rogers and Philbrick describe the reaction of a young girl named Nancy to an episode of *The Three Stooges* television program in which the Stooges are shown harming a dog. "I want to go into the television and help it [the dog]," Nancy says as she burrows her face in her mother's lap, "but I'm afraid that they will hurt me too." Rogers and Philbrick use this anecdote to lead into a larger discussion about young children's perceptions of the actors and scenarios they view on the television screen. They note Nancy's "deep emotional involvement" with the encounter on the screen and how her mother was taken aback by her daughter's reaction. "The young child's limited experience and immature perceptual system," they

write, "makes it difficult for [her] to separate fantasy from reality."
They continue:

> The vivid images presented by the television camera make it even
> more difficult for him when these images are violent and fright-
> ening, the child faces an *additional dilemma*. Since television is
> a piece of furniture, placed in the home by parents, it is endowed
> with an air of parental sanction. Children witness their parents
> firmly terminating a sibling battle, but sitting and staring in appar-
> ent unconcern while a bloody slaughter takes place on television.
> This presents *deep confusion* for the child who perceives one
> incident to be as real as the other. Much public concern has been
> expressed over the effect that the *content* of violent television pro-
> grams ha[s] on children. We also need to be concerned about how
> these programs affect the child's *relationship* with the people who
> present them.[1]

In this rich and revealing paragraph, Rogers and Philbrick
communicate the complexities involved in the then novel process
of children's televisual reception and communication. In their
analysis, they make an original link between the lived emotion
felt by the child and her ethical sense of this emotion as it calls for
action to resolve the conflict. Nancy cannot stop the beating of the
helpless dog, of course, because she cannot enter the contiguous
and yet impossibly distant space depicted on the screen. Reveal-
ingly, Rogers and Philbrick speak of the child's dilemma, which in
and of itself addresses the "ethical emotionality" that underscores
the creative fabric of *Mister Rogers' Neighborhood*. Adding to the
dilemma of the child's original response to the ethical imperative is the fact that the parent, by not intervening, seems to the
child to be condoning the unethical events that have now entered
their family dynamic. "As adults," Rogers and Philbrick write,
"we may feel that we 'permit' the happenings on the television

screen because we clearly recognize them as unreal."[2] They are, of course, speaking of the adults' learned ability to compartmentalize so that while they intervene in conflict within the family system, they allow for representations of conflict on television to go on unmitigated. To the child, this compartmentalization represents an emotionally distressing and puzzling behavior, for the ethical emotionality attendant on the experience of viewing the beating of a dog goes unaddressed.

This understanding of the ethical emotionality embedded in television programming, further compounded by the reality that this medium operates within the home space of the family, serves as the key point of inflection in Rogers's television creation. His emphasis on the ways television interacts and interferes with the actual human relationships in the family home is one of the unique and most innovative aspects of Rogers's philosophy and approach to his own television program. In almost every document he produced that develops the main ideas and framework for the program, Rogers emphasizes the significant location and proxemics of the television set as existing within the domestic space of the family home and thus embedded in the family communication culture. At the same time, Rogers's analysis of television is deeply grounded within and influenced by a troubled popular discourse on television and children rooted in concern over the new medium's effects on emotional development, social life, morality, and human behavior. Trained as a musician and composer with former Presbyterian ministerial ambitions, Rogers, who entered the new industry of television as an NBC production assistant during its initial exploratory and experimental phase, moved quickly from critic to producer, asserting that the new medium could be used to display and promote more elevating, ethical, and nurturing ways of being and behaving.

Rogers, in identifying the vast communication opportunities that the new television technology created to reach a wide net of

Americans in their familial environment, and in trying to counter what he perceived as representations of callous and debased behavior displayed on the new medium, set out to employ television to communicate, through dialogical and theatrical pedagogy, a set of anthropocentric behavioral, ethical, and cultural values that he hoped would contribute to the stabilization and formation of postwar subjectivities in a rapidly changing and culturally contested period.[3] In this regard, he aimed to perform a pedagogical intervention in the public sphere by privileging a televisual interpersonal communication ethic, with an emphasis on mutuality, the management of feelings, and the maintenance of ethical social relationships, in order to counter the industry's increasing privileging of commercial, vaudevillian, and slapstick entertainment forms.

TELEVISION, INFLUENCE, AND INTERPERSONAL CONNECTION

When the television set was sold as piece of furniture within the home, it was intended by manufacturers to blend with other objects in the "living" (familial social) space of the home. As such, it transformed the previous intimacy of the home, as it provided an opening for "strangers" to occupy a space previously restricted to only those of kinship. Thus, television is not an extension of the cinema, in part because of its location within family life. Film is viewed in the darkness, in a public space with unfamiliar surroundings. The screen is large; its size and that of the images depicted on it can overwhelm the viewer. Characters rarely appear in more than one film. In contrast, television is viewed in the familiar space of the home, usually with the lights on, and in the presence of family members. The screen is small, indeed smaller than a child. And the same characters appear week after week in series programming. Newscasters appear daily. "Children," Grant Noble notes, "report that they answer the talking head when it simulates face to face interaction."[4] These characteristics are of critical importance for understanding how television functions on an interpersonal and familiar social level.

In 1985, communication scholar Joshua Meyrowitz noted that "much more than in print, electronic media tend to unite sender and receiver in an intimate web of personal experience and feeling" due to the embodied, oral nature of human representation on the screen.[5] He contrasts the discursive nature of print communication, in which messages are communicated through the use of language or language-like symbols, and the "presentational" nature of electronic media, in which embodied human expressions dominate. Written language "communicates," Meyrowitz writes, while electronic media is characterized by "expressions." Expressions are personal and idiosyncratic; in contrast, communication can be about anything. Meyrowitz relates these two contrasting styles—communication and expression—to Erving Goffman's back and front regions of the brain: "Discursive and presentational forms are so distinct that they are apparently produced and perceived primarily by different hemispheres of our brains."[6] Print media, Goffman posited, have a "front region bias,' meaning that the brain processes this information within the context of a conception of public life. In contrast, electronic media, characterized by "expressive," embodied communication practice, have a "back region bias." That is to say, this form speaks to the part of the brain that connects with the personal or the familial. It is due to the embodied nature of electronic communication—its orality, physicality, and expressive quality—that a more personal, elementary kind of response occurs within listeners and viewers. Thus, if this form of media is brought into the home, it makes sense that those communicating on the device could become integrated into the family communication culture, which is constituted by an embodied togetherness in the home space in which communication is primarily oral.[7]

In a speech he delivered at a Yale symposium on young children and television in 1972, Rogers says that "television, whether
by intent or accident, is now an essential aspect of practically
every home. Even families without telephones have television
sets—consequently, the attitudes expressed by us or anyone else
on television become involved in family communications."[8] Rogers
emphasizes the interpersonal aura and function of the television,
a consistent theme in his writings. It is from this critical observation that Rogers builds his program's approach to educating both
young children and their parents. As we will see, his program is,
at its core, an interpersonal, dialogical, and familial endeavor, in
which Rogers, the host, ritually establishes and reestablishes an
intimate, parasocial relationship with his intergenerational viewers in order to reassure them about their worth, the stability of the
world around them, and the importance of creating and maintaining a life-giving ethos with both themselves and others.

In his Yale speech, Rogers asserts that any person delivering
messages on a consistent basis through the television medium
will almost "organically" become incorporated into the communication culture and interpretive meaning-making processes of the
family unit. Although his analytical assessment of television reit-
erates the prominent cultural understanding of television's unique
position within the family institution, Rogers's articulation of the
penetrating significance of this positionality in regards to the
ways that televisual communication functions *within* the family
communication culture itself offers a nuanced perspective on the
phenomenon in its implied personification aspects of television
technology.[9] Rogers asks, "Have you ever observed a baby at her
mother's breast? Did you notice how carefully the baby watched its
mother's face as it sucked and drank her milk? Do you ever notice
a similar sight with people watching television? Older children
eating popcorn and [drinking] Cokes, younger ones sucking on
their fingers. If this association is by any means a valid one, then

television viewing must be considered as having its roots at the very core of human development." Rogers follows this analytical analogy by noting that the difference between looking at most mothers and looking at television sets is that "a human mother can help the baby develop active modes with dealing with what he or she is feeling, while the television set invariably presents some kind of stimulation and lets the viewers drink it in as they will." He thus concludes that the effects of television viewing should be considered with specific regard for the possibility that child viewers "are exposed to experiences which may be far beyond what their egos can deal with effectively," as in the case of young Nancy watching the dog being abused by the Three Stooges. Here, Rogers reveals the grounding philosophical and psychological positions from which his sociopedagogical project departs; he is questioning not only the content of television programs but also the damaging neglect on the part of those who create and produce television for children. He calls on producers to address the subjectivity of the child as different from the subjectivity of the adult. "Those of us who produce television must assume the responsibility for providing images of trustworthy, available adults who will modulate these experiences and attempt to keep them within manageable limits," he asserts. Rogers's visionary directive here illustrates his focus on providing a sense of security, responsibility, reassurance, and "appropriate" content to children via television.

Both the Yale speech and the narrative he authored with Philbrick for the Pittsburgh Area Preschool Association publication illustrate Rogers's keen analysis and insights into the visceral communicative power of televisual representation. Both are also suffused with Rogers's deep sense of care for the child's emotional and developmental wellbeing and thus inscribed with an overarching ethical imperative for adults (and parents especially) to understand their role in mediating the child's viewing experience.

As such, they demonstrate the primary social-emotional concerns that drive Rogers's efforts in television production, his prescient understanding of the interpersonal connections made between screen players, events, and viewers, and his understanding of his project as a kind of family intervention. In later chapters I will show how, indeed quite remarkably, *Neighborhood* captures and enacts in televisual form Rogers's initial understanding of and vision for his project as an intervention in childhood culture and pedagogy.

But I first want to open a window into national discussions of the postwar period regarding television and its categorical connection to the placement of machines into domestic spaces, including anxieties surrounding the potential threats of the new television device and the ways that domestic machines were resemanticized with anthropomorphic qualities—qualities that ascribed to television an aura of familial membership. Rogers can be placed within a rhetorical tradition of pastoral ideal concerned with the technological sublime and the machine's challenges to a once dominant agrarian culture in which values of community, creative work, and social-emotional bonds were of primary importance for human health and survival. *Neighborhood* as "middle landscape," as Leo Marx would have it, embodies the artificiality of the city and cultivates the naturalness of the pastoral such that threats of the wilderness are safely avoided.

The middle landscape/Arcadian village of *Neighborhood* and its emphasis on the "invisible essentials"—community building, creative work, and the development of social-emotional bonds— characteristic of its way of life can be seen as a response to the frustrations and anxieties at work during the postwar period of the 1950s and 1960s. In the face of the increases in alienation, destruction of community bonds, rampant narcissism, unbridled consumption, and flattening of the individual perceived to be taking place at the time, *Neighborhood* offers a quiet, calm, interpersonal, and inventive environment in which to restore an affective sense of self-worth and human connection in the mind of the viewer.

Rogers, as both a television artist and a Presbyterian minister beginning in the 1960s, straddles the line of public life and acceptable religious expression during a period that many scholars might label as the beginning of the post-Christian era in the West. In the context of a Protestant establishment fighting to maintain its cultural dominance within a rapidly changing early mid-twentieth-century environment characterized by urbanization, industrialization, increasing mobility, immigration, and pluralism, Rogers's vision fits into a lineage of American Christian concern with theatrical content and efforts to address such concern that ranged from censorship to proactive intervention. Rogers and his lead consultant, Dr. Margaret McFarland, understood their project as a pedagogical family intervention; this intervention, I will demonstrate, takes its place within a progressive approach to achieving educational equality at the national level—PBS. With the new television technology, traditional educators and "cultural elites" like McFarland and Rogers could administer a finely tuned cultural and educational program that taught the insights of child development psychology "inside" the most important pedagogical system of the family. Rogers's solution to the problem of exposing children to representations of images and human behavior that they are not emotionally or cognitively equipped to process reveals his insightful and critical perspective on the medium's reception. For one, he asks producers to become more aware and self-critical of the programming destined for the child viewer, whose cognitive and emotional abilities are significantly distinct from the adult viewer. Second, he posits that in watching such disturbing content on television with the child, the adult is essentially condoning the behavior depicted on the screen.

In a document that appears to have been written prior to

the inception of *Neighborhood*, "Children's TV: What Can the
Church Do about It?," Rogers decries the ways that television programming and its antieducational, debased content are quickly
becoming a dominant cultural force in children's lives. If, Rogers
seems to posit, television is added to the existing pedagogical
sites such as the church, family, and school, then children's programming should be subject to a standard regime of carefully
prescribed emotional and ethical staging. From the Victorian
period on, adults had been in charge of exposing the young to
various forms of socioethical knowledge and assisting them in
intellectually and emotionally grasping concepts and phenomena.
In his assessment, Rogers appears to be alerting his audience to
the fact that television transmits content to whoever is watching,
without any local system of adult censorship or chaperoning.[10]
Further, viewers perceive the human activity on the screen in ways
similar to that of real life and the process of watching at home
arguably creates a more intimate and personal relationship with
screen characters who appear every day or every week in their
homes. It is thus irresponsible, Rogers argues, for adults charged
with instructing and caring for the younger generation to allow
children unbridled and unaccompanied viewing of representations
they have not yet reviewed and deemed worthy of consumption.[11]

   In addition to his perspective on the radical changes television
brings to the lives of children in regards to content exposure and
adult supervision, Rogers details how television's representation
of human life appears to affect individuals in an interpersonal,
almost familial way by likening images of people watching television to that of a baby nursing at the breast of her mother.[12] Rogers's
analogy configures an understanding of the dynamic between the
screen and the viewer that can be understood in relation to Horton
and Wohl's concept of the parasocial relationship. In this relationship, they write, characters portrayed in audiovisual media like
television "come to life . . . in an especially vivid and arresting

way." The parasocial experience entails the erasure of the line
that separates reality from fiction such that the viewer becomes
mesmerized by events that transpire in the televisual space and
therefore develop a kind of "real" relationship with the characters.
This interpersonal way of connecting and relating, brought about
by the power of orality that television revives, bears relating to
Walter Ong's observations of orality and the sacral power of the
spoken word that binds individuals into communities. "Because in
its physical constitution as sound, the spoken word proceeds from
the human interior and manifests human beings to one another
as conscious interiors, as persons, the spoken word forms human
beings into close-knit groups. The interiorizing force of the oral
relates in a special way to the sacral, to the ultimate concerns of
existence."[13] When Rogers notes that those watching television
behave similarly to babies who are sucking from their mother's
breast, he alludes to the essential, organic, and material process
of bonding and interpersonal formation that is the very essence of
human social life. It is the formation of these close-knit bonds that
constitute what Émile Durkheim identified as the sacramental
bonds of community, which he posited emerge from religion and
the concept of the sacred. Indeed, Ong points out that "in most
religions the spoken word functions integrally in ceremonial and
devotional life" because the voice emerges from the materiality of
the human body.[14] In this light, Rogers appears to identify in television the very fundamental communication pathways that allow
for the development of significant human bonding and community
formation in which he will make an intervention.

THE CONTROVERSY OVER TELEVISION

At the turn of the twentieth century, progressives grew increasingly concerned about the "dehumanizing effects of machines."
Tasks previously performed by individual labor and the physi-

cal work of human hands were transferred to new technologies, resulting in the machinization of human work.[15] The idea of having machines regulate relations in the family domestic setting was met by ambivalent response in many American homes as long-held agrarian ideals informed the collective imagination and challenged the emerging mechanized world.[16]

The new invasion of household machines contributed to what Ruth Cowan Schwartz calls a redefinition of the concept of family leisure from the Victorian understanding of spiritual development that prepared members for daily duties to a modern and more secular one designed to "liberate" subjects from the toils of work life. In this new industrialized domestic setting, everyday domestic duties such as the washing of clothes, as well as traditional leisurely pursuits such as playing the piano or reading stories aloud, were reassigned to the work of these household machines (e.g., electric washing machines, radio). Interestingly, although household machines were promoted as devices that would reduce the laborious manual work of women in the home, "they reorganized the work processes of housework in ways that did not save the labor of the average housewife."[17]As such, a tension ensued in American culture between a celebration of new pleasures and an anxiety about the reorganization of time and relationships being spelled out by the machines. Suffice it to say that there were notable variations across different areas and regions of the country in these overall patterns.[18]

As the economy shifted from production to consumption during the early part of the twentieth century and mass production in particular removed productive work from the private sphere, persuasion agents of the new consumer economy set out to ease anxiety over the vast social and economic changes that the new household technologies brought about. In this new environment there emerged a new subjectivity of the consumer, who, "courted by new kinds of advertising, purchased new kinds of goods at new kinds of stores," culminating in the "wholesale transformation of most Americans' daily life from near-subsistence farming to mass participation in the money economy both as workers and consumers."[19] Because of their reimagined role as keeper of a household in which using and overseeing the work of machines was key, women were targeted by advertisers as a primary audience for the marketing of such devices.[20]

By the 1950s similar efforts were made by industry agents to refamiliarize the population with the new machine of television. Many popular magazines described the television device as a "newborn baby," a "family friend," a "nurse," a "teacher," and a "family pet," tension giving way to a resemanticization of the domestic machine, which has moved from the position of a stranger, intruding upon the family space, into a constitutive and subordinate member of the family.[21] While citizen groups and others interested in the public good (e.g., journalists and activists) remained suspicious of the presence of this machine in the home life, advertisers, for whom the television was poised to become indispensable, sought to neutralize its negative image by incorporating a rhetoric of the technological sublime in its messaging. For example, a 1951 newspaper advertisement by the Admiral Corporation, a maker of televisions, features an image of a seductive, ethnically ambiguous, exotic, and glamorous woman with long eyelashes, dressed in an off-the-shoulder top, looking off into the distance as she rests her chin on her gloved hand. Her grand presence is set just behind a smaller television device that features an image of a white man and woman, most conventional in appearance, singing. The visual rhetoric lends a sense of conventional, Americana familiarity within the frame of the television "box," while at the same time emphasizing the abilities of television to transport its owner to larger-than-life exotic and seductive places and peoples. In a mix of script and print, the ad headline reads, "Built for the Future: Admiral 20" TV." Just below the set in smaller letters it states, "World's Most Powerful TV: Ready for UHF Stations."[22] Such ads focused on the device's ability to broadcast both the glamor culture of Hollywood and the more conventional Americana musical entertainment shows into the home space.

On the other hand, Spigel notes how advertisers, perhaps attuned to discourse that anthropomorphized the device, often conjured the relational image of master-servant to assure potential consumers that the device would operate as other machinery in the house did and with the primary purpose of serving family, household needs. A 1952 newspaper advertisement for Magnavox television sets features a photograph of a young boy standing next to a large television set and manipulating the channel-changing knob. He smiles while exerting his control over the depiction on the screen—a clown in full makeup and red nose who appears as if he is staring right back at the boy. Notably, the boy looks down at the clown, whose head is tilted upward to see him. The image displays a high power/low power dynamic in which the boy holds the higher status.[23]

Within a discourse of threat and warning, popular magazine writers posited the idea of a "technology out of control" that had the potential to wreak havoc on family life. In 1956 prominent critic Jack Gould of the *New York Times* noted that while television broadcasters should not be expected to "solve life's problems . . . they can be expected to display adult leadership and responsibility in areas where they do have some significant influence." Gould went on to decry the promotion of performer Elvis Presley, whom Gould described as partaking in "strip-tease behavior," to a teenage television audience. Gould places the phenomenon of television with a host of other early to mid-century developments that were uprooting young adults from the traditional dwelling places of home and school: "With even 16-year-olds capable of commanding $20 or $30 a week in their spare time, with access to automobiles at an early age, with communications media of all kinds exposing them to new thoughts very early in life, theirs indeed is a high degree of independence. Inevitably it has been accompanied by a lessening of parental control." Gould prefaces this concern over the lessening of restrictions for young adults by noting that "family counselors" have "wisely noted" that the culture is in a period of "frantic" and "tense" transition.[24]

In addition to the threat of the television machine dominating and destroying an idealized harmonious family life, there was concern about its "encouragement of passive and addictive behavior."[25] A page from a 1950 issue of *Ladies' Home Journal* on the "Telebugeye" illustrates this concern with passivity and distraction. The copy presents a profile drawing of a small child slumped on a stool watching the television set. Her eye is attentive, large, and fixated on the screen; her hair is scraggly, and she does not wear shoes. The copy below the drawing reads: "This pale, weak, stupid-looking creature is a Telebugeye, and, as you can see, it grew bugeyed by looking at television too long. Telebugeyes just sit and sit, watching, watching. This one doesn't wear shoes because it never goes out in the fresh air anymore and it's skinny because it never gets any exercise. The hair on this Telebugeye is straggly and long because it won't get a haircut for fear of missing a program. What idiots Telebugeyes are."[26] Discourses emphasizing the phenomenon of television "addiction" suggest ways that the device inspires antisocial behavior. Indeed, popular wisdom of the time often connected "addictive" television viewing to aggressive behavior in children. Such concerns followed theories resulting from social-scientific experiments on children and media, such as the Payne Fund Studies of the 1930s, which characterized mass media as injecting their ideas into passive victims.[27]

In *The People Look at Television: A Study of Audience Attitudes*, a 1968 social-scientific research tome commissioned by the Bureau of Applied Social Research at Columbia University, Gary

A. Steiner notes themes of violence, education, and babysitting in adult audience responses on television and the family. He cites an article in *Ladies' Home Journal* calling television a form of "American brainwashing" and asserting that television is a device of social pressure that leads young minds to conclude that violence is a socially acceptable way of life. Steiner also found, parallel with many responders' concerns about representations of violence, that parents generally worried that television was exposing their children to "things they shouldn't see," contributing to a broader fear of television's "bad influence." He quotes one parent as stating, "You read in the paper where the kids are shooting each other or hanging by the neck, that they've seen on TV." On the more positive side, Steiner reports, viewers note that parents who favor television find that the device can be intellectually educational for their children.[28] Other parents emphasize that they are able to find freedom and relief for themselves in the domestic sphere by occupying their children with television programming. Some expressed pleasure in the idea that the television keeps the children in the safety of the home and away from possible trouble outside of it.

Within this kind of cultural discursive space, in which both anxiety and curiosity regarding the effects of mass media coalesced with advertising efforts to promote the new medium and its products, Rogers developed his own views and perspectives on the subject. Rogers, dedicated to understanding the ways that the new technology of television affects ethical and emotional development, culture, community, and human relationships, appears to view media with an air of both skepticism and wonderment.[29]

REDEPLOYING THE PASTORAL IDEAL

The contrast between the television as the "nurse" or "new baby" in the family and the "Telebugeye" can be understood in the context of discourses of praise and concern regarding the emergence of industrial machines. Writing in 1964, Leo Marx examines Perry Miller's concept of the "technological sublime" in his book *The Machine in the Garden: Technology and the Pastoral Idea in America*.[30] Marx looks at how canonical writers dealt with the machine's challenges to the dominant agrarian/pastoral ethos. Focusing on nineteenth-century technologies such as the locomotive and the telegraph, he posits that they were viewed as "sublime" because they at once appeared to overshadow and dominate both the individual and the vast, romanticized American pasture.[31] This overshadowing and domination of the individual was of special concern in regard to conceptions of work, an aspect of human life ascribed with the highest virtue in several American Protestant traditions. Thus, as industrial machinery took human creativity and reward out of the working person's experience, concerns arose about the dehumanizing effects of such mechanized jobs and the replacement of the worker by a machine. Could the worth of each individual be seen in factory settings where industrial machines performed the work formerly done by human hands and manual labor? How could a hardworking individual find satisfaction and value in a system where his everyday work practices were reduced to unskilled, repetitive actions ostensibly mimicking the movements of industrial machines? The question raised by radio and television—as machines within the family that do not perform work like a washing machine but that entertain and disseminate information—constitutes a radical shift from the concerns of industrialization. The insertion of this "domestic machine" in the intimacy of the home marks a qualitative shift from a consideration of a machine engaged in doing work to a machine engaged in the construction of subjectivity. While one could argue that this domestic artifact is not unlike the book in its ability to construct and influence subjectivity, radio and especially television are markedly different from the literary medium in their orality and the visceral, socioemotional power of such embodied communication.[32] Those who praise, as well as those who suspect, the power of this new machine recognize in it its potential for supplanting teachers and parents in the production of the "subject."

The replacement of the worker by the machine provoked a romanticization of an agricultural society in which the relationship of the producer and the object produced was not mediated by the machine. Thus, the relationship of the artisan to the production of his craft is praised and highlighted as the preferential option in comparison to the mechanized worker, who is now tied to the machine, and whose work involves zero individual creativity or craftsmanship. In this sense, the neighborly, small-town setting of *Neighborhood* is linked to the idealization of a society in the early stages of industrialization where the relationship of the worker to the factory has not yet reached the generalized impersonal relationships of the advanced industrial age. A kind of simultaneous effort to place value in the integrity of human work while embracing new industrial technologies can be seen in various elements of Rogers's philosophy and programming as he clearly rejects the alienating conditions of the worker as an appendix to the machine.

Rogers is artfully expressing what Marx identifies as "the middle landscape," or, in modern capitalist times, "the garden." As Marx explains, the middle landscape belonged to the topography of the pastoral scene famously described by Virgil in the *Eclogues*, where a shepherd tends to his flock in pastures between the city and the natural wilderness. Man here lives in nature, but a cultivated nature set apart from the chaotic and threatening wilderness. It is here, in this middle landscape, that, as expressed in literary works up until the eighteenth century, serenity lies. In the beginning of the eighteenth century, Marx tells us, these depictions begin to change: instead of Virgil's pasture, we see the appearance of the garden. The garden thus becomes a space where the two polarities of men in the Western philosophical tradition—the rational and the animalistic, wild, and emotional—can find reconciliation.[33] Indeed, this analogy works quite well for thinking about *Neighborhood*, a space where children are called to visit to participate in their own kind of "taming." The garden appears to correlate with the primary aim of Rogers's *Neighborhood*, which he articulated in 1969 as a project that could do a great "service for mental health."[34] *Neighborhood*, as middle landscape, embodies both the artificiality of the city and the cultivated naturalness of the pastoral, leaving out the wild threats of the wilderness. As such, it is an ideal stage for the project of "taming" the young.

As *Neighborhood* illustrates, Rogers's understanding of the relationship of the human subject to work offers a countervailing sense of the value of the person in relation to work. Rogers places the person at the center of production, above both the machine and the object produced. It is useful to detail part of the structure of a standard episode here, to demonstrate how Rogers routinely illustrates the value of human work. After Rogers begins the episode with his invitational song, "Won't You Be My Neighbor?" he enters a conversation with his viewer in the living room of his home. Such conversation often centers on an object that he has brought in for discussion and investigation. After initial understanding and curiosity about the object has been established through Rogers's inquisitive and dialogical speech, he will usually move to learn more about the purpose and meaning of the object by asking his "Picture Picture" wall frame to play a short film about the object. The film runs through moving pictures of the object as it is employed and understood by various people, while Rogers performs a voiceover with his own interpretive and descriptive narrative of the object and the ways people construct and use it. Musical director Johnny Costa's instrumental dreamscape adds another layer of wonder to the progression of the film in the eye of the viewer. There are times, too, that Rogers chooses instead to visit a business or other locale, such as a factory, where the object is either constructed or used by humans. Factory visits to see "how people make sneakers," "how people make wagons," "how people make plates," and "how people make crayons" are some of viewers' most beloved scenes from the program.

Hedda Sharapan, a longtime producer of *Mister Rogers' Neighborhood*, has highlighted the way Rogers celebrated the role of the person in industrial and creative production in both demonstrations of play and visits to adult workplaces such as factories and small businesses. She recalls that during an early program in which Rogers visits a crayon factory, he introduces the segment by saying, "Let's see how crayons are made." Soon after the production of this segment, she noted that he shifted his language to make the human person the agent of action in workplace visits. "He started saying, instead of 'how sneakers are made,' it was 'how people make sneakers.'"[35] Rogers makes an effort toward a kind of anthropocentric industrialism, in which new technologies are embraced, but the worker remains centrally valued as the primary contributor to the material creation. This understanding of work and its connection to the person seems to harken back to the American small-town mythos, in which industry had not yet displaced the artisan and where personal relations among the members of the community offset any kind of deep alienation present in the "Telebugeye" illustration.

Rogers's sense of the person was no doubt influenced by his formative years growing up in the small town of Latrobe, Pennsylvania, where his elders were highly active and well regarded in community life. Latrobe was founded in 1852 by a civil railroad engineer named Oliver Barnes, who bought a 140-acre farm from Thomas Kirk in the hopes of connecting the eastern part of the state with the city of Pittsburgh. Although the city of Latrobe is a phenomenon of industrialization, the Latrobe area is, like much of western Pennsylvania, constituted by old, agrarian farming communities. Barnes donated three acres of his land to establish a railroad station, a water tower, and a hotel. The city's proximity to the railroad and to Loyalhanna Creek helped attract the interest of industrial businessmen who quickly established a paper mill, tanneries, distilleries, and breweries.[36] Both Rogers's father and grandfather were industrialists, well regarded for their treatment of workers and for their active and personal engagement in the community of Latrobe's well-being.

Rogers's iconographic use of the "neighborhood," aesthetically expressed in the setup of small houses and cottages, constitutes the program's outer set concept and can be understood to some extent within the context of an American mythos that romanticized a return to nature. In the late nineteenth and early twentieth century, upper-class Americans began building homes outside of the city, in the country, where they sought privacy and aesthetic beauty. Middle-class men and women gradually followed this exodus just as mass public transportation provided them with the opportunity to live farther and farther away from their places of work.[37]

In his book *American Dreamscape*, Tom Martinson identifies three kinds of freestanding suburbs that emerged in the late nineteenth century—"the isolated refuge of the Nobility and Gentry," the company town, and the Arcadian village—the latter of which appears to be most relevant to our discussion of Rogers's romanticized, neighborhood environment. The Arcadian village was intended to be peaceful, simple, and unadorned. Martinson calls it "an archetypal yeoman environment" in which comfortably sized houses were set on relatively large lots. Like Rogers's "television home," Arcadian domestic structures usually have front and side porches (Rogers has a large front porch with a bench swing) and are set back from a street landscaped with lush bushes, grass, and trees. Martinson describes Arcadian neighborhood blocks as "peaceful and inviting" and asserts that Arcadian villages are "highly romantic environments, in part because of the relaxed visual interplay between house and landscape." The idea that the everyman, or the "yeoman," as Martinson calls him, could settle in the kind of picturesque, naturalistic, and peaceful neighborhood of an Arcadian village was made a reality in this nineteenth-century moment in which a kind of American suburbia inspired by the romantic movement led to the creation of land plots "featuring large individual lots for the so-called common man—the Yeoman."[38] Indeed, *Neighborhood* is rooted in the aesthetic and discursive values of this "American dreamscape," its picturesque simplicity and its egalitarian sense of social, cultural, and economic attainment.

Mister Rogers' Neighborhood is set in Rogers's modest house. The surrounding neighborhood, we learn from a camera pan of a model Arcadian neighborhood at the beginning of the program and during subsequent visits to neighborhood locales, is composed of houses, small businesses, and civic spaces (the library, the police station, parks) and an imaginary, fantasy realm called the Neighborhood of Make-Believe (NMB), which constitutes the middle segment of the program. The NMB set mirrors Rogers's surrounding neighborhood on a much smaller scale, with fantastical animal puppets and their toylike homes, which distinguish it from reality. *Neighborhood*'s primary environment, the home of Mister Rogers, seems most appropriate for viewing by very small children, as it reflects the child's world—centered within and on a safe, modest American home. The program also emphasizes the presence of a larger outside world, similarly safe and modest, in its articulation of the neighborhood—the community within which the family home resides. In all of these ways, the neighborhood exudes the celebrated ethos of this particular American dream, articulated exceptionally well by Scott Russell Sanders when he says that the "deepest American dream is not . . . the hunger for money or fame; it is the dream of settling down, in peace and freedom and cooperation, in the promised land."[39]

It is this concept of the American dream, presented in the American village ideal and captured in the architectural and planning aesthetic of the Arcadian village, that *Mister Rogers' Neighborhood* depicts. In the simplicity of the neighborhood-oriented lives of Rogers and his "neighbors," in the slow and manageable pacing of the program embodied in Rogers's speech patterns and in the steady and easy movements of people and events, this manageable village life is created on screen. Interestingly, such a setting seems characteristic of the collection of neighborhoods that make up the city of Pittsburgh or, perhaps, Latrobe itself with its surrounding pastoral and agricultural makeup. Martinson writes that in both symbol and fact, the Arcadian village was esteemed as an "ideal environment" by millions of Americans: "This widespread conviction—whether in rural areas, small towns, or suburbs—reflected a powerful mixture of contributing influences, ranging from the Yeoman's desire for personal space, to the metaphysical value attributed to nature by the transcendentalists. For the average American, hopeful that the new republic was indeed a better place, an appreciation of the preeminence of nature went hand-in-hand with the characteristic optimism of the romantic movement and its emphasis on creative exploration and personal freedom."[40] The interplay of these American idyllic virtues of "creative exploration" and "personal freedom" and their embeddedness within this presuburban, romantic aesthetic is recognizable in the visual, performative, and discursive rhetoric of *Neighborhood*.

These ideals were indeed thriving in Western Pennsylvania at the time when Rogers came into the world. Born in 1928, Fred McFeely Rogers was the only son of James Hillis Rogers and Nancy McFeely Rogers. He was raised in the Presbyterian church, where both his mother and father were highly active.[41] James was an elder of the First Presbyterian Church's board of trustees. After a short career in business, James became president of the First National Bank, owner of his father-in-law's McFeely Brick Company, and owner and president of the Latrobe Die Casting Company.[42] The family was very prosperous, valued hard work, and made an effort to treat their workers well. According to Sharapan, James Rogers "was known as someone in the community who really respected and cared for his workers. I think the word was that every now and then there were thoughts about union but they trickled away because he was so caring to them. . . . That whole sense of caring for and respecting your workers—Fred grew up in that world."[43] Nancy Rogers was well known in the community for her volunteerism and concern with social justice, eventually becoming a nurse's aide. She knit sweaters for the American troops during the war.[44] According to Fr. Douglas Nowicki, the current archabbot of Saint Vincent College and a longtime friend of Fred Rogers, the college had a large fire in 1963 to which James and Nancy Rogers responded by creating a foundation to help people in need in the community.[45]

Set in the nearby, larger city of Pittsburgh in the 1960s, *Neighborhood* depicts elements of both industrial and agrarian culture and values. Rogers's now famous handmade cardigan sweaters, which he wore in every episode, are notable as a fleeting piece of residual, preindustrial culture wherein everyday attire was often made by mothers and grandmothers rather than by textile machines. In fact, all of the sweaters Rogers wore on *Neighborhood* were made by his mother and given to him as Christmas gifts throughout his life.[46]

A communicative ethos that juxtaposes the fast-paced nature of industrial life with the slower-paced living characteristic of an agrarian culture is also resonant in *Neighborhood* and represented most clearly in the figure of Mister Rogers's mailman, Mr. McFeely, named for Rogers's maternal grandfather, Fred McFeely, with whom Rogers was very close during his childhood and upbringing.[47] McFeely makes visits to both Rogers's home and the fantasy world of the Neighborhood of Make-Believe on nearly every episode. His imminent arrival is often communicated to the audience and to the host character of Mister Rogers by a change in background music from a settling and moderately paced piano overlay to a staccato, upbeat, piano-led interlude.

McFeely announces himself by repeating the phrase "Speedy Delivery" in an urgent, almost anxious manner. The juxtaposition between Rogers's slow, calm aura within his modest home and McFeely's excitable entrance onto the scene at the front door is somewhat startling, but Rogers always reacts to McFeely's arrival with a smile and a hint of excitement to reassure his audience of the nonthreatening nature of his fast-paced guest. He treats McFeely's arrival not as an unwelcome disturbance, which would be easy to do given the interruptive nature of the event, but rather as a moment that calls for a disciplined social adjustment wherein Rogers calmly and graciously turns his attention from interpersonal dialogue with the viewer toward greeting McFeely at the door, all the while maintaining an inclusive discourse whereby he holds both McFeely and the viewer in his communicative gaze. Rogers greets the mailman with a warm smile, indicating his pleasure at seeing McFeely. The two have a brief exchange wherein Rogers receives the mail and McFeely emphasizes that he is on a schedule and must soon be on his way. They say goodbye to one another, Rogers smiling genuinely throughout the exchange, and McFeely exits the scene.

The presence of the mailman is a sign of those outside the walls of the home and surrounding neighborhood that is the program's imagined community. As such, the mail system puts people in contact with those who are not physically present. Historically speaking, Rogers appears to be recapitulating here an iconic scene of the arrival of mail via the train, which disrupts the rhythms of the older, sleepy agrarian community. Rogers's joyful reception of the messenger who brings news from those who are not physically present enlarges the child's imagined community and constitutes a significant representation and intervention of the industrial characteristics of modern life, such as imagined community, speed, and the collapsing of time and space through rapid communications.

Although McFeely brings messages to Rogers from persons who are outside the purview of Rogers's home, Rogers and McFeely have a substantial, embodied relationship. They know one another, greet each other with the proper "How are you?" and engage in small talk. Though their relationship is constituted by labor and service, they treat one another as neighbors; they acknowledge each other's personhood and express care and concern for the other's wellbeing. The symbolic representation of this interaction can be read not only as a contrast between a fast, industrial culture and an older and slower agrarian one but also as a pedagogical representation of the demarcation of home/private and public life—a divide carried over from Victorian culture where the home space is characterized by peace, quiet, intimacy, the spiritual, and relief from the rapid pace and high demands of public life.[48] Still, the relationship is a fixture of the program and as such serves to connect the two worlds in a human and neighborly way. In a neighborhood, people know one another by name and engage with each other when they have encounters. This contrasts with the alienating forces of urbanization and industrialization in which individuals tend to live in varying degrees of anonymous isolation.

The simple, pleasant, and manageable villagelike iconography of *Neighborhood*, the straightforward and neighborly behaviors of the characters, and the moderate pacing of human action appear designed to quell human anxieties faced by children in their efforts to master "healthy" behaviors and ways of being during their early development. They also appear poised to provide relief for adults navigating a complex, postindustrial world in which stressors resulting from urban isolation, longer workdays, the destabilization of the family (e.g., increasing divorce rates), and Cold War anxieties created collective and individual unease.

Rogers tries to integrate industrialism with the American pastoral ideal, perhaps most significantly in his visits to factories, where he provides a kind of anthropology of how people make things. These film clips that detail the various mechanical production mechanisms and human work in places like a crayon factory are interspersed with B-roll of craftspeople and artisans, seemingly with the hope of calling forth the anthropocentric elements of material creation in both types of human production. Both depictions emphasize the work of human hands and the dignity of human work. Yet, as we know, the alienation of the factory worker from the product he makes and from the buyer of his product is not experienced by the artisan/craftsman. Further, the kind of satisfaction that is derived from creative, noncommodified crafting does not result from factory work.

In *The Machine in the Garden*, Marx discusses the powerful generation and regeneration of the concept of American pastoralism within the collective imagination and thus the language of cultural symbols in the United States. It is important to underscore that around the time that Rogers went into television, Marx was writing his book, describing the "uses of the pastoral ideal" in the construction and reconstruction of the American experience. Marx is particularly interested in identifying the ways that this ideal "has been incorporated in a powerful metaphor of contradiction—a way of ordering meaning and value" that elucidates the zeitgeist and inconsistencies of the postwar period. "What possible bearing can the urge to idealize a simple, rural environment have upon the lives men lead in an intricately organized, urban, industrial, nuclear-armed society?" he asks.[49] The idea that pastoralism serves a therapeutic function for moderns persuasively responds to Marx's question if we consider that the pastoral imaginary has been articulated in such American classics as Henry David Thoreau's *Walden*, the poetry of Ralph Waldo Emerson and Walt Whitman, Herman Melville's *Moby Dick*, and Henry

Adams's *The Education of Henry Adams.* This point appears most relevant to our understanding of Rogers's project in its discursive efforts to present to young and older viewers alike, a world that is human-centered, manageable, deeply connected to nature, and full of wonder in its ability to nurture curiosity and creativity.

Rogers's redeployment of the American pastoral includes an attention to the moral, emotional, and spiritual benefits that agricultural life and culture convey to the individual. David Danbom identifies "romantic agrarians," ostensibly disciples of Thoreau, who concentrate on the "moral, emotional, and spiritual benefits" that agricultural life and culture convey to the individual. The ideology of romantic agrarianism has been employed as a vehicle for criticizing industrial capitalism. It became extremely popular at the turn of the twentieth century, when American culture was undergoing a vast "sea change" in which the dominance of factory work and commercial values were bleeding into human relations in every sphere of life. As when new technologies of communication were introduced—radio, television, film—many accepted and welcomed such changes, while others resisted it. Part of the resistance took place by way of a framework of romantic agrarianism, which promoted a return to traditional values. Another took the form of unionizing. Some became radicalized. Others embraced Populism, which was agrarian, to a fault.[50] Rogers expresses this *romantic* agrarian view of life that has been developed and intertwined with an industrial, postwar suburban ethos. *Neighborhood* seems to embrace the nostalgia of romantic agrarianism as a subset of its redeployment of the American pastoral.

RESPONDING TO EXIGENCIES IN POSTWAR AMERICA

Rogers's emphasis on helping children (and adults) "manage" their feelings should be understood not only from a child development perspective but also from this broader social, economic, and

cultural context.[51] Rogers created *Mister Rogers' Neighborhood*
during an increasingly tumultuous time in modern American
history—the 1960s. As Todd Gitlin keenly summarizes in *The
Sixties: Years of Hope, Days of Rage*, the disruptive movements
of this decade—the birth of the New Left, the hippies, the civil
rights movement, the assassinations of key public figures on the
left, the sexual revolution, youth rebellion, and second-wave feminism—grew out of an immediate postwar decade characterized
by affluence and abundance.

During the 1950s a rhetoric of renewal and rebirth was
trumpeted by a mass media made increasingly influential by
the introduction of the television into the home environment. A
return to the intertwining of a cultivated nature and civilization
was embraced by the creation and settlement of suburbs, which
sought, once again, to offer relief from urban life. Shopping centers and automobiles brought about the possibility of unlimited
consumption. Improved roads promised to finally unite the large
landmass of the country and inspired a sense of endless individual
freedom of movement. A "flush of prosperity," an unprecedented
acquisition of consumer goods, and a thrill of military victory combined to produce a zeitgeist of national glory, success, wealth, and
freedom from the fears and anxieties brought about by the Depression and Second World War. "The idea of America had long been
shaped by the promise of opportunity in a land of plenty, but at
long last the dream seemed to be coming true," Gitlin writes.[52]
But underneath the surface of this "affluent state of mind" and
the rewarding payoffs for hard work and a willingness to accept
authority lay anxieties and frustrations about the changes and
costs of the new status quo.

Bestselling books of the period written by prominent social
critics reflected the more distressing phenomena of the new
mass culture. In 1950, David Riesman's book *The Lonely Crowd*
decried a new shift in the American social character in which he

posited that individuals were relying less on the influence of the
past authorities in their kin/group to inform their own conduct
of affairs and more on that of their peers. Gideon Lewis-Kraus
writes that Riesman thought that "contemporary society . . . was
best understood as chiefly 'other-directed,' where the inculcated
authority of the vertical (one's lineage) gives way to the muddled
authority of the horizontal (one's peers). The inner-directed person
orients herself by an internal 'gyroscope,' while the other-directed
person orients herself by 'radar.'"[53] Riesman's critique speaks to
a number of emerging characteristics of mass society, including
a deterioration of tradition, the decreasing authority of the family,
the increasing authority of the mass media, and the decline of
intergenerational interactivity. Indeed, the less radical critics of
the period were in agreement that "authentic community and tradition were being flattened by a mass society"—an issue Rogers
seeks to addresses on *Mister Rogers' Neighborhood* through the
representation of the "neighborhood" as community.[54]

In addition to the "flattening" of the sense of community
was an equally important concern about the "flattening" of the
individual. While earlier decades brought about anxieties over
ways industry was doing this to workers, especially in factories
where individuals performed like cogs in a larger machine, 1950s
corporate culture was producing a similar type of numbing of
middle-class, white-collar workers. The banality of a work life
in which one's work is not one's own but instead belongs to an
autonomous company who essentially owns one's time and labor
was producing what C. Wright Mills calls the ebbing of a once
independent middle class. In his 1951 book, *White Collar*, Mills
laments the rise of a sales mentality in which a deadening culture
of rationalization and bureaucratization reigns, and the death of a
middle class formerly employed by more entrepreneurial practices
such as small manufacturing, retail, and farming. These former
middle-class professions, Mills decries, have been replaced by

managers, salaried professionals, salespeople, and office work-ers—all of which require these middle-class workers to forfeit their liberty and authority to those higher on the corporate ladder. As articulated by Steven Rytina, "the angst of the frontier-bred free spirit pounded into the corporate cage made a timely theme" for Mills and other critics identifying these new, constraining structural changes in society that were affecting people at both the individual and collective levels.[55]

Later in the decade, muckrakers like Vance Packard, John Keats, and John Kenneth Galbraith criticized the rise of a con-sumer society. In *The Hidden Persuaders*, Packard exposes the manipulative strategies of advertising executives who exploit con-sumer anxieties. Keats critiques the 1950s "chrome car culture" and its celebration of the period's arguably irrational consumptive practices of the middle class in *The Insolent Chariots*, by show-ing how the average man earning less than $5,000 per year paid something like $1,250 per year in car payments.[56] That same year, Galbraith hoisted a critical spear into the "giddiness" of the cul-ture of abundance in his *The Affluent Society* by illustrating how while the United States was becoming more wealthy in the private sector, it continued to be poor in the public sector, charging that public services were being starved.

Rogers does his own work of social critique in *Neighborhood* by emphasizing the importance of human relationships and creative work over displays of wealth, glamor, and automation. In contrast to the glossy portrayals of the culture of affluence in the visual media of the time, *Neighborhood* exhibits an aesthetic of simplic-ity, frugality, and moderation. Each episode focuses on creative abilities of persons, with Rogers introducing an everyday object to the viewer on nearly every episode and then showing how it can be manipulated and interpreted within the social context in several different ways. No object is branded and, due to the noncommer-cial uniqueness of the initial PBS project, no advertisements were run before, during, or after the program. Moreover, Rogers often makes a point of tracing the object back to its origins in nature, celebrating the natural world and its gifts. Few, if any, consumptive practices are evident on the program.

In addition to object use and manipulation, Rogers celebrates the performative arts, such as music, dance, and theater, by showcasing a plethora of visiting artists who not only discuss their art form from the perspective of personal origins and cultural relevance but demonstrate it on screen. The focus on these enriching and rewarding human activities contributes to an emphasis on the range of creative expressions—expressions that take form without any need to buy something—that constitute the program's ethos. Such emphasis certainly works to counter the practices and values of "organization man," described in William H. Whyte's bestselling book, *The Organization Man* (1956), whose banal office tasks and focus on a dehumanizing obsession with productivity arguably contribute to the flattening and narrowing of human subjectivities.

Another of Rogers's aims is to provide viewers with models for coping in this dramatically changed and changing postwar world.[57] He does this not only through empathic verbal messaging and a focus on creative work, which we now know reduces the levels of cortisol (stress hormone) in the brain, but also through the visual rhetoric of the show's pastoral-inspired, neighborhood setting.[58] Visually, *Neighborhood* focuses less on elements of busy images of urban, industrial life, and more on the quiet and peaceful space of the home during daytime hours. Through this lens of the home as refuge, the program is constituted as a tranquil and friendly space inside of a quiet, slow-paced village attuned to the speed and rhythms of the body. It is a village in which people walk, ride bikes, or hop on the sole trolley that navigates the neighborhood streets. There seems to be a "soft veil of nostalgia" operating in *Neighborhood* that, while not a complete return to the pastoral, functions in dialogue with it.[59]

The interweaving of the American pastoral imaginary with the galloping growth of industrial life is historically tied to the rise of political Progressivism during the mid-to-late nineteenth century. The heart of this political movement sought to employ government as an agency of human welfare in addressing the problems caused by industrialization and urbanization.[60] Indeed, Barbara Ehrenreich and Deirdre English note that even "revolution" in the term "industrial revolution" is "too pallid a word," as "people were wrested from the land suddenly, by force; or more subtly, by the pressure of hunger and debt—uprooted from the ancient security of family, clan, and parish."[61] In response to this widespread uprooting and the embodied feelings regarding the loss of the old world, the antimodernist back-to-the-land movement critiqued urban-industrial society and its impact on human happiness and "right living." Through the publication *The Craftsman*, proponents of this movement urged Americans to leave their cities and purchase acreage in the country, arguing that rural living would foster a "restoration" and recapturing of "a free and natural existence that had been lost." In 1907 Bolton Hall, the author of *Three Acres and Liberty*, wrote, "We want to check . . . needless want and misery in the cities," pointing to the harsh conditions of urban life and the creation of consumer desires by commercial interests.[62] During the same period, sociologist Kenyon Butterfield, of the country life movement, celebrated the freedom of the farmer by waxing poetic about his ability to "read God's classics, listen to the music of divine harmonies, and roam the picture galleries of the eternal."[63] Similarly, rural journalist Liberty Hyde Bailey describes the city as "parasitic . . . elaborate and artificial."[64] Missing from Leo Marx's understanding of these pastoral movements is the reality that the prominent country life movement recognized the advancement of urban, industrial society as an unalterable reality. As such, they did not hope to eradicate it from existence but rather to reform rural life to the extent that it could and would remain a "vital and vibrant" sector of American society in order to "continue to serve the social and economic needs of an urban nation." In order to achieve these aims, country lifers aimed to make the countryside more like the city in regards to its efficiency, sophistication, organization, and mechanization and commercialization of operations. These steps, they thought, would help preserve "the essence of rural life."[65] Clearly, in the understanding of Rogers, whose father and grandfather were industrialists in a once dominantly agrarian community, the tension between industrialization and the social and ethical values of the agrarian community could be reconciled and negotiated in a kind of third way.

The transition from agrarian culture to industrial life meant significant changes for the structure of family life and the conceptualization of the child. As Spigel writes, while the child in agrarian culture was essential to the family income, industrialism shifted the societal understanding of children, as they were no longer directly essential to the economic survival of the family. In this new context, the child was reimagined as a "new sociological category in whom the middle-class adult culture invested new hopes and dreams."[66] Under the influence of Darwin's evolutionary theories, the child came to play a critical role in human evolution and as such, its habits and activities were no longer considered trivial matters. Rather, children became of critical importance to the survival of the entire species due to the fact that the old rural society was diminishing and a new society centered in cities and constituted economically by a new world of professions was forming. In a world changing every day due to the rapid developments in science and technology, the child, in her ability to quickly learn new information and skills, became more important than ever for the survival and success of the family and family name into the new century. In this new setting, the former educational methods of imitation that take place within the family setting (and are heavily reliant on the mother and her natural abilities) are no longer relevant; instead, pedagogy occurs outside, and a sense that the "child cannot be left to women" arises and power over the education of young children is seized by "child experts."[67]

At the turn of the century, as birthrates and infant mortality rates dropped, parents began to view their children more as individualized persons with distinct personalities in need of moral support and guidance. Simultaneously, child labor practices among black, immigrant, and working-class families became widespread as a way to achieve some measure of familial income security. Out of this milieu, "child-saving" movements emerged out of the larger Progressive movement that attempted to address industrial practices of employing children, labeled as child abuse, through the proposal of broad political reforms for children of diverse races and classes.[68] This sentimentalization of the child, or as Viviana Zelizer conceptualizes it, "sacralization," was a relatively new phenomenon in the collective structures of feeling that took place at the turn of the century. Notably, this new sacralization of the child led to new measures to protect children from harm, which resulted in their increased domestication and supervision—a legacy that carries into *Neighborhood*, which occurs ritually inside the safe space of the home.

At the heart of this new social shift, children were viewed as both innocents and arbiters of progress; as such, their image "was not only at the center of power struggles at home" but also served to "legitimate the institutional power of scientists, policy-makers, and media experts who turned their attention to children's welfare."[69] Such developments contributed to even more accumulation of power for men, whose occupations in the public sphere now reached into the realm of childhood, a space formerly governed by women, and the domestic realm. "Now it is as if the masculinist imagination takes a glance over its shoulder and discovers it has left something important behind in 'woman's sphere'—the child. This child—the new child of the twentieth century—is not valued,

like the child of patriarchy, simply as an heir. The child is conceived as a kind of evolutionary protoplasm, a means of *control*
over society's not-so-distant future."[70] This emerging social interest
in the child was thus capitalized upon by men in the medical and
other scientific professions who presented themselves as experts
in child-raising and child development. Through sustained efforts
of persuasion, in which they "wooed their female constituency,"
these agents effectively turned motherhood into a science and redirected its origins away from the innate process led by women in
the home and community, toward a scientific model of expertise
led by male doctors and researchers.[71] The relationship between
such self-appointed experts and the mothers who listened to them
was never one of equality, as it "rested on the denial or destruction
of women's autonomous sources of knowledge: the old networks
of skill-sharing, the accumulated lore of generations of mothers."[72]
Within this context, women found themselves in crisis, confused
about their role in the new modern world, questioning the knowledge passed along to them during their upbringing, and finding
themselves with little authority in any realm of the social order.

This is the framework into which, decades later, Rogers,
McFarland, and the *Mister Rogers' Neighborhood* television project fit. Rogers, who became a child development expert himself
in order to gain legitimacy as a producer of educational children's television (and other multimedia material, including books,
records, and pamphlets), envisioned his program as a pedagogical
endeavor aimed at providing a "healthy" alternative to the content
and values prominently displayed in commercial, vaudevillian, and
slapstick television entertainment of the time. Moreover, he seems
to be interested in providing a model of interpersonal communication exchange rooted in an older, agrarian network of human
interaction in which cultivation of land, stability, continuity, and
community maintenance foster the practices of neighborliness,
friendship, and cooperation are reasserted as the order of the day.

Such an ethos appears aimed to counter an ever-emerging zeit-geist constituted by the production of a competitive, survivalist world of individual achievement characteristic of 1950s corporate culture and the age of abundance. In this context where "an old world was dying and a new one was being born,"[73] Rogers appears steadfast and keen in his discursive project to recover for himself and others the human-centered social dynamics of this old world some seventy years into the new American order of industrial capitalism, and to display this dynamic on the screen.

CHRISTIAN BELIEFS AND MASS ENTERTAINMENT IN CONFLICT

Beyond identifying Rogers's project as a redeployment of the American pastoral, given the cultural anxieties brought about by galloping industrialization, it is important to situate Rogers within the cultural and political lineage of the debates that took place between intellectuals, Christians, and the entertainment industry. The struggle over the evolution of American theater involved an alliance between religious citizens and the educated wealthy elite that was held together by the dominant Victorian social system.[74] In response to the emergence of theatrical and later cinematic entertainment that featured vaudevillian forms of artistic representation, these dominant forces in American life often came together to critique and decry what they often viewed as the transmission of undesirable values and tastes.[75] As William Romanowski has observed, "cultural elitists derided popular culture on grounds of aesthetic taste; religious moralists feared its influence and yearned for disciplinary control."[76] What resulted from this ongoing struggle during the mid-to-late nineteenth century was the discursive creation of the categories of high and low culture by "the arbiters of culture" who sought to categorize and differentiate types of fare and assign them as appropriate or inappropriate to different social groups of people.[77]

According to Lawrence Levine, these arbiters "were convinced that maintaining and disseminating pure art, music, literature, and drama would create a force for moral order and help to halt the chaos threatening to envelop the nation."[78] William D. Romanowski is careful to note that these categories do not merely describe created products. Rather, they are "ways of thinking that affect the policies, practices, and institutions" (such as schools and museums) of modern society.[79] "The new industrial democracy," which included an emerging culture of abundance, popular culture, and mass entertainment, rivaled the older Victorian cultural model for dominance. This tension is illustrated well in Levine's descriptions of Henry James's observations of a changing America represented in the face of the non-English-speaking urban immigrant of the late nineteenth and early twentieth centuries. Upon visiting Boston's Athenaeum, James came away with the following feeling of disgust: "This honored haunt of all the most civilized— library, gallery, temple of culture" had become "completely out of countenance by the mere masses of brute ugliness. . . . It was heart-breaking."[80] To cultural arbiters of a formerly predominant singular, homogenous American Victorian, Anglo-Saxon culture like James, Levine notes, "it was not merely tradition that was in danger but taste itself."[81] It is within this conflicted setting of emerging ethnic diversity and cultural multiplicity that film, the phonograph, and the radio were born and that Victorian intellectual and religious agents experimented with different and varied ways of negotiating their cultural dominance inside this new shifting terrain of mass culture.

At the beginning of the twentieth century, the notion that the United States was a "Christian nation" was a standard, foundational given for most Americans. Protestant leaders saw themselves as setting the norms for American public life, "relish[ing] their status as the established religion." These leaders' sense of authority "came with a God-given responsibility for the moral and religious character of the nation and a sacred duty to work toward its improvement."[82] In general, the Protestant establishment of the early to mid-twentieth century identified its core values, with an ardent emphasis on the conscience of the individual, justice, and stewardship as part and parcel of American democratic values. The preservation of these values, along with the institutions that supported and purveyed them, was of key importance to ensure the cultural reproduction of a Christian-American ethos. These dominant, but not necessarily hegemonic, goals contained in them profound contradictions that would prove difficult to negotiate when dealing with the challenges of what would arguably become the most powerful influencing tool ever known to man—cinematic and televisual technology. According to Romanowski, the Protestant establishment "wanted social control and individual freedom, progress and traditional moral purity, corporate profits and the common good," unaware of the fact that these binomial objectives contain irresolvable contradictions at their very core.[83] Questions about how to go about ensuring the reproduction of Protestant culture in America in the face of the dual rise of cinema and cultural pluralism were prominent among these groups during the earlier part of the century.[84]

Romanowski notes that when cinematic content challenged the normative Protestant values, most mainline leaders and believers did not partake in boycotting or censorship efforts as some of the more conservative ones did. Rather, because cultural separatism was not a practice typical of most Protestants, and because they understood themselves largely as "cultural caretakers responsible for securing a fitting place for movies in American life," mainline Protestants took an integrative approach to the challenges posed by the new medium.[85] This approach is in stark contrast to the efforts of the American Catholic church, who saw its population gain in numbers at the beginning of the twentieth century, and whose leaders actively spoke out against representations of "immorality" in cinema, organizing efforts to censor the public displays of countless Hollywood and foreign films.[86] Like such Catholic leaders, however, Protestant leaders perceived early on the ways that cinema was becoming a critical tool for socialization. Since there already existed a deep desire on the part of such Protestant leaders to integrate Protestant teachings into all aspects of American life, it follows that such leaders were eager to see movie producers work "in harmony with the home, school, and church to promote a truly healthy Americanism." Romanowski points out that "even if they were not always frequent moviegoers themselves, the Protestant elite recognized that film contributed to the marketplace of ideas. They saw legal censorship as un-American, undemocratic, impractical, unnecessary, and prone to political graft and corruption. At the same time, they believed that a reasonable measure of self-restraint on the part of moviemakers was acceptable—even necessary—to protect the public welfare."[87] Clearly, the Protestant establishment did not see the depth of the dilemma that was beginning to emerge between the principles of freedom of speech and artistic expression, which involved the expression of values, and their desire to see the continuation of the dominance of the Protestant ethos.[88] In the crux of this dilemma Rogers managed to make a televisual intervention that remained true to his Christian convictions within an increasingly secular and pluralistic public sphere.

During the decades that *Neighborhood* ran on PBS, Rogers responded to questions regarding what television shows he viewed by noting that he did not actually watch television. In autobiographical recollections of his upbringing, he notes his study and playing of the piano; his special relationship to his grandfather Fred McFeely, who encouraged him in this practice; his role as newspaper writer for the high school paper; his election as senior class president; and the bullying he endured as a young boy. His family was highly active in the Presbyterian church and it was expected that after graduation from college, Rogers would go into the seminary to become a Presbyterian minister. His path made a slight turn after his sophomore year of college at Dartmouth, when he realized that he wanted to major in music instead of Romance languages. He then transferred to Rollins College, a school with a more robust music program. Still, his track to seminary school continued and by his senior year in 1951 he was accepted to Western Theological Seminary in Pittsburgh. It was not until he watched television for the first time that year, during a break from school, that he realized that he wanted to pursue creative work options in the new medium. His initial perception of television as being exciting as a new medium and at the same time distasteful in its imagery provided Rogers, he remembers, with the motivation to pursue a career in the industry in order to create better programming. If we consider his response within the context of his religious, elite, upper-class upbringing, Rogers appears to be a descendent of the intellectual, Protestant establishment perspective wary of mass entertainment forms.

In "Children's TV: What Can the Church Do about It?," Rogers discusses his project from a religious, ministerial perspective, asking his readers if they are aware that children see and hear an average of three thousand hours of television before they begin their schooling and that by the time they finish schooling they will have spent more time "with the television than they have in the classroom."[89] He then asserts that, in regards to the content they will have consumed by this point in their lives, children will have seen mostly "charmingly cynic, sardonic, sadistic animated tripe with slick puns, inversions and asides."[90] The negative characterization that Rogers gives to this children's programming exceeds his earlier concerns about pie throwing. These programs, according to Rogers, are downright insidious and seductive. Here, he is clearly raising an urgent alarm and attempting to awaken an audience that may be confusing the charm of animation and human performance with benign entertainment. "To the occasional viewer and listener children's tv fare may seem 'harmless' enough: but a steady diet of the weak always magically winning and the villains always being the big ones, of people getting flattened out one second and popping into shape the next, of conniving and teasing and hurting and belittling and stopping tears with elaborate gifts . . . is a steady diet of this what we would choose to feed our children's needs?"[91] Rogers poses for his audience a cascade of questions designed to prompt the church to face the facts of a now dominant televisual culture, which it seems to continue to ignore and deny. Are parents aware that they are condoning the behavior depicted on the screen? he asks. "Without knowing it," he writes, "we are encouraging our children to disrespect, disobey, dispel much that we feel is important in our heritage. Are our children (and the children whom the Church has never been able to reach), being fed a slick stimulating sound-tracked trash 1,000 hours a year while our Church schools try to teach the opposite with posters, crayons and paste in one tenth the time?"[92] Rogers's fears regarding children's consumption of television are centered upon the fundamental concern that the representations depicted on the new device undermine the education and values disseminated to children by traditional institutions—institutions that were established, in part, to communicate certain sets of knowledge to young people to aid in their development and upbringing.[93] He has clearly already made the decision to move into this cultural vacuum left by the church's misunderstanding of the situation and inaction.

Rogers's concern here addresses, like many critiques of the time, the undermining of the social and ethical lessons and values taught in schools and the church. Employing a tone of deep urgency and concern, uncharacteristic of his television persona, he writes, "We must know this . . . we must know that we're failing our children but, either we won't let ourselves admit it, or we think that there's nothing we as the Church can do about it." Employing the persuasion technique of problem-solution organization, Rogers, with fervor, offers a bold solution. For its values to regain a platform in American culture, the church must move beyond the limits of its institutional, historical tradition. The church can no longer represent its values as solely the values of the Protestant tradition or the values of an unquestioned, dominant worldview. It must reach beyond religious, class, race, and economic differences and approach a universal child for whom it deeply cares.

> There *IS* something we can do! But, it's not so simple (or cheap) as writing letters of complaint! Irate parents who by the thousands have written to local tv stations bewailing the frenetic inferior children's fare have repeatedly received courteous curt replies: "You can always turn your television set off!" That may be true—but you can't do it without becoming the ogres in the house: just as tv has been intimating to your child that big people are! But we as the Church <u>CAN</u> do something very effective. We can begin to *produce* and promote television programs for children as an expression of caring for the children of the whole country. We can communicate to a child that he is accepted as he is: happy, sad, angry, lonely, exactly as he is. We can do what commercial broadcasters fail to do over and over again and that is to give the child a healthy choice on the television dial. I say we <u>can</u> because some of us already <u>have</u>!

Rogers's exhortation to action is not in the least utopian. He offers the church not only a plan of action but the experience (10-plus years) that he has already gained. He calls for those in the church to get involved in television production by describing the "overwhelming" positive responses his program has received since he began his work with *The Children's Corner* in 1954. In an appeal to maintain the attention of his readers through a dire sense of urgency, Rogers prefaces his call to action with testimonies of public praise for his efforts to produce wholesome and interpersonal programming. "Please make your program longer"; "You're the only tv person who treats my children like real people"; and "You're my favorite," he quotes viewers writing to him.

Rogers does not point to explicit religious instruction—nor does his program. Rather, he urges readers to get involved in making programming that communicates care and worth to young audiences, leaving out any connection of such care to the Divine. That is to say, he removes the signifier of the divinity (Christ) from the gospel message. By breaking out of the confines of the explicit, traditional language of Christianity, Rogers frees himself to blend gospel teaching with a modern understanding of child development to construct a pedagogy and rhetorical framework that meets the exigency of the historical and cultural moment as he perceives it. His primary aim thus becomes helping children to feel loved and accepted as they exist within the array of emotional states experienced by all persons living in the world. Rogers could be trying to motivate Christians to support his media forays into the child developmental psychology of the period that appear geared more toward liberal secularized ethics than conventional religion. Rogers's explicit project is to set a countervailing force against the charming cynicism, sadistic puns, and inversions and asides that he feels do not mitigate anxiety and confusion but actually foster it.

Rogers's rhetorical choices are notable in several ways. For one, as I mentioned above, they are devoid of the explicit religious language of piety that one might expect given the fact that he is addressing an church audience. That choice could reflect the growing exclusion of religion from the public square and the postwar emphasis on pluralism. It could also likely be that Rogers continues the approach of the social gospel tradition, which was not pietistic. Elsewhere, Rogers does not shy away from religious language; in a 1975 transcription of a *Protestant Radio Hour* featuring Rogers, he ties his messages of love, forgiveness, acceptance, neighborliness, and care directly to the gospel. "It seems to me that one of our most important tasks as parents and Christian educators is to help and encourage both children and their adults to discover their own unique ways of expressing love," he begins. Later in the document he discusses how Jesus inspires acceptance and emphasizes the importance of loving a person for who they are "on the inside." "Christianity to me is a matter of being accepted as we are. Jesus certainly wasn't concerned about people's stations in life or what they looked like or whether they were perfect in behavior or feeling. . . . Children often show me the clothes they're wearing and tell me that their pants or their dresses are new. After I tell them that I like their clothes I often add, 'But you know the part of you that I like best; it's the person *inside*!'"[94] Here, he ties his core beliefs to the teachings of Christ and notes the ways that he tries to model Christ in his behaviors and attitudes. He does so on a religious radio program, despite excluding religious language in secular spaces in order to reach a broader audience.

Second, Rogers's rhetoric regarding care, affect, and its connection to "health" is deeply engaged with the contemporary theories of child-rearing and child development stemming from the work of Erik Erikson and popularized by Dr. Benjamin Spock. In this rhetoric, language of health replaces language of grace and salvation.[95] Thus, he advocates for his readers to come together to produce "healthy" programming choices for children, in contrast with the commercial stations' "trash." Such a rhetorical move is indicative of the ways Rogers sees his project as allied with the interests of the church and its behavioral and cultural curricula, a perceived need on the part of Rogers to speak the values of Christian ethics through secular language, and Rogers's attempt to integrate Christian ethics with child development understanding of the time.[96]

Finally, Rogers addresses the question of funding and the church's either inadequate resources or insufficient commitment. Thus far, his program has had to rely on the budget of educational television or the support of a local department store to underwrite his program: "The Church has always had to retreat to radio jingles and spot quilt makers." This funding situation cannot be the basis on which to launch a project that calls for a "long-range excellence in children's television." Rather, such a ministry would be fulfilled only if secure funding for long-range television production were made possible. This is Rogers's challenge to the church should it want to have agency and influence in this cultural moment. Only then, he implies, would there be a choice in the television market for viewers. With passion, he tells the church that this is practically its last chance to assert both paramount values to their tradition—individual freedom (here in relation to consumer choice) and social influence. "The time of speaking to our children in an entertaining yet SANE way through television has never been more appropriate. It is not fair for parents (and children) not to have a choice. It is evident that the commercial telecaster will not give this choice. The Church *can* offer that choice by recognizing what we already know: that television *is* the major source of broad communication in our world today. Let's find the money to produce, and promote long-range excellence in children's television. What a magnificent ministry it really can be!"[97] As an alternative to writing letters to broadcasters in order to censor displeasing television content, Rogers suggests creative action by offering his work as a model of success in this new cultural setting. In order to influence the behavioral and cultural instruction of the young to ensure the maintenance of once dominant Protestant values, Rogers proposes an alliance between individual agents such as himself and the church. He sees in the church an old and successful institution that can swerve into a new field of cultural and political action and construction of consciousness. From this perspective, we can view Rogers as part of a tradition of more liberal mainline Protestants working within media to promote the maintenance of traditional cultural and ethical values in American society.[98] Rogers seeks to empower his Christian peers to assert themselves more directly into the production of television. He hopes that taking this action will lead to the development of choices in television programming that reflect his values, which he feels are not currently represented on the small screen.

BLURRING BOUNDARIES: TELEVISION AND FAMILY COMMUNICATION

Rogers's perspective on the family's critical position as educator of the young, as constituted by the deep and essential bond created by constant contact and communication, is informed by his advanced academic studies with University of Pittsburgh child development psychologist Dr. Margaret McFarland. McFarland asserted that all education in our society is founded upon in the interactions of infants and young children and their parents. As such, the family, she wrote, "is the primary educational institution."[99] Indeed, she criticized the development of a primary educational system that avoids the family altogether as an educational unit. McFarland and Rogers saw an opportunity with television to make a cultural and pedagogical intervention into the American family unit, especially with regard to its educational role in child development and upbringing. Television, like radio before it, thus posed opportunities to transcend the former institutionalized educational system hindered by its nonfamilial organizational model, class-structured economic inequalities, and curriculum differences.[100]

Through collaboration with McFarland, Rogers developed a deep understanding of how adults could communicate with children by taking into account not only the capacity of television for the production of communication with the wider public but also the new understanding of the child's consciousness as an amalgam of cognitive and affective development, which involves specific stages. Drawing from Erikson, whose work observing and working with children produced breakthrough understandings of the development of personality, McFarland and Rogers attempted to translate their knowledge about healthy child development through the new medium of television.

Writing in 1950, Erikson details new conclusions in psychology about how persons develop neurosis. Whereas previously, "psychopathology" professionals pondered whether neurosis resided in the individual or in his society, new research had produced a nuanced consensus that held that "a neurosis is psycho- *and* somatic, psycho- *and* social, and *inter*personal."[101] Such a conclusion shifts attention away from the individual himself and emphasizes instead his psychological development within the larger social system—the most important and influential of which is the family unit. Erikson's groundbreaking therapeutic approach stresses a process of observing the child in his family environment to gain greater understanding of the child's internal conflict, engaging in interpersonal talk therapy with the child to assist him in articulating his feelings, dialoguing with all family players about the new breakthroughs in understanding the child's perspective, and figuring out ways, collectively, to manage and resolve the problematic dynamic. Erikson's discoveries were adopted and employed by McFarland and Rogers on *Neighborhood*. As we will see, this perspective arguably served as the foundational footing for *Mister Rogers' Neighborhood*. Rogers had been instructed by his Pittsburgh Theological Seminary professors during his final semesters there to do research in the field of child development at the Arsenal Family and Children's Center.[102] In planning the structured contents of each program, Rogers worked closely with McFarland, his primary consultant and mentor. The two worked to construct scenarios, stories, and messages keenly tailored to the educational and psychological needs of children as understood by the Arsenal Center's founders, Spock, Erikson, and McFarland herself.[103]

Reading magazine articles by such scientific "experts" became a nationwide practice among women. The new child psychology was a "child-centered model," which called for mothers not only to care for her child's body and health but for the mind "and its rate of development."[104] As a result of these additional pressures, along with the increasing stress on the importance of early life and its connection to raising a well-adjusted child, mothers found themselves in a role with more pressures and yet lacking in the specialized knowledge needed to succeed in their changing role.

Within this sphere of heightened anxiety regarding child-raising, Dr. Benjamin Spock stepped in to quell some of the collective parental distress by reassuring mothers (and fathers) that their natural instincts were more than likely correct and thus empowering them to redevelop confidence in their abilities. With this new outlook and in other ways that broke from early twentieth-century psychological consensus on parenting, Spock's intervention into the sphere of child-raising advice with the publication of his 1946 book, *Common Sense Book of Baby and Child Care*, marked a deep break with the predominant thinking in the field of child raising during the pre–World War II period. In contrast to expert John B. Watson's theories on child-rearing, which emphasized the treatment of infants and toddlers as small adults who should never be kissed or hugged, Spock argued that children needed love, not coercion.[105] In *Baby and Childcare*, he encourages parents to trust their instincts and preaches that traditional disciplining methods, which he equates to punishment, are far less effective than the modeling of good behavior by parents in raising well-adjusted, emotionally and socially healthy adults.[106] "Discipline comes from the word 'disciple,' and really means 'to teach'.... the main source of good discipline is growing up in a loving family—being loved and learning to love in return," writes Spock.[107]

Spock's approach to child raising integrated psychology, educational theory, and pediatrics; he was especially influenced by Sigmund Freud and shared Freud's assumption that the early years of life determined the personality of the adult.[108] He also was inspired by John Dewey's democratic educational approach. Through this integration of psychology, education, and medicine, combined with his personal and practical experience, Spock advised mothers and fathers how to prevent their children from developing antisocial and emotionally impaired habits of being. His key pedagogical points instructed parents to respond to their child's needs, to foster a close, secure attachment with the child, and to give and model love within the entire family.[109]

As a pediatrician, Spock was beloved by mothers and children alike. Part of his charm had to do with his other-oriented dynamic that stressed mutuality and respect. A 1998 *New York Times* obituary of Spock states that part of his success was due to his concern for the feelings of his patients and their parents, noting that he wore business suits to work instead of the traditional white coat in order to make his visitors feel more relaxed.[110] Spock's focus on mutuality, concern with the feelings of others, and practice of making others feel comfortable in his presence harkens to the style and approach of Rogers, who emphasizes his show's offering of ritual expressions of care for his television viewers.

By 1952 *The Common Sense Book of Baby and Child Care* had sold more than four million copies, demonstrating an enthusiastic reception by a public that could not get enough advice texts.[111] Like his predecessors in the area of giving advice on child-rearing, Spock published widely in women's magazines such as *Redbook* and *Ladies' Home Journal*, offering his democratic, "common sense" style of parenting. One could argue that the magazines and books proffering advice on child-rearing acted as a precursor to the televisual presence within the family of a credible male stranger, who communicates with mothers in a helpful, authoritative way. In contrast to the presentation of textual advice, the television, which does not require the skill of reading in order to be understood, allows such authorities to, in a double irony, speak directly to the child, bypassing both mother and father as the primary educators. Prior to Spock, the primary assumption that undergirded such practices was that both the child and the mother were passive receptors, that the expert knew best, and that therefore it was the responsibility of the lay adults, as led by the "experts," to "generate moral values in the young by guarding the gates to knowledge."[112] Although Spock still assumed a position of "expert," his primary message to readers placed agency and confidence in parents by encouraging them, in overarching fashion, to trust their own lay knowledge and biological instincts. Spock's discursive intervention marked a sharp turn within expert consensus—and, with the success of his book, society at large—in regards to child-rearing approaches and practices.[113]

Examining and analyzing these documents and placing them in the sociocultural context of the discussions regarding television and the family, the rhetoric of the "technological sublime," the cultural critiques of the 1950s and 1960s (regarding alienation, rampant individualism, loss of community bonds, unbridled consumption, etc.), Christian responses to mass entertainment, and postwar child development theory, contextualizes and situates the approaches and aims of Rogers and McFarland in ways that reveal the curious paradox of the television medium's parasocial affects. In an increasingly alienating, advanced capitalist society, television promises to bring people closer together and to transcend the physical and temporal divides that exist in the new mass society. So too, the then novel theories on child development during the period stress the importance of creating and nurturing interpersonal bonds between adult caregivers and children. While Rogers and McFarland emphasize the unique teledialogical opportunities for human connection that television affords and attempt to capitalize on such knowledge, that paradox of the simulacra—the perceived feelings of closeness and community that television inspires juxtaposed with the reality that real connections between screen actors and viewers are not actually being made—remains. Indeed, Rogers and McFarland made a unique and revolutionary discovery in the moment when they understood the parasocial capacities of the medium for teledialogism with the family—an understanding that came to inform their conception of the program as a pedagogical intervention in the family.

2

 Creating the Dialogic

CHRISTIANITY, CHILD DEVELOPMENT,
AND THE PARASOCIAL

IN A DECEMBER 1, 1966, letter to Margaret Rasmussen, editor of the Association for Childhood Education International, based in Washington, DC, Margaret McFarland asks for the association's help in notifying parents in select cities (Boston, New York, Chicago, Philadelphia, Schenectady, and San Francisco) of the debut of the new educational television program *Misterogers Neighborhood*.[1] McFarland praises Rogers as both a "talented dramatic artist" and "musician," and calls particular attention to his studies in child development in her own graduate program at the University of Pittsburgh. She notes Rogers's studious efforts to learn about child development "in order to make his communication with children appropriate for them" and specifically cites his direct work with children at the Arsenal Child Study Center as informing the quality of his television programming.

According to McFarland, when Rogers first came to the graduate program, she found him "unusually observant and empathic with children," noting that he wrote "songs that spoke deeply to them." She explains the center's interest in Rogers's programs "as a mode of studying the significance of training in the dynamics of child development for the creative artist who is communicating with children." From her perspective, the "only way to combat inappropriate television for children is by the availability of good programs" like *Misterogers Neighborhood*, and she describes Rogers's creation of the program as a promising example of television artistry informed by new work in child development. In light of this, she asks Rasmussen if communication could be sent out to local groups of the Association for Childhood Education International to help create an audience for the new program. She follows this request with another: to encourage parents and children to write either to Rogers or to their local station offices once they have watched. This gesture, she notes, should help in maintaining interest in "the development of such programs on a national basis." Further, she states, the evaluations of professionals who work with children are "helpful if written to Mr. Rogers at WQED," as "he is very eager to supply whatever insight is available to him in subsequent programs."

McFarland's letter captures well the collaborative and dialogic nature of *Neighborhood*'s beginnings and the dynamics at work in Rogers's professional life. Rogers studied child development at an advanced level with rising experts in the field such as McFarland and Erik Erikson—then and now considered groundbreaking and still relevant to contemporary understandings of the needs of children. Rogers became McFarland's student while studying pastoral counseling at the Pittsburgh Theological Seminary, where he attended graduate classes during his lunch break at Pittsburgh's new community broadcasting station, WQED. In this period, Rogers was engaged in a multidisciplinary dialectical practice of learning that simultaneously involved television production and creation, child development theory and observation, and theological and pastoral study.

In this chapter, I focus my analysis on Fred Rogers's visionary and retrospective writings and articulations on television, children, and his televisual creation, *Mister Rogers' Neighborhood*, in order to ascertain how his understanding of the program is nourished by the discoveries made in the observational settings of the Arsenal Family Center. In this novel approach led by Arsenal founders McFarland, Erikson, and Benjamin Spock, the teacher learns from observing how the child develops in her own subjectivity and social competence. The child-centered observational approach of Arsenal constitutes the fulcrum of Rogers's new understanding of communication with children that could be deployed via the television medium. In particular, Rogers's understanding of Erikson's "8 Ages of Man" and the guiding presence of Erikson's theory of child development at Arsenal provide the theoretical and practical ground on which Rogers develops his vision of an adult ("Mister Rogers") who plays a primary role in building trust with and a sense of autonomy and initiative in the child viewer.

Rogers's profound understanding of the power of dyadic communication—characterized by acceptance, affirmation, compassion, and mutuality—was born of two defining moments in his young life, in which he found healing through the development of an "I-Thou" relationship of mutuality and care. Both instances, one defined by his relationship to God and the other by his relationship to an adolescent peer, serve as foundational parables and meaning-making narratives in Rogers's life. Rogers integrates novel child development theory on the importance of helping children develop a greater sense of awareness and self-worth with a Christian understanding of the human being as created in the image of God and thus fundamentally creative, life-giving, and designed for social life. I further connect Rogers's philosophy of education to the ideas of John Dewey, who believed in the uniqueness of the individual and in an education imperative that directs learning toward the subject's dialogical participation in democratic life. Rogers reworks Erikson and Dewey's understandings of personhood and especially of young people through an incorporation of unconditional love and service to others in the Christian sense. In doing so, Rogers lays the groundwork for a pedagogy that positions adults as child educators whose primary role must be to encourage creativity and foster the unique abilities of the individual within an ethos of community membership. Moving away from a theocentric rhetorical orientation within the Presbyterian Christian framework, Rogers's practice of listening and responding, inspired by his Protestant, democratic, American belief in individual freedom and the worth of the individual, is in fact anthropocentric.

As part of his pedagogical communication strategy of dialectic interaction, Rogers developed a sense of the parasocial with his viewer. From the foundation of a dynamic and sophisticated understanding of the needs of children, Rogers frames his overarching aim as showcasing the simple acts of finding wonder in life's experiences and places this aim in stark contrast with the commercial fare of the time, which he characterizes as escapist and violent.

Rogers created a third way response to his keen reading of the spirit of the times. In rejecting the theocentric approaches of both the Pietist and neo-orthodox wings of the contemporary American Presbyterian church and by creating a theologically sound practice of healing hearts through an anthropocentric orientation characterized by I-Thou communication, Rogers was able to make a significant cultural intervention on a mass scale that reflects his own negotiation with a new postwar, increasingly secular, cultural environment. Rogers's inchoate search for an effective means of communicating with children, as bearers of a unique subjectivity, found its answer in the empirically based methodology of Arsenal. In this disciplined observational setting, Rogers not only discovered Erikson's theories of child development but also had an opportunity to experiment with different communication approaches with actual children at Arsenal. In these interactions, and in reflexive dialogue with McFarland, Rogers discovered that his own lived experience of drawing upon the pain of his childhood wounds in order to heal others constitutes the core of his artistic power and creativity.

Rogers's quest for the transformation of the Presbyterian ministry into a practice based on an I-Thou model coincides with discussions that arose during the 1950s and 1960s at the Pittsburgh Theological Seminary. In a collection of handwritten notes dated 1984, he wrote that "those who preach to broken hearts will remain relevant in contemporary life" while "those who wed themselves to the spirit of the times will find themselves widowed."[2] Here, he intervenes in discussions concerning the mission of the church in the current historical moment. While avoiding taking sides with either the traditional Pietists or the neo-Orthodox reformers in the church, who constitute the two primary poles of the discussion, Rogers offers a third way. While affirming the reform spirit of the social gospel branch in celebrating the timeless relevance of the gospel's directive to minister to broken people, he warns his audience against the lure of becoming too attached to the messages and spirit of the times. His third way, based on the I-Thou relationship of Christian care, sets up a general societal milieu of values that arguably addresses the problem of poverty and isolation in society at large through a social pedagogy that stresses an ethic of care as practice (rather than as a set of rules). This pedagogy includes both acts of caring and habits of mind, which he models on *Neighborhood*.[3] Thus, the ministry need not duplicate the work of the state, nor should the church blindly follow the tenets of "sociological urban, and psychological concerns."[4] The approach to ministry should not be to "sell our theology to people," Rogers writes. Rather, its mission should be grounded in the question, "How can I help you?"[5]

Rogers parts with both the theological and the social activist approach to ministry. Instead, he develops the concept of an anthropocentric approach to human suffering. This anthropocentric approach to addressing the condition of human suffering appears in notes found at the Fred Rogers Archive, in which Rogers ponders the wisdom of psychology and modern Protestant theologians. In this chapter, I show that Rogers's anthropocentric approach—his third way—enables him to produce a television program for children that is deeply rooted in foundational gospel messages of love and care and is simultaneously free of christological language and iconography.

DIALOGIC BEGINNINGS

Prior to the creation of *Neighborhood*, Fred Rogers produced and costarred (behind the scenes as a puppeteer) in the WQED children's program *The Children's Corner*. He cowrote both the scripts and the music with the program's star, Josie Carey. The program consisted of conversations between Carey and Rogers's puppets—Daniel Striped Tiger, Henrietta Pussycat, King Friday, and Xscape Owl—who later carried on their respective roles in *Neighborhood*. In 1955, the show, which launched in April of 1954, won a Sylvania Award for the best locally produced children's program in the country. Later, Rogers and Carey produced a similar show for NBC Saturday morning distribution.[6]

Starting in 1954, while working full-time producing *The Children's Corner*, Rogers took courses for his master's degree in divinity on a part-time basis at the Pittsburgh Theological

Seminary. It was through his seminary study that Rogers began his relationship with Dr. Margaret B. McFarland. The seminary eventually required that he take a course in counseling for his degree, and when he communicated his interest in working with children, the course instructor suggested that he contact McFarland, who was a professor of both early childhood development and psychology at the University of Pittsburgh and the director of the recently established Arsenal Family and Children's Center. For eight years, Rogers's course of study at the seminary overlapped and comingled with his empirical studies on children and child development at Arsenal. It is not surprising to see an amalgam of his study in both institutions in his television ministry.

Arsenal provided a space where graduate students could study child development, and McFarland encouraged Rogers to employ the center for this task. He subsequently spent many hours watching, listening, and learning from the children at Arsenal.[7] Arsenal's methodology, based on theory and practice, relied on the close observation of children.[8] The center was set up as an educational laboratory where adult caretakers taught and learned from the very young children: children attended school at Arsenal, while teachers, scholars, doctors, and graduate students taught and observed them in order to gain further understanding and to formulate and reformulate child development practices. The pedagogical phenomenon occurring at Arsenal was innovative in many ways, but its most distinctive characteristic was its dialogical setup: the teacher learning from observing how the child develops in her own subjectivity and social competence.

As a graduate student, Rogers's engagement with the children at Arsenal was informed by McFarland's expertise in the field and functioned as an ongoing case study. The framework of Arsenal's model consisted of participant observation practices followed by dyadic and small group meetings between McFarland and Rogers (and sometimes other graduate students) in which oral debriefing and analysis would occur, resulting in an ongoing, dialectical form of experiential and dialogic education. In this environment, communicative learning and meaning is the result of the interplay between communication and action.[9] At its heart, the engagement at Arsenal was a foundational, dialogical education process in which adults learned from children through interaction and observation and then convened to discuss what they had learned. In both steps, all persons involved—Arsenal's preschoolers, scholars, psychologists, and graduate students like Rogers—learned through a process of dialogue and conversation. With this practice at Arsenal, Rogers and the other adults there reversed the traditional pattern of learning in which children simply received information and therefore learned what the adults wanted to teach them. At Arsenal, the adults were learning how children learn in order to better interact with them so that children could be not just passive receptors of instruction but agents in the learning process. It was within this practice of learning and meaning creation that *Mister Rogers' Neighborhood* developed, evolved, and was practically maintained over the years. Indeed, I maintain that it is one of the secrets of the immense success of the program not only with children but adults as well.

The dynamic between adults and children at Arsenal gave voice and worth to young children within the educational realm and enabled them to make sense of everyday life, in contrast with the dominant child-rearing advice given by John Watson and others in the late 1920s. In Watson's view, the child did not have the capacity to make sense of his experience. Because of this, the meaning of life had to be transferred from adults to children in learning environments where adults had control of all aspects of learning. Watson wanted to impart to children bits of learning derived from the wisdom of adults, and to develop a scientific study of human behavior, which he called "behaviorism."

In contrast with Watson and in consonance with Rogers's philosophy as developed at Arsenal, Paulo Freire identifies the first characteristic of antidialogical setup as "the necessity for conquest." For Freire, the act of conquest, "which reduces persons to the status of things[,] is necrophilic."[10] He posits that liberating action is "dialogical in nature" and argues that dialogue cannot take place without critical thinking, a process that empowers and inspires agency and worth among those involved. Critical thinking, which is achieved through dialogue, yields an indivisible solidarity between the world and people. Further, such thinking generates a perception of reality as transformation and process rather than as stasis. This outcome is key to learning and growing processes to which those at Arsenal appear dedicated. In this framework, relationships are organized within a "with-and" dynamic, in contrast to Watson's hierarchical one.[11] Such reliance on persons in dialoguing relationship with others has been later discussed by Ronald C. Arnett. Following Freire and Martin Buber, Arnett observes that the use of "the term *conversation* in conjunction with education suggests that dialogic education is a collective and active process, not one conducted in isolation."[12] Education thus can never be conceived of as a solitary activity but rather as requiring the "bringing together of ideas, relationships, and values within an organizational culture in symbolic interaction with the goal of transmitting and understanding information."[13]

In *Communication Ethics Literacy: Dialogue and Difference*, Arnett and his coauthors expand upon his earlier analysis on the question of pedagogy and ethics in a way that sheds light on Rogers's early praxis. The key characteristic of the dialogic approach to communication ethics, according to Arnett, Janie Harden Fritz, and Leeanne Bell, is the primary importance of "meaning that emerges in discourse between persons." Although *Neighborhood* is not a referent for Arnett, his findings from classroom experience coincide with Rogers's own vision for a communication ethics.[14] According to Arnett, "a dialogic communication ethics acknowledges multiple goods that give rise to and emerge in ongoing conversations, protecting and promoting the good of learning. A dialogic approach to communication ethics, or a dialogic ethic, recognizes that human beings live within an ongoing conversation that began well before a specific interpersonal interaction begins and is never concluded. Such an ethic protects and promotes the unexpected revelation that emerges between and among persons, a revelation owned by no one and meaningfully important to many."[15] Rogers took intentional measures to insert himself and the characters on his program within a family dynamic through a dialogic and interpersonal communication ethos in which he presented himself in respectful and caring conversation with one viewer. Rogers was also careful to maintain this conversational language and tone throughout the program, asking his listeners questions and prompting them to reflect on the ideas and questions he has posed. At the end of each episode, he offers a song of temporary farewell, singing, "I'll be back when the day is new / And I'll have more ideas for you, / And you'll have things you'll want to talk about. / I will too."[16] Here Rogers makes clear that his conversation with the viewer is ongoing and emphasizes the relationship of mutuality that binds them together as communication partners in a dialogic dyadic journey of making meaning out of the everyday encounter between people and the world.

In an interview with Karen Herman of the American Academy of Film and Television, Rogers tells the story of his friend Jeff, a mentally disabled man who worked in the pool area of the recreation center where Rogers swam. Rogers describes Jeff's recent and intense interest in the untimely death of John F. Kennedy Jr. in July of 1999. He recalls asking Jeff on the very morning of the interview why he was so interested in all the media coverage regarding

Kennedy's death. To this Jeff responded, referring to the Kenne-
dys, "Well, I grew up with them. I was nine years old when his
daddy died." Rogers then asked Jeff how old he was when his own
dad died. "Eleven," responded Jeff. Rogers then offers Herman his
own analysis of this interaction:

> I think that what I want to say about all of that is that television
> is an exceedingly personal medium. It reflects the story back to
> us. And the story we bring to the screen, whatever we happen to
> be watching, we bring our own story to the screen. And so con-
> sequently, it's like a dialogue. And there are those people who
> sometimes say that television doesn't affect us all that much. Well,
> all I can say is then why would advertisers pay so much money
> to put their message on a medium that doesn't affect us all that
> much? I do feel that what we see and hear on the screen is part of
> who we become.[17]

From this anecdote, Rogers draws two key analytical points that
guide the conception and vision of *Neighborhood*. The first is that
despite the technological aspect of television's mass communication, it is in fact "an exceedingly personal medium." The second
is that the medium "reflects the story back to us" and provokes
a dialogue due to the fact that "we bring our own story to the
screen." In a way, Rogers is recovering for the analysis of television the old Aristotelian theory of catharsis, in which people can
see the drama of their own lives in the play (theater). With the
identification of these two analytical points, particularly the last
one concerning the establishing of a dialogue between viewer and
messenger, Rogers seems to understand that the dynamic at play
involves processes of coding and decoding.[18]

Meaning making, as Bakhtin has observed, is a subjective
process that occurs in a dynamic, interactive communication
exchange in which readers bring their own knowledge and

experiences to a text, like Jeff with the televisual story of the Kennedy family, resulting in a diversity of interpretation and meaning making through textual engagement. In this way, Rogers sees himself as entering a dialogue with each viewer, who comes to him with his or her own story, experiences, and understanding of life and the world. The genius of Rogers's program is the ability to connect with the different and yet the same human yearnings for meaning making.[19]

This dialogic model of communication poses a challenge to the idea that television reception is a matter of consumption, a view that minimizes the creative part of the human communication process. Indeed, we now understand, as John Fiske wrote in one of his most important studies on television reception, that "popular culture is not consumption, it is culture—the active process of generating and circulating meanings and pleasures within a social system."[20] Indeed, Fiske's analysis of television (as popular culture) seems to match that of Rogers when he writes that "popular culture has to be above all else, *relevant* to the immediate social situation of the people."[21] Concerned about the rise of a coarse popular culture, Rogers recognizes the process of meaning making through televisual interactivity as early as the 1950s. He took great care to construct an interpersonal dynamic between himself and the viewer, perhaps with the hope of breaking through a cacophony of voices in popular culture so as to more effectively capture attention and deliver his countercultural ethos. By employing a form of dialogical, invitational rhetoric, a technique that allows him to break the fourth wall and connect interpersonally with his audience, Rogers hopes to contribute his voice to the circulation of meanings and pleasures within the cultural realm of discourse.[22]

The interpersonal and dialogical communication method in which Rogers grounds the program appears to be an extension of his own social behaviors in everyday life, and vice versa. Rogers's method, especially his portrayal of "Mister Rogers" on the show, is illuminated by Donald Horton and Richard Wohl's concept of the parasocial. They write that "for a brief interval, the fictional takes precedence over the actual, as the actor becomes identified with the fictional role in the magic of the theatre. This glamorous confusion of identities is temporary: the worlds of fact and fiction meet only for the moment. And the actor, when he takes his bows at the end of the performance, crosses back over the threshold into the matter-of-fact world.[23] However, as if attempting to contravene the dynamic of fusion and confusion between the actor and the character, Rogers insists on "playing it straight." He refuses to play a different role on his television show other than his real-world self. He has developed a character based on himself that is also an artistic creation, not unlike a painter's self-portrait. This choice has psychological consequences for viewer perception in regards to understanding the ways that the parasocial interaction between Rogers and his viewers developed.

The parasocial experience, as in any other social concurrence, is likely to be accompanied by an "immediate sense of mutual awareness and mutual attention with the TV performer."[24] During the time Rogers spent at Arsenal, where he engaged in communication with very young children, he was able to hone a particular style of address that reached this underdeveloped group with remarkable efficacy. There he did not develop a "fictional character" designed for interaction with children. Informed by his interactive and observational work at Arsenal, where he engaged in group and dyadic communication with children, Rogers developed on *Neighborhood* a dialogical ethos in which he attended to the inner needs and desires of small children through conversation. In a 2015 Public Radio International article, *Neighborhood* producer Hedda Sharapan is quoted saying, "What made Mr. Rogers' Neighborhood so different is the time Fred spent listening to children and trying to understand, what are they worried about? What are they thinking about? What helps them feel better?"[25] In this way, he reenacts conversation with viewers on his program inspired by dialogues based on his empirical interactions with preschoolers at Arsenal. Rogers's cultural intervention follows his recognition that entertainment is, in fact, a pedagogy. In this conflated space of entertainment and pedagogy Rogers's radically new understanding of child subjectivity as a developmental process that engages both cognitive and affective dynamics abides.

McFarland notes that contemporary wisdom on early childhood education neglects the importance of the family as an educational unit, promoting instead the assembling of young children for exclusive instruction by "teachers or child care workers."[26] "There is much to be said for preschool education when the teachers are well qualified and basically concerned for the development of the children but such groups are a family supplement and not a family substitute. . . . It is possible that society would be able to obtain a richer return on the public investment in the development of children if a greater portion of the available resources were applied to enhancing the family as an educational group." From this position, McFarland moves to discuss the new phenomenon of television and its location within the center of family life. She identifies the rise of television communications in the 1960s, noting that the device has become "an integral aspect of family experience." Further, she decries the fact that no national plan exists for enriching the education of those considered "deprived of stimulation and meaningful exposure to cultural influences" through the employment of the new technology.[27]

McFarland notes that this new exposure of children to "dramatized situations" on television has the potential to confuse the child's sense of reality and thus can have a negative influence on her development.[28] As a corrective, McFarland urges the development of child-friendly and educative programming, emphasizing the new technology's capacity to extend "the educational experience of all children regardless of the economic circumstances of their parents, the socio-cultural identity of their families, the type of community in which they live or other factors by which we define segregation."[29] McFarland's ideas about the potential of television to reach and educate the lower classes were held by many progressive educators, such as *Sesame Street* creator Joan Ganz Cooney, also an early children's programmer for National Educational Television (NET), which later became PBS.[30] Compulsory literacy had already shown that school attendance diminished regional, class, ethnic, and racial differences and disseminated an American norm based largely on white, middle-class values and aspirations. Rogers and his collaborators made an effort over the years, like *Sesame Street*, to include racial diversity on *Neighborhood.*[31]

McFarland's argument appears to integrate the structural perspective that supports the promotion of state-funded education models as a solution to social and economic inequality with more culturally focused arguments that place primary responsibility on the family institution in regards to socioeconomic uplift and success. In essence, McFarland posits that the television device creates a unique communication environment for learning to occur in which educators can ostensibly insert themselves into the communication culture of any given family. If, as McFarland argues, the family is the most important educational institution that exists in human culture, the television allows for external agents and experts in the area of child development and education like her and Rogers to enter into family discourse with their educative curricula with the hope of conveying "better" values and practices. Such intimate communication not only with children but with the intergenerational family unit appeared to hold great promise for educating the underprivileged inside McFarland's coveted family sought-after dynamic setting.[32]

McFarland's letter next points to *Neighborhood*, a relatively new program at the time, as an example of how television can be used as a pedagogical tool for fostering healthy child development. She notes that *Neighborhood* is directed toward children in their preschool and "early school years" and draws an explicit connection to the then novel Head Start program, which targets children of the same age. Having established the intended educational value of *Neighborhood* by comparing it to Head Start, McFarland describes the unique personality and talents of Fred Rogers. Highlighting Rogers's pedagogical and professional credibility, McFarland writes, "Mr. Fred Rogers, the creator of this program, is not only a talented creative artist, he is a well-qualified child-development specialist." She then moves to deepen and add further dynamism to the reader's impression of Rogers by noting that he "has a unique capacity for interpersonal relationships with children" and is "deeply empathic with their needs and feelings, and their perceptions of the world around them." Here we can see the influence of Spock, who asserted that a baby who is lovingly cared for, appreciated, and encouraged to explore the world will grow to become a confident and well-adjusted adult.[33] McFarland provides testimony of Rogers's talents and expertise as well as an account of child viewers of *Mister Rogers' Neighborhood*. She notes Rogers's dynamic and broad cultural knowledge, praising him as the primary source for *Neighborhood* programs. She stresses his "basic concern for the welfare of children and the clarity of his professional identity as an adult responsible for making a positive contribution to the development of children."

Finally, she describes in detail her experience observing "Mr. Rogers" interact with children. "Children seem to regard Mr. Rogers on the television screen as a trusted person, related to them in an interpersonal way. Their responses to this program are different than to the usual television entertainment for children. Children tend to talk to Mr. Rogers during the program, their faces are mobile reflecting varied feelings, they are prone to get up and respond actively to suggestions." Further, she writes, when Rogers says goodbye at the end of the program, child viewers react "as though they had been separated from a meaningful adult."[34] It would seem that Rogers, in his direct interaction with children at Arsenal, had discovered the power of face-to-face dialogical communication. It is this communication dynamic that he sought to transfer to the interaction between the television persona of "Mister Rogers" and his child viewers.

As McFarland was a professor of psychology and child development, her analysis of children's reactions to the program hold immense weight in assessing the program's educational worth. She notes how the original songs Rogers sings on the program refer to the elements of life that are very important to children. "Reference to the natural feelings of childhood evokes the children's awareness of their inner experience. The artistry of the program stimulates children's interest in the world around them and therefore fosters their learning," she writes.[35] Here McFarland points to two fundamental aspects of the program—assisting in articulating children's "natural" feelings in order to help them acknowledge and understand them (which Rogers refers to as "coping" in his Yale speech), and representing in dramatic form various everyday aspects of the child's world in order to promote learning and the development of healthy and nonthreatening relationships with others. McFarland's appreciation of Rogers's artistry concurs with his own sense of the objectives of his creation. "Our program is not designed to avoid all anxiety-arousing themes," Rogers writes. "We deal with the beginnings of life as well as life's closure and many of the feelings in between."[36] Rogers thus models behaviors on his program that allow children and adults to deal with difficult and conflicting emotions and to choose nonviolent behaviors. Indeed, he seems to have discovered how to touch what is "invisible to the eye"—that is to say, the child's inner world and experience. McFarland's multidimensional analysis of the children's behavioral responses to the show's intimate communication efficacy demonstrate the detailed intellectual and holistic perspective that she deployed in contributing to and understanding the program and its effects on children.

In perhaps the most persuasive and revealing part of her letter, McFarland discusses her observations of children watching *Neighborhood*. By describing how children tend to respond to Rogers's directed questions by speaking to the television set, she provides evidence that Rogers's interpersonal approach is, in fact, effective and not simply a theoretical communication strategy on the part of the show's producers. In confirmation of Rogers's achievement of the dimension of communication theorized by Horton and Wohl as the "parasocial," she further notes that when Rogers says goodbye at the end of the program, children respond with behavior similar to when they are separated from a "meaningful adult." Horton and Wohl note that when parasocial interaction occurs "the conditions of response to the performer are analogous to those in a primary group. The most remote and illustrious men are met as if they were in the circle of one's peers; the same is true of a character in a story who comes to life in these media in an especially vivid and arresting way."[37] In McFarland's letter, however, she seeks to demonstrate that Rogers's relationship to his viewer is unique, while Horton and Wohl argue that this interaction seems to be happening at a broader level.

According to McFarland and other colleagues of Rogers at Arsenal, such interactions are driven by a striving to meet the young child where he is, and to provide for him an attentive, dialogical adult response with the intention of building greater understanding and trust, and of learning from the interaction. In her letter, McFarland notes how empathically Rogers behaves with his viewers as well as the ways that Rogers's "artistry" stimulates his viewers' curiosity about the world around them. What does it mean when McFarland notes that when the program ends, children behave as if they have just been separated from a "meaningful adult"? This detail refers the concept of "attachment," which emerged out of studies in the late 1960s by John Bowlby and Mary Ainsworth. Bowlby described the concept of attachment as a context of development necessary for children to experience healthy growth. It understands the early parent-child relationship as critically important to child development and calls attention to the ways that transactions between the individual child and her multiple primary relationships and contexts influence development.[38] Within this model of understanding, the first five years of life are the most rapid period for development and thus critically important because "it sets either a strong or fragile stage for what follows."[39]

Bowlby described the attachment process as having three primary functions for child development—it provides a crucial sense of security, it assists in the regulation of affect and arousal, and it promotes the expression of feelings and communication. Attachment develops through relational transactions between infant/ toddler and the parent during which the infant communicates an essential need—to be fed, to be played with, to be comforted— and the parent responds. When proceeding in the best possible way, these transactions will be mutually reinforcing, synchronous behaviors by the parent and infant; they will have a high degree of "mutual involvement;" they will be attuned to one another's feeling states; and attentiveness and empathy will be consistently expressed by the parent.[40]

What is key here in thinking about the performance of Mister Rogers, as noted in McFarland's letter, is that he *enacts* this role as a trustworthy adult-parental figure on the screen. As we will see further in our examination of *Neighborhood* episodes, Rogers is caring and careful to speak to his viewers in an empathic way that involves mutual recognition combined with a soothing message and tone. In a secure attachment, the mutual recognition of arousal by the parent helps the infant/toddler to develop her own ability to regulate her arousal. It is thus through this experience of empathy, mutual recognition, and soothing that the infant/toddler internalizes strategies for self-soothing. Such successful self-reg- ulation of emotions helps the child to feel capable and confident in controlling distress and negative emotions.[41] All this is part and parcel of Rogers's objective of teaching the child "healthy" coping strategies.[42]

With this understanding of the critical elements of attachment as it relates to healthy child development, we can see the ways in which Rogers's efforts on *Mister Rogers' Neighborhood* aim to provide very young children with a primary adult relationship in which the adult, "Mister Rogers," offers the viewer affirming attachment responses to his viewers on a daily, ritualized basis. McFarland's identification of Rogers's ethos of dyadic mutuality, encouragement of play and curiosity with the world, empathic tone, involvement, and attunement serve to emphasize the critical ways in which he performs, from a child development perspective, the role of an assuring, ideal primary caregiver for his viewers.

Though Spock, writing in the 1940s, did not use the term *attachment*, he asserted that "the foundation of a healthy person- ality" begins with the formation of a close, secure bond between child and a caregiving adult (not only the parent but professional caregiver).[43] As Spock, Bowlby, Erikson, McFarland, and Rogers all stress, the primary role of the parental figure in the very young child's upbringing is to make the child feel safe and secure in the world in order to help the child eventually self-manage any emotional stress he experiences. In this model, success in devel- oping the underdeveloped mind of the young child comes through "nurturing, guidance and instruction," rather than the domination practices of old.[44]

Informed by Arnett's discussion of dialogic communication

ethics, we can see that in this situation, meaning is created in discourse between persons, and both knowledge and the path to understanding are found within the unique subjectivity of each participant. The first episode of *Mister Rogers' Neighborhood*, from 1967, which addresses the question of change, is exemplary of this dialogical meaning making. After Rogers's opening greeting, which would be repeated every episode for more than thirty years of the show, he informs his audience that something has changed in the arrangement of furniture in his kitchen. He asks his viewer directly, "Do you like change? What do you think of change?" Indeed, the theme of change is interwoven in each segment of the five episodes that compose the first week of the program, from the periodic visits with mailman Mister McFeely to the invited artists who come and sing about change to the drama that ensues in the Neighborhood of Make-Believe, when the puppet Lady Elaine is found to have made changes to the landscape of the neighborhood without consulting the neighbors. Each character in the first five episodes comes to grips with the question of change, big or small, personally or virtually, and gains an understanding of the concept.

Rogers often examines a problem throughout a series of shows through either conversational song, dramatization in the Neighborhood of Make-Believe, or dialogue with the viewer and/or other actors on the show (e.g., Lady Aberlin, Chef Brockett, Mr. McFeely, Mrs. Saunders). In such a communication ethic, primary import is given to the actions of listening and response. In particular, for Rogers, both at Arsenal and in *Neighborhood*, value and power are bestowed upon the child interlocutor whose unique subjectivity is praised and regarded as special.

THE WOUNDED HEALER AND THE MUTUALITY OF HOLY GROUND

In several speeches and interviews, Rogers reveals formative stories from his childhood and adolescence that situate the importance of an ethos of mutuality and dialogue in his life. His transfer of social and pedagogical power to the viewer/student of his program, traditionally the less powerful person in the relationship, appears to be a position of critical importance to Rogers for personal reasons. In a 1997 commencement speech Rogers gave to the Memphis Theological Seminary, "Invisible Essentials," Rogers, writing at the age of sixty-nine, reflects back on the critical moments in his life when he found his calling as a communicator. In the middle of this speech, Rogers breaks into a parabolic anecdote. He recounts times when, as a young child, he was bullied. As a boy, he was overweight and timid, and afraid to go to school each day. One day, after being released from school early, he was walking home and soon noticed that he was being followed by a group of boys who gained on him and began taunting him verbally. "Freddy, hey, fat Freddy," they shouted, "We're going to get you, Freddy." Rogers recalls breaking into a sprint in the direction of the house of a widowed neighbor who he hoped would be home. There, Rogers found "refuge."[45] This concept of refuge would be established as the sine qua non of his television show.

In *Neighborhood*, Rogers introduces himself and greets the viewer in every show with a song that proclaims the beauty of the neighborhood and offers an invitation to spend time together. "It's a beautiful day in the neighborhood . . . / Would you be mine? / Could you be mine? / Won't you be my neighbor?" This invitation to be a neighbor, to be *like each other*, is one of the primary reasons why viewers were so moved by and devoted to Rogers and to *Neighborhood*. Amy Hollingsworth speculates that Rogers's understanding of what it means to be a neighbor owes much to his friendship with the Benedictine monks at Saint Vincent Archabbey in Latrobe, Pennsylvania. She writes that the monks used to visit Rogers's grandparents and parents when he was growing up, and that "it was through the monks and *their* work in his community of neighbors that a young Fred Rogers learned to heed Saint Benedict's call to respect and revere the whole of God's creation because 'the divine presence is everywhere.'" She adds that "for Fred, and for Mister Rogers, this was the work of God: seeing the eternal in your neighbor, that divine presence that allows us to show mercy to our neighbor—and to receive it."[46]

Rogers reflects on the resentment and pain he harbored for years after his childhood experiences of bullying. He writes that although the authority figures in his life advised him to ignore the taunts and to act as though the insults did not bother him, Rogers came to realize that denying his feelings betrayed the authenticity of his experience. "What I actually did was mourn. I cried whenever I was alone."[47] Such "mourning," as he describes it, set him on a path of profound introspection, in which he found in music the possibilities for genuine expression and transformation. "After a lot of sadness," he wrote, "I began a lifelong search for what is essential."[48]

Rogers writes that he came to realize that acknowledging the pain he felt as a result of bullying was critical to his own healing and development. "Somehow along the way," Rogers writes, "I caught the belief that God cares, too; that the divine presence cares for those of us who are hurting and that His presence is everywhere."[49] Although Rogers in his public persona does not often emphasize his faith in God, his life, philosophy, and artistic production were led by his belief in a caring and merciful divinity: "I always pray that through whatever we produce (whatever we say and do), some word that is heard might ultimately be God's word. That is my main concern. All the others are minor compared to that."[50] To the postmodern sensibility rooted in suspicion, Rogers's spirituality might seem unsophisticated, if not naïve. The fact remains, however, that the "caring nature of God" serves as the foundation of Rogers's life and work—and the thirty years of *Neighborhood* programming.

Rogers has stated that he saw the production of his children's television show as a space infused by the Holy Spirit where he, as a servant of God, strove to minister to children's deepest and most essential need—to be loved and accepted just as they are.[51] In this sense, Rogers appears to understand the relationship between God and human beings, and the relationship between Martin Buber's "I and Thou," as a Bakhtinian dialogical process of communication in which both sender and receiver are engaged in a mutual dynamic of discovery. "I'm not that interested in 'mass communications,'" Rogers wrote. "I am much more interested in what happens between this person and the one watching. The space between the television set and that person who's watching is very holy ground."[52] Rogers envisioned his program as a possible space for giving birth to that "holy ground" of communication—a space between any two people in which each is accepted "just the way you are." This is the space that is essential, Rogers asserts, and yet "invisible to the eye." Rogers pulls this phrase from Antoine de Saint-Exupéry's *The Little Prince*: "Here is my secret, a very simple secret: It is only with the heart that one can see rightly; what is essential is invisible to the eye."[53] In other words, that which is invisible is the disposition of the soul. It is this kind of affective, relational sensibility that Rogers embodies in the form and content of *Neighborhood*. This relational spirit animates the show.

Through his own search for healing, Rogers discovered that for him, the healing process was not just a question of speaking about one's wounds but included an understanding of the divine as caretaker. In *The Wounded Healer*, Catholic priest and psychologist Henri Nouwen—a public theologian, intellectual, and friend of Rogers—suggests that ministers make their own emotional wounds known as a source of healing for those under their care, thus proposing a necessary mutuality of "I and Thou." Nouwen writes that "Jesus made his own broken body the way to health, to liberation, and new life. Thus like Jesus, he who proclaims liberation is called not only to care for his own wounds and the wounds of others, but also to make his wounds into a major source of his healing power. . . . Words like 'alienation,' 'separation,' 'isolation,' and 'loneliness' have been used as the names of our wounded condition. Maybe the word 'loneliness' best expresses our immediate experience and therefore most fittingly enables us to understand our brokenness."[54] Indeed, the most memorable psychological and spiritual wounds from Rogers's childhood come from the alienation and isolation of bullying, itself an expression of alienation and shame. Consequently, his program and life project are concerned with providing everyday acts of healing to those who experience such fundamental wounding of the human spirit. "It may seem strange," he noted in a speech delivered at Saint Vincent College, "but the more I live, the more I find myself feeling gratitude for the tough times I've been through—not that I would have asked for them—but they turned out to be times in which God's presence was so clear—so real that it felt like Mrs. Stewart [the neighbor who welcomed him in when he was being teased by bullies] opening her door and taking me into her safe home."[55] The instrument Rogers uses to minister to those experiencing the great wound of alienation is his own wounded person—his body, articulating a message of acceptance and inclusion in an everyday ritual of television performance.[56]

The artistic elements of Rogers's performance of acceptance are not incidental. Rogers's narrative goes on to detail how he found relief from the bullying only by acknowledging his hurt and expressing his wounded emotions through playing the piano—a transformative and healing way of processing pain. Accepting the wound, in combination with the emotional expression of piano playing, reveals a creative space that allows Rogers to grow beyond it. Instead of becoming aggressive, scarred by shame, retaliating against those who bullied him, he becomes the "wounded healer," transforming his pain into a form of *caritas* in imitation of Christ. His primary interest thus becomes providing care for others who are experiencing difficulty and/or pain through an aesthetic, artistic practice that focuses on creative transformation and social emotional bonds.[57]

In a 1994 interview for the *Christian Century*, Rogers told reporter Lisa Belcher-Hamilton that his beloved seminary professor William F. Orr introduced him to a conviction that he came to embrace. Rogers describes Orr's conviction in saying, "Evil is the accuser and Christ is the advocate. Evil wants us to look at ourselves and others with accusing eyes and hearts, while Christ encourages us to look at ourselves and others with the eyes and hearts of love."[58] In his "Invisible Essentials" speech, Rogers notes that while Orr rarely spoke about evil, the few times he did hear Orr discuss the matter he was very clear about the way it operated in intrapersonal emotions and human behavior. According to Rogers, Orr told him, "Evil will do anything to make you feel as bad as you possibly can about yourself. Because if you feel the worst about who you are, you will undoubtedly look with evil eyes on your neighbor and you will get to believe the worst about him or her. Accuse yourself. Accuse your neighbor. Get your neighbor to accuse somebody else, and the evil thrives and spreads."[59]

In contrast, Rogers juxtaposes Orr's description of evil with his description of Christ, "the Advocate": "While on the other side—way on the other side of evil—is Jesus the Christ who is our Advocate. He will do anything to encourage us to know that God's creation is good, that we, His brothers and sisters, can look on each other as having real value. Our advocate will do anything to remind us that we are lovable and that our neighbor is lovable too!" These antithetical figures and the behavioral choices that characterize their respective interactions with others illustrate well Rogers's philosophy for acting in the world in imitation of Christ.

Critically, and in ways that relate to Rogers's bullying experience, Orr describes these two oppositional forces in the Christian religion with reference to shame, one of the most common emotional responses to bullying. In Orr's assessment, evil brings about a feeling of shame by encouraging the individual to feel "the worst about who you are." In contrast, Orr describes Christ as an advocate, who protects the individual from the destructive emotion of shame, encouraging persons to look upon themselves and others as having value and being lovable. This focus on the psyche of the person and the power of rhetoric to affect one's emotional life further points to Rogers's interest in assisting children in learning to manage their feelings. "You've made this day a special day by just your being you," he repeatedly tells his viewers on each episode of *Neighborhood*. This ritualized statement expresses Rogers's optimistic belief in the goodness of things and people as created in the image of God, who is good. This trust in the goodness of God is confirmed in Rogers confiding in Hollingsworth that he prays every day before entering the studio with the following invocation: "Dear God, let some word that is heard be Yours."[60]

Having identified his television program as his ministry when he was awarded his MDiv in 1963, Rogers assumes the teaching, ministerial role of Christ by modeling his behavior and communicating the fundamental message of the gospel in everyday language. The historical Christ speaks as a teacher, not as a savior, and thus his message is more anthropocentric, Rogers would say, than theological.[61] Rogers likewise communicates primarily with everyday people and in everyday, storytelling language. He does not make huge theological statements; rather, he speaks about loving one's neighbor as thyself, which requires the utmost command and management of one's feelings. Rogers's teaching, like Christ's, is a pedagogy of affects and ethics in which he primarily sets out to help his viewers learn how to manage their fears and anxieties. Integrating Christianity and child development psychology, his specialized areas of knowledge, Rogers engages in a careful performance with the intention of providing emotional and spiritual care for those watching his program. Just as Christ reassured his followers to "be not afraid, I walk beside you," Rogers invites viewers to be his neighbor and sings:

> We're not to be afraid of anything
> Of anything at all
> We're not to be afraid
> We're not to be afraid
> The king says fear nothing at all.[62]

Alluding to Christ through the verbal code of "the king," Rogers reassures his viewers of Christ's message to have no fear. The concept of neighbor functions on a dual religious and secular level. It was Rogers's childhood neighbor who offered him sanctuary and safety from the bullies out on the street. Reciprocally, as the "wounded healer," Rogers offers his television home as a place of refuge for *Neighborhood* viewers. Although Rogers may not have been conscious of these choices during the early years of his program, he seems to have recognized much by the time of his "Invisible Essentials" speech.

Playing the role of the "wounded healer," Rogers reenacts rituals of spiritual healing on each *Neighborhood* program through the act of dialogue and expression of genuine feelings with the viewer. In a powerful way, as a kind of covert minister in the character of "Mister Rogers," Rogers creates and enacts a fatherly, Christ-like, adult male figure who cares for his "children," as articulated in the Christian theological narrative. "In the light of the Gospel's teaching," writes religion scholar Judith Gundry-Volf, "Christians are called to make a place for children in the fellowship of believers as coparticipants in the gifts of salvation through Christ, and also learn from children how to participate in God's reign."[63] Through this healing, Christ-like figure of the minister, who speaks to listeners from a place of authenticity of feeling and understanding and who bestows empathy on his interlocutors, Rogers works to endear his television audience to him by offering them a space of spiritual relief grounded in merciful connectivity.

Another story that demonstrates this critical positioning of mutuality and affirmation through dialogue is Rogers's recollection of his high school classmate Jim Stumbaugh. Asked by Herman about his high school years, Rogers notes that he was an active writer for the school newspaper and president of the student council. But he quickly moves from that statement of pride and accomplishment to a place of humility, acknowledging that at first he was neither confident nor successful as a high school underclassman. "I was very, very shy when I was in grade school and when I got to high school I was scared to death to go to school." This all changed when Stumbaugh, described by Rogers as a "big man on campus" and a star of various sports teams, was injured at a football practice.[64] The injury put Stumbaugh in the hospital for several weeks, and Rogers was instructed by one of his teachers to deliver Stumbaugh's homework to him there. According to Rogers, the two began to talk and, as Rogers describes it, he began to see "what substance there was in this jock." Correspondingly, Stumbaugh "could see what substance there was in this shy kid," Rogers tells Herman. Later, when Stumbaugh returned to school, he praised Rogers to the other students, saying, "That Rogers kid's okay." This act, according to Rogers, "made all the difference in the world" for him. "Just somebody saying to the others, 'That Rogers kid's okay.' It was after that that I started writing for the newspaper, got to be president of the student council. What a difference one person can make in the life of another. It's almost as if he said, 'I like you just the way you are.' And for me to be able to pass that kind of acceptance on through this wonderful medium, that's been a real blessing for me."[65] Rogers reveals the powerful meanings that the two created in their interpersonal and subsequent group interactions. The two first discovered one another through interpersonal dialogue and mutual recognition, and find in this interaction acceptance, appreciation, and a sense of their common humanity. Most significant, perhaps, is the way that dialogue, in this instance, transcends difference and transforms Rogers's sense of self. A childhood acquaintance of Rogers, E. Kay Myers, wrote in 2009 that "the friendship of the athlete [Stumbaugh] and the fat kid [Rogers] ended the school teasing that long had plagued Fred."[66]

The relational qualities detailed in these recollections of Stumbaugh and Rogers's dynamic exemplify Buber's understanding of the powerful elements of a dialogical orientation and communication ethic. In their discussion of Buber's psychotherapeutic analysis of dialogue, Mick Cooper, Amy Chak, Flora Cornish, and Alex Gillespie note the "thou-ifying" qualities of the dialogical relationship. Buber conceives of dialogue as a form of communication "where each of the participants really has in mind the other or others in their present and particular being and turns to them with the intention of establishing a living mutual relation between himself and them."[67] Thus, for Buber, the first and most basic action or movement that occurs in any given dialogical engagement is a "turning" toward the other, which includes "an attentiveness, receptivity, or responding to their Being."[68] Specific to Buber and critically useful in thinking about Rogers's project is the idea that essential to this basic dialogical movement is that "this turning is toward the *particular* Being of the Other—their unique and individual existence—the one that is concretely and existentially in the situation made 'of flesh and blood.'"[69] This identification of the other, Cooper, Chak, Cornish, and Gillespie assert, is contrasted with the abstract experiencing of the other as perceived in law. Buber's understanding of dialogue experientially "requires an *I-Thou* attitude toward the other" as opposed to an *I-It* attitude.[70]

For Buber, the I-Thou attitude is characterized not only by this relating to the Other in their particularity but also a "standing alongside" the other, and an experiencing of them as a fluid, freely choosing subjectivity. In contrast, in the I-It attitude, the Other is experienced as a static determined "thing," something that can be broken down into parts, and surveyed, studied, or measured.[71] Essential for understanding the transformative dialogical relationship between Stumbaugh and Rogers is Buber's assertion that the I-Thou attitude is characterized by a *confirmation* of the other. This confirmation is essentially an act of love.[72] This identification of dialogue's first position of turning toward the unique other and second position of existential confirmation contributes greatly to our understanding of Rogers's perception of the process of dialoguing and befriending he experienced with Stumbaugh. Clearly, in this parable, Rogers is inscribing an understanding of the I-Thou dialectic, which has gained, of late, great acceptance in secular spheres.

STAGING EARLY CHILDHOOD DEVELOPMENT

During his early period at Arsenal, Rogers was invited by Nancy Curry, a psychologist and instructor of preschool-aged children at the center, to bring the puppets he had made and operated on his earlier WQED television program, *The Children's Corner*, into her classroom. In the 2014 documentary *Lessons from Mister Rogers*, Curry describes the scene between Rogers, the puppets, and the children during these visits as "magic moments." According to Curry, Rogers had the children "mesmerized" by the puppets as they all gathered together in conversation. "He and I had eye contact," she says, "and when something special would happen with one of the children, we would just be so excited." Curry tells of a memorable moment when Rogers's puppet King Friday, a character on *The Children's Corner* who would later become a fixture on *Neighborhood*, spoke to a little girl in the class. "Do you know what?" the little girl asked Friday, "I'm going to move to a new house."

"A new house?" Friday responded. "How wonderful! Are you going to take your toys with you?" Rogers moved Friday up just a few feet in front of her face, creating intimate space between the two.

"Yes," the little girl responded with a smile.

"Are you going to take your mommy and daddy and brother and sister?" Friday asked.

"Yes," she responded.

"Wonderful!" he pronounced as she cast a wide smile and stared into the puppet's face.

In recollecting this dialogue on camera, Curry notes that Rogers "was being empathic" with the little girl. She chuckles and says that he had a kind of "mini-therapy session with that girl." She then notes how "happy" she was to have Rogers in her classroom and confesses how each week she would anticipate the day that Rogers would come for a visit. "The kids loved it; I loved it; I felt like a child myself," she says. "I think that was—is one of the things about Fred—that he can reach to the child in you even if you are a grownup."[73] This last observation reveals a very important aspect of Rogers's dialogical communication—his ability and intention to communicate not only with the child but intergenerationally.

At Arsenal, Rogers was also able to attend guest lectures by world-renowned psychologist Erik Erikson, a cofounder of the center.[74] Although Erikson did not complete his doctorate because he wanted to learn solely from interaction with and observation of children, his theories on psychosocial development were groundbreaking at the time and are still influential today.[75] Erikson emphasized learning from children through direct contact and observation. "You see a child play, and it is so close to seeing an artist paint, for in play the child says things without uttering a word," Erikson once said. "You can see how he solves his problems. You can also see what's wrong. Young children, especially, have enormous creativity and whatever's in them rises to the surface in free play."[76]

Erikson called his prominent theory on the life cycle the "Eight Ages of Man."[77] In his theory, Erikson posits the defining problematic of each of his categorical stages of psychosocial development. For Rogers, Erikson's discussions concerning the early stages of life were of critical interest. Erikson first proposes a stage from infancy to the second year defined by the pairing of basic trust versus mistrust. The most prominent feeling the child experiences during this stage is "Can I trust the world?" In this phase, the most significant relationship is with the mother, as the child relies on her to meet his fundamental needs of eating, sleeping, and bowel relaxation. The experience of "mutual regulation" is key to healthy development, as it helps the child to balance the discomfort he feels as a result of the "immaturity of homeostasis with which he was born."[78] The infant's first achievement is to let his mother out of sight without "undue anxiety," trusting that she has left him in a safe situation to which she will eventually return.[79] Erikson sees in the passage from one stage to the next a moment in which a virtue develops—in this case, hope. This presentation of the need to learn to cope with anxiety is an overarching objective of Rogers's program. He makes concerted efforts to serve as a trusted adult, accompanying the child during the "television visit" as the two explore the social and material world together. Twice a month, Rogers reviewed scripts with McFarland, who identified and analyzed how language, aesthetic, and other choices Rogers made would likely be perceived and understood from the young child's perspective.

Erikson sets up the second stage problematic as "autonomy vs. shame and doubt" and assigns to it the ages between two and four. In this stage, the child's leading existential question is "Is it okay to be me?" The toddler must internalize a basic faith in his existence. "As his environment encourages him to 'stand on his own feet,' it must protect him against meaningless and arbitrary experiences of shame and of early doubt."[80] Like the "trust vs. mistrust" phase, the "autonomy vs. shame and doubt" phase is critical for the child to develop in a healthy way (i.e., with minimal development of neurosis). Shame, Erikson writes, is a dangerous emotion, "rage turned against the self." The child who does not develop a sense of confidence in his abilities during this stage (by way of efficient mastery of toilet training and clothing himself, for example), will, according to Erikson, overmanipulate himself and develop obsessive, repetitive behaviors. "He who is ashamed would like to force the world not to look at him, not to notice his exposure. He would like to destroy the eyes of the world."[81] The damaging effects of this kind of unhealthy development seem destructive and antisocial. If the child develops in a healthy manner during this stage, he will develop the virtue of will, according to Erikson.

When Rogers sings words of encouragement and acceptance to his viewers, he appears to be tackling both of these early problematics. In each and every episode Rogers tells the viewer, "You are special" and "I like you just the way you are," which can be taken as a response to the child's predominant question during the first stage—"Is it okay to be me?" Below are excerpts from two songs, "I'm Proud of You" (which first aired on episode 1131 in 1971) and "It's You I Like" (which aired on episode 1133 in 1971), that also answer this question. The second song, "It's You I Like," subtly combats feelings of shame; Rogers sings that he is not interested in the "things that hide you."

I'm Proud of You

I hope that you're as proud as I am
I'm proud of you
I'm proud that you are proud and that
You're learning how important you are
How important each person you see
    can be
Discovering each one's specialty
Is the most important learning
I'm proud of you[a]

It's You I Like

It's not the things you wear,
It's not the way you do your hair
But it's you I like
The way you are right now
The way down deep inside you
Not the things that hide you
Not your toys, they're just beside you

But it's you I like
Every part of you
Your skin, your eyes, your feelings
Even when you're feeling blue
That it's you I like
It's you yourself
It's you
It's you I like.[b]

NOTES

a. "I'm Proud of You" first appeared on *Mister Rogers' Neighborhood*, episode 1131 (1971). Provided courtesy of the Fred Rogers Company.
b. "It's You I Like" first appeared on *Mister Rogers' Neighborhood*, episode 1133 (1971). Provided courtesy of the Fred Rogers Company.

In Erikson's schema, the second stage is followed by the preschool stage of life, ages three through five. In this third stage, the child's existential question becomes, "Is it okay for me to do, move, and act?" The pairing here is "initiative versus guilt." This problematic builds on the development of autonomy from the previous phase in the form of quality undertaking, planning, and addressing a task for the sake of acting and moving on. The child is engaged in a process of experimentation in which she attempts to master the material world around her. During this stage, she learns to take initiative, take risks, and develop independence. Children may feel guilt when their initiative does not produce their desired results. Rogers articulates feelings of frustration with such tasks in his song "It's No Use."

> It's no use,
> No use trying
> 'Cause it's no use
> No sighing
> 'Cause I can see
> That it never will be
> I hope hopelessly
>
> It's no use,
> No use crying
> 'Cause it's no use
> No use denying
> It's time that
> I just stop trying
> Because it's no use.[82]

Here he models the articulation of frustration for his preschool viewers, who by their age have developed increasing linguistic sophistication that permits them to communicate their needs and feelings more accurately than that of a toddler.[83] By communicating his frustration, Mister Rogers simultaneously shows empathy for his viewers and helps them to see that such frustration is something experienced by everyone. Rogers's artistic creation thus creates rhetorical ways of addressing Erikson's stages of development by speaking to the struggles and feelings that come with each stage in a productive and processual way.

CREATIVITY AS LAYERS OF THINKING AND FEELING

The education Rogers received through observing children at Arsenal, in discussing his observations with McFarland, and in other readings and lectures, provided him with foundational perspectives for understanding and communicating with young children and the larger family unit on his television program. In a 1969 address at Thiel College titled "Encouraging Creativity," Rogers points to Erikson's writings on the ways that youth develop strength and confidence in their own talents and creativity. According to Erikson, Rogers states, "in youth, strength emerges from the sense that society recognizes the young individual as a bearer of fresh energy and that the individual so confirmed recognizes society as a living process, which inspires loyalty as it receives it [and] honors confidence as it demands it."[84] From Erikson's assessment, Rogers posits his own thesis—that education must have as its primary goal *helping* students develop greater awareness of "their own unique selves" such that they "increase their feelings of personal worth, responsibility, and freedom."[85] Rogers explicitly identifies a certain kind of mutuality in a relationship as the launching point of the self, as it exists within a world of others. Rogers applies this fundamental interplay between self and society/other to the language and philosophy of education, suggesting a radical change in the way we understand the role of teacher and the institution of school, as well as of the parent as the first teacher.[86]

Before making this assertion, Rogers deliberates on the standard methods for and discursive consensus on improving instruction and curricula in American schools. He begins with the premise that every child comes into the world with a "unique endowment" that grants him the chance to create something "entirely different from everybody else in the world."[87] From this starting point, he asks his audience what happens to children who hear that their creations—such as a mud pie—are not good, or that their block building, for example, holds no importance or worth. "What do you think happens to that something from inside—that SELF which was trying itself on the world for size?" he writes. In reply to his own questions, he states that as a result of this "degradation," and if constant in its articulation, the child is likely to feel unaccepted and may carry such feelings with him as he grows into adulthood. Noting to his audience that most of them are likely appalled by the notion that any adult would degrade a child's creation in such blatant and cruel fashion, Rogers points to the ways that such communication is employed in both implicit and explicit ways in the culture. "What about people who have developed the machines for teaching human children which when a child presses the button for a wrong answer the machine gives off an unpleasant response?" he asks. "Children, like laboratory rats, can learn quickly not to experiment with wrong answers."[88] Although Rogers's critique is now "commonplace, it was novel at the time. His reverence for the importance of making mistakes as part of the learning process is most notable in his speech as he advocates for compassion in a way that addresses the pragmatic concerns that undergird and drive the systems of measurement and achievement developed by those who work for educational interests. This is not to be confused, however, with a communication process that demeans the child. The question is how to communicate to the child that the building he built with blocks is not designed to hold weight in language that still upholds the worth of the child's endeavor.

Rogers decries the postwar educational approach in which children are treated as future cogs in a machine. He argues that this kind of educational approach undercuts one of the most fundamental aspects of a child's basic humanity—the ability to produce new creations and insights. He notes how more and more, the practices of educators focus on methods and techniques that seek to shape students to fit a particular type of rigid subjectivity assessed by IQ tests and multiple-choice exams for "computerized industry potential." Activities that constitute early learning environments, such as "block building, 'homemaking' and drama, are labeled 'EXTRA curricular' in schools beyond the preschool level. It's as if we, the educators, were saying to the developing person 'From now on, young people, the way we tell you to do something is the way you must do it or you won't pass,'—and, by the time those children hear 11 or 12 years of that, is it any wonder that they have trouble knowing who they are?" Rogers's pedagogical aims stretch far beyond his immediate interests in the very young child. Indeed, in a 1969 statement he made to a congressional committee dealing with whether to fund educational television, he notes how, in the long run, his program will perform "a great service for mental health."[89] He thus views his project as part of larger societal issues on how best to nurture human creativity at both the personal and institutional levels in order to produce emotionally and spiritually healthy subjects. In fact, in this same speech, he blames the kind of rigid programming of individuals practiced at schools for the rebellion of adolescents and young adults emerging in the 1960s counterculture. "Our young people are weary of being programmed and pigeon-holed," he states, "and, those whose creativity has not been encouraged are rebelling."[90]

In many ways, Rogers's critique of education is informed by John Dewey's progressive education reform movement. Dewey, writing at the beginning of the twentieth century, finds the traditional American schooling system limiting in its rote learning model, perhaps best described by Freire some fifty years later (though in reference to Brazil) as the "banking model of education." Dewey's pragmatic approach focuses on the problem of how we think. For Dewey, all thinking is situated in a problematic solution, "and is brought to a conclusion within a context that shapes the thinking and determines the relevance, and, indeed the truth of the conclusion."[91] Thus, for Dewey, knowledge is what we seek in attempting to resolve a problem, and truth is the answer that "satisfactorily solves the problem." Such a trajectory emphasizes the contextual complexities involved in any given human endeavor and thus highlights, as Rogers does in his speech, the need for an educational practice that places value on human creativity. In addition to this fundamental and novel idea, Dewey developed in his later writings the concept of value in human life, which he identifies as *growth*. The point of living, for Dewey, is growth, which implicitly means that if we are to continue living over time, we must encounter problems "if we are to realize the full richness of life."[92] Neither Dewey nor Rogers is interested in bringing up children who do not encounter problems as a measure of their happiness. Quite to the contrary, they both understand that encountering problems is inevitable and learning to solve them is indispensable.

Indeed, identifying growth as an increased ability to resolve problems is one of the major themes on *Neighborhood*, and although Rogers does not discuss it explicitly in "Encouraging Creativity," he alludes to it throughout his speech in the ways he calls for the continuous development of human expression through the encouragement of each person's inherent human value. "Our job in life is to help people realize how rare and valuable each one of us really is—that each of us has something which no one else has—or ever will have—something inside which is unique to all time. It's our job to encourage each other to discover that uniqueness, and to provide ways of developing its expression."[93] While embracing these primary philosophies of Dewey, Rogers adds another critical element to his pedagogy that is singular to his program, and arguably the most compelling aspect of *Neighborhood*. In his speech, Rogers argues that compassion, and respectful and affirming recognition of the other, are essential components in the process of nurturing creativity and growth, which he defines as the primary goal of education.

Dewey's essential philosophical principles are "that the learning process occurs within the context of concern and challenge, and life takes on values as long as this continues as an active process."[94] As discussed, Rogers's educational approach follows much of Dewey's progressive educational philosophy, but it also expands and reworks Dewey's principles through an incorporation of the concept of love, which, he posits in "Encouraging Creativity," expanding upon Dewey's progressive principles. Rogers proposes that love is a critical component of education. "We also need to help people to discover the true meaning of love," he asserts toward the close of his speech. "Love is generally confused with dependence," he declares. "Those of us who have grown in true love know that we can love only in proportion to our capacity for independence. We must be able to be ourselves in the face of love for our love to have meaning. Only by understanding our own uniqueness can we fully appreciate how special our neighbor really is. Only by being aware of our own endowments can we begin to marvel at the variety which our Creator has provided in men."[95] Rogers's conclusions link his discussions on the role of education in the lives of youth to a concept left out of discussions on education and society. He characterizes the act of encouraging creativity as essentially an act of love. Like encouraging creativity, love is the act of bestowing worth on the other, which can only take place, he argues, when an individual receives love from another. Love is thus an endless, dialogical process of giving and receiving genuine appreciation, in which one experiences "the joy and dignity of being truly human."[96] Love can even serve as a platform for the lessons on international hostilities of the Cold War. It is, in essence, a priori to all other essentials for learning and creativity and is "invisible to the eye."

Rogers begins the speech with the identification of the unique creativity of the human person as inscribed from birth and thus essential. In doing so, he posits creativity as fundamental to the person and gives it moral weight by ascribing goodness to it. In doing this, he lays the groundwork for advocating for the protection and fostering of creativity. This is the duty of the parent and the adult educator, he says: to call children and adults into relation with one another, into a relationship of I and Thou. In this relation, the act of protection and fostering comes in the form of the dialogic. The child creates something and shows it to the adult. The adult, Rogers says, must respond by validating the worth of the child's creation through language, in conversation. In this sense, Rogers personalizes Erikson's theory, which asserts that "society" grants youth strength and a sense of self-worth, by detailing which persons—parents and teachers—are largely responsible for such protection and fostering. Rogers's language brings Erikson's societal and theoretical language into the reality of everyday life in American society at large.

As he moves outside his concise critique of the American school system in an effort to connect creative learning to the larger world, Rogers tells the story of the American pianist Van Cliburn, who made several appearances on *Neighborhood*. In 1962, Van Cliburn traveled to Russia for a Tchaikovsky competition to which the Russian Ministry of Culture had admitted thirty-two American musicians.[97] The competition was broadcast via television throughout the world. Van Cliburn apparently told Rogers how, after each session, people would await their favorite performers outside the venue, on the streets, in order to embrace them and tell them how meaningful the performances were to them. Rogers recollects reports that Russian pilots announced the final scores of the competition on their flights on the day the results were publicized. In this Cold War atmosphere, Rogers is prompted to argue, if more creativity were encouraged, perhaps war would not seem always imminent. "Isn't it possible that we in America have underestimated the role of the creative artist in international affairs? Isn't it possible that we might do well to encourage people to develop from within—and help them to feel confident of the worth of communicating their inner selves to the world of others rather than insisting that a person's worth is to be measured only in how many right answers he can recite?"[98] Moreover, he states, there are no right answers around a place such as the Paris Peace table. What matters in that setting, he says, is solutions to problems. This example points to the ways in which creativity functions in human life in a range of highly important arenas.

Rogers's critique of the American school curriculum and its exclusion of the creative arts involve an identification of an educational system interested in the atomization of subjects. In "Encouraging Creativity," Rogers implicitly asks, what kind of human beings are educational practices like this producing? Though once again operating in a rhetorical schema in which he is the subject speaking to a group of people, Rogers employs a Socratic, dialogical communication strategy in which he calls his viewers to adopt a critical stance to matters of community affairs that concern their wellbeing. His critique of school curricula extends the less overtly political messages on his program, which, through specific rituals, practices, and discourses, stress values of community, the unique worth of the individual, creativity, and relationships.

PARASOCIAL INTERACTIVITY AND THE BIRTH OF "MISTER ROGERS"

In 1961 Rogers was contacted by Fred Rainsberry, the director of children's programming at the Canadian Broadcasting Corporation (CBC). According to Rogers, Rainsberry said something like, "Fred, I'd like you to come up here and do a fifteen-minute program for children. Would you do it? I've seen you talk with kids,

Fred. I want you to translate that to television."[99] Rogers agreed
to the project and recalls the CBC experience as the first time he
looked directly in the camera and said, "I'm glad to be with you."
At the CBC he developed the program *Misterogers*, which would
later, for a US audience, become *Mister Rogers' Neighborhood*.
Nancy Curry recalls her reaction to watching Rogers speak to the
camera for the first time during a taping of *Misterogers*. "When
they trained the camera on him," she says, "he began to glow. It
was just hard to explain but he had that kind of presence in front
of the camera that brought it out in him and then it was like he was
talking to each child individually." Rogers credits his adaptation of
this interpersonal communication style to actor Gabby Hayes, who
hosted a western series called *The Gabby Hayes Show* on NBC
from 1950 to 1954. Rogers often floor-managed this show when
working in television, in a variety of different production roles,
after graduating from Rollins College. In *Lessons from Mister
Rogers*, he recalls asking Hayes, between shots, "Mr. Hayes, what
do you think of when you look into the camera and you know there
are so many people watching you?" According to Rogers, Hayes
responded, "Freddy, I just think of one little buckaroo." To Rogers,
this was "superb advice for anybody who would ever be thinking
of television. It's a very, very personal medium."[100]

From the perspective of Horton and Wohl, the kind of direct
address employed by Rogers's character on the show defines the
program's genre as a "personality program." Horton and Wohl
contrast the "personality program" to the "drama," asserting that
it is "especially designed to provide occasion for good-natured
joking and teasing, praising and admiring, gossiping and telling
anecdotes, in which the values of friendship and intimacy are
stressed."[101] Excluding acts of teasing and gossiping, Rogers's
televisual performances on *Neighborhood* fundamentally include
all of the social-communicative elements of Horton and Wohl's
"personality program."

Within this media matrix of direct "sociability," Horton and Wohl note that typical of the "personality program" is a sense that those being interviewed by the host are treated as "persons of consequence." For example, they note that in interviews that hosts undertake with "non-professional contestants," such subjects are often praised for having children or for their "youthful appearance." This treatment of ordinary persons is, in a sense, redirected on Rogers's program in a most meaningful and dynamic way. On *Neighborhood*, the viewer, whose representation on the actual screen is visually nonexistent, is treated by Rogers as a "person of consequence." Horton and Wohl argue that "personality programs" in which hosts interact with everyday persons on the show itself leave viewers with a sense that if they so wished, they too "could appropriately take part" in the kind of social solidarity that these programs espouse through their inclusion, albeit brief, of "ordinary" people.[102] In contrast, Rogers, through a technique of direct "sociability" with the viewer, effectively eliminates the step in which viewers are prompted to imagine that they "could appropriately take part" in social solidarity with him. Instead, his primary and ultimate concern in every episode is undeviating attention to and connection with the viewer himself.

In an early documented consultation conversation between McFarland and Rogers, in which the two are videorecorded sitting at a desk, McFarland tells Rogers that "the real difference between [Rogers's] program and most television for children is that it is less a *show* for children and more *real communication* with them."[103] She recounts to him how, when Rogers does live meeting events with the viewers of his program, the children run up to Rogers, throw their arms around his legs, and call him "my Mister Rogers" in anticipation that Rogers will recognize them as they recognize him. "To the child," McFarland tells Rogers, "the television program between you and the child is a real relationship and . . . you are speaking to the child."[104] She tells him that her former secretary has told her that her child gets up from her seat and speaks back to the character of "Mister Rogers" when she watches him on the television screen.

This interaction between McFarland and Rogers reveals much about the significance of their working relationship and McFarland's involvement with the development and maintenance of the program. McFarland acts as an analytical agent, offering a child development reading of the program. In this regard, she translates her everyday psychoanalytical practice from the Arsenal laboratory with Rogers the graduate student to Rogers the television producer. In much the same way that she would watch Rogers interact with children at the center and then meet with him afterward to offer her observations and insights, she would read a script or watch an episode of *Neighborhood* and then provide critical feedback with Rogers one-on-one. According to Rogers, the two met for script-draft analysis and other program-related consultation once a week. The two discussed the techniques, messaging, and other pedagogical phenomena that Rogers intended to produce or already produced, including children's reactions to *Neighborhood*.[105]

PUBLIC PEDAGOGY AND *NEIGHBORHOOD* INTERVENTION

In what we may presume to be a grant letter, McFarland places significant emphasis on the identification of the family as the primary educational agent in society, and on television as a media technology whose discursive power is designed to function within the family communication system.[106] The ethic Rogers and McFarland developed at Arsenal found public expression of its central family communication tenet in the establishment the National Education Television network in 1952.[107] Unlike the corporate-profit-driven economic framework of the reigning commercial networks (NBC, CBS, and ABC), NET was funded by the Ford

Foundation, whose liberal and progressive philanthropic mission was to advance human welfare. Organizations like Ford and the Carnegie Foundation began to focus on the prospects of an educational television network in the 1950s and 1960s as an alternative to commercial programming. The Public Broadcasting Act of 1967 "granted state sanction to the idea that commercial TV had failed to serve the interests of the American people," according to Anna McCarthy. Further, "it enshrined in media infrastructure the idea that the most effective means for activating TV's promise as an instrument of self-governance was to offer viewers a prosocial, culturally diverse complement to the degraded fare offered by the networks."[108]

In his 1969 address to Congress advocating for government funding for his and other PBS programming, Rogers tells Senator Pastore that he "is very concerned, as I'm sure you are, about what is being delivered to our children in this country." Those in children's television production, he argues, criticizing vaudevillian cheap thrills, need not "bop someone over the head to create drama on the screen." He then details how his program deals with the authentic dramas of childhood "such as getting a haircut, or the feelings about brothers and sisters, and the kind of anger that arises in simple family situations." On his program, he says, "we deal with it constructively." Rogers notes how viewers in Boston, Pittsburgh, and Chicago actively requested the development of more *Neighborhood* shows when they learned that the program might be cut due to lack of funding. "We've got to have more of this expression of care," he characterizes them as saying. Then, he confirms their description. "This is what I give . . . an expression of care every day to each child." Finally, after recounting the lyrics of one of his program's standard songs in which he tells his viewer that he likes him or her "just the way you are," he says, of the effects of his program, "If we in public television can only make it clear that feelings are mentionable and manageable, we will

have done a great service for mental health."[109] Here, in addressing a congressional assembly, Rogers ties his program and its
pedagogical framework to the civic realm, detailing how his program assists in the healthy emotional development of American
children.

Rogers was also keenly mindful of the rapidly growing consumer cultural ethos in the 1950s and 1960s, created by an
advertising culture that had infiltrated both print and electronic
media. He very consciously constructed his program according to
a different value system, arguably rooted in a residual Protestant
and agrarian ethic that emphasized the importance of frugality,
hard work, family, and community. In a 2011 panel at the University of Pittsburgh on the legacy of *Mister Rogers' Neighborhood*,
which featured former producers of the program, several panelists
noted that Rogers consistently rejected any proposals to mass
produce and commodify in toy form any characters or artifacts
from the program. Bill Isler, current CEO of The Fred Rogers
Company, spoke about Rogers's emphatic rejection of Isler's prop-
osition to manufacture toy trolleys modeled after the trolley on
Neighborhood. According to Sharapan, now the director of early
childhood initiatives for the Fred Rogers Company, Rogers never
"wanted parents to think that he was exploiting them."[110] Moreover,
Rogers rejected the idea of replacing his handmade puppets with
more polished, machine-made versions because he wanted child
viewers to get the sense that they could construct similar, simply
crafted puppets of their own to play with. Rogers instead wanted
to maintain the show's iconography at an artisanal level, rejecting
the commercial model that Henry Giroux shows eventually gained
dominance.[111] In his verbal Senate testimony and a document he
wrote titled "Philosophy," we can see how Rogers sets up his project as a sort of antithesis to the dominant commercial ethos of
popular children's television programming of the time and as such
can be read as a countercultural effort.

ROGERS'S "PHILOSOPHY"

Drawing from his work in television at NBC and WQED, his theological studies, his study with McFarland, and experiences at Arsenal, Rogers developed *Mister Rogers' Neighborhood*. In "Philosophy," an undated document presumably written during the developmental stage of *Mister Rogers' Neighborhood*, Rogers makes explicit his vision for the program. This vision was well thought out and meticulously articulated in a typed document. The first "premise" establishes that the program does not conceive of children as isolated individuals; rather, it stresses the child as embedded in a social and psychological family dynamic that spans at least two generations. The second "premise" calls for the television artist to become a participant in the viewer's family dynamic. As Rogers breaks the fourth wall and speaks directly into the television camera, saying, "You are a very special person and I like you just the way you are," he becomes part of the child's immediate, yet virtual, social environment, and thus a participant in the child's world of family relationships. In the third and final premise, Rogers envisions that each show will center upon a theme that correlates to "everyday growing experiences."[112] Here, the emphasis is on finding wonder in life's everyday experiences rather than the absurdist and escapist violence of slapstick comedy prominent in the commercial children's television of his time.

The second section in the "Philosophy" document focuses on what Rogers and his colleagues call the "elements" of the program that Rogers regards as indispensable to the framework of *Neighborhood*. The list begins with "Adult to child relationship," which asserts that Rogers will "play it straight"; that is, Rogers will not play a character other than his "real life" identity. As such, Rogers presents himself as a caring and reassuring parental figure, ensuring that the act of communication, which involves conversation, characterization, and situation, revolves around aspects of "everyday family life" as understood by 1960s norms. The presence of this "real life" parental, neighborly, adult, figure feeds into the next "element" of the show—respect for the "integrity of feelings."[113] Rogers's objective is to demonstrate to the viewer that her feelings (fear, anger, anxiety, sadness, joy) are identifiable, mentionable, and manageable.[114]

Rogers's role as himself, a calm and caring adult figure, contrasts with much of the vaudevillian and burlesque entertainment styles of network children live action television programs of the time such as *The Howdy Doody Show* (1947–1960), *The Pinky Lee Show* (1954–1966), *Lunch with Soupy Sales* (1952–1962), *The Soupy Sales Show* (1964–1966), and others. In these programs, some of the adult characters clown around by imitating the behavior of the child; as a result, these programs are perceived as humorous. Such shows were characterized by several entertainment commentators of the time as "hyperstimulating" and are likely what Rogers referred to in his Senate testimony when he referred to children's television as "bombardment."[115] Rogers tries to provide a gradual slowing down for a viewer who is likely tuning in to his program after watching a fast-paced program. He once said, "There is so much that's so fast about television. Wherever you're placed on the television schedule you know very well that there's going to be some hyper thing before you, and it goes off in a very hyper way, so we have some music and movement right away to help make the transition."[116] There were other exceptions to the hyperstimulation model in period television programs. Captain Kangaroo, played by Bob Keeshan on the program by the same name (1955–1984), is one. Rogers and Keeshan paired up for a 1979 PBS special, *Springtime with Mister Rogers*. Keeshan has stated that due to the strong profit motive, broadcasters are less likely to hand airtime over to children's television programs with adult hosts.[117]

In *Mister Rogers' Neighborhood*, the adult remains an adult and the child learns from the caring relationship with this adult. Indeed, in one of many recordings of Rogers and McFarland in conversation during the early years of the program, McFarland stresses that the real difference between *Neighborhood* and "most television for children" is that *Neighborhood* is "less a show for children and more real communication with them." To this, Rogers responds, "I am an adult in relationship to the child, not working out some of my old needs in front of a group of children." McFarland confirms, "That's right," articulating that the difficulty involved for persons creating programs for children lies in the fact that the creative process itself is rooted in one's own "experiencing of childhood." She continues, "but to be able to differentiate one-self from the watching child is an essential part of making it an adult-child relationship."[118] Here, McFarland stresses the behavior necessary to create and maintain Rogers's role as adult in relation to his child viewers. This choice appears to be rooted in the inten-tion to keep the program grounded in everyday reality.

One of the most important "elements" articulated in the "Philos-ophy" document is Rogers's emphasis on the distinction between reality and the imaginary, fantasy world of children. "Each show is conspicuously composed of reality and fantasy segments," the document states. According to the "Philosophy" document, there are many psychological lessons at work in a fantasy environment. "Make-Believe," according to Rogers, "serves as a laboratory of the imagination from where children can test options in behavior."[119] In the "Reality-Fantasy" section of "Philosophy," Rogers writes that "reality provides *real* norms against which one's progress can be compared and gauged; and reality provides a basis for what to expect in the future. Fantasy is the playground of the imagination from which creative ideas and fine distinctions can be drawn and understood; and the ability to distinguish abstract notions such as 'good'and 'bad' adds to the quality of real life."[120] It is important here to note that fantasy is not divorced from reality. Fantasy, in this sense, does not refer to something false or delusional.[121] Instead, Rogers demonstrates his understanding of child development: the primary target audience for his program is children at the pre-school age, who, more than any other age group, live to engage in individual fantasy play as well as dramatic play with their peers. As for the older toddler, play fosters skill development, reality exploration, and mastery of anxiety. The established consensus in child development holds that "imaginative play takes center stage in development, becoming an essential vehicle for constructing and understanding the world as well as facilitating cognitive and socio-emotional growth."[122] These well-established theories of fantasy/imaginative play originated with child development philosopher Jean Piaget, whose 1920s writings were translated into English in the 1940s and widely read in American child development and psychology programs in the 1950s and 1960s.[123]

The show opens with Rogers coming into his "television home." He then greets his television audience; together they exist on the same level of reality in the material world, in the entryway of his home. "Routinely," Rogers writes, the program "opens in the 'real' NEIGHBORHOOD with Mister Rogers entering his television house as though returning from the office," indicating that he has an adult life that he attends to outside of the home.[124] After this entrance, Rogers takes off his formal shoes and puts on his sneakers in an effort to indicate to the child viewer that he is entering a time and space where he is fully attentive to him. In this space he refamiliarizes himself with the viewer in conversational dialogue that introduces the ideas that will serve as the episode's themes. Then, after a discussion of such ideas, perhaps followed by an activity either in Rogers's home or neighborhood, there follows an invitation by Rogers to both imagine and visually travel to a story that is unfolding in the Neighborhood of Make-Believe, a theater in which puppets and human actors mingle in a drama.[125] As a child development specialist, McFarland no doubt taught Rogers about the importance of transitions in the child's everyday experience. Because transitions usually involve a great deal of cognitive, emotional, and physical effort for young children, signposts like the entrance of the trolley into Rogers's home help children to prepare for the transition by signaling its impending arrival. McFarland considered transitions one of "the most important aspects of people's lives."[126] In a modern world that values fast-paced movement and rapid production, Rogers tries to provide a more anthropocentric speed of life that allows people to sustain concentration and manage tasks and events in a less rushed fashion. We tend, he says, "to hurry through transitions and to try to hurry our children through them as well. We may feel that these transitions are 'nowhere at all' compared to what's gone before or what we anticipate is next to come."[127]

Finally, the "Philosophy" document allows us to see the unexpected and defining role that music plays in the program. Rogers, who graduated from Rollins College with a degree in music composition, wrote every song that was performed on *Neighborhood*.[128] The document reveals that he believed that music offers "a mode of affective expression" and creative channeling for one's inner feelings.[129] As we saw earlier in his "Invisible Essentials" speech, Rogers used music as a young boy to process his difficult and volatile emotions prompted by those who bullied him on a daily basis. "The insides of me," says Rogers, "from the very beginning, have been connected to music."[130] As Roderick Townley has observed, Rogers uses music on the show primarily as a transitional device. "I've always had the analogy of moving from one key to another in the program," Rogers said. In this way, he "modulates" from the entryway to the living room to the Neighborhood of Make-Believe. The music reflects the kind of shift in feeling that comes with the change in environment and task. Rogers has described the ways that he plays with keys in transitioning from the living room of his home to the Neighborhood of Make-Believe, saying that "you want to find as many notes in the new key that are the same as the notes in the old key. And you play with those and almost imperceptibly get into the new key." For example, he says, in the modulation going from the key of C to the key of F, only the B-flat is a new note. Thus, "there are a lot of notes you can play as if you were playing in both keys. So little by little you get to F."[31]

This use of music demonstrates Rogers's interest in maintaining the child's trust, an essential act that must consistently recur on show after show in order to reestablish Rogers as a reliable fixture in the child's life. Secure attachment relationships between primary caretakers and the child are necessary for the child to feel safe and venture into the world of play and learning with confidence and emotional strength. In his book coauthored with Barry Head, *Mister Rogers' How Families Grow*, Rogers discusses "a child's transition from the oneness with the mother to relationships with a world full of people—first other people in the family, and then all those people beyond."[32] Townley observes the ways that this model functions on the neighborhood, in which Rogers gradually expands the child's social familiarity from the primary relationship with him in the home, to the recurrent neighborhood characters such as Mr. McFeely, Betty Aberlin, Joe Negri, and others, to irregular "drop-in guests" like Tony Bennett or Yo-Yo Ma. Such a dynamic mirrors the kind of concentric circles present in a child's life starting with the primary relationship in the home, branching out to the neighborhood community and school, and then moving beyond into interactions with strangers.[33]

AN ANTHROPOCENTRIC, CHRISTIAN-BASED INTERVENTION

Rogers's articulation of foundational Christian values such as simplicity, honesty, love, and the unique value of human beings and their relationships with one another undergirds and directs his communication project. Yet while Rogers is clear about the influence of Christian precepts on his understanding of human life and behavior, his modern, pluralistic approach to his "ministry" significantly departs from more traditional, Pietistic Christian practices and expressions. In a collection of notes he dated September 19, 1984, Rogers jotted down the following "secrets of success":

> Find a need and fill it.
>   "   " hurt and heal it.
>   "   " problem and solve it.
> Success will always be unselfish.
> Success cannot tolerate alternatives.

He continued in his musing with the following progression:

> We must never use t.v. to manipulate the minds of people to vote the way "we" vote. We must preach to broken hearts. If we do we will always be up to date.
>
> Who marries the spirit of his age will soon find himself a widower.[134]

> What are the classical human universal personal needs?
>
> What is the ultimate need that transcends all others (it's anthropocentric not theocentric)
>
> Church has abandoned the human being to the psychologists. We must listen to the cry
>
> WILL TO MEANING FEEL I HAVE VALUE (self esteem, self worth)
>
> The function of the church is not to sell our theology to people. It's to say "How can I help you?"

> Freud: deepest human need is the will for pleasure
> Adler: "   "   "   " to power (to feel you're in control)
> Victor Frankel: " "   " to meaning (he then wrote Logo Therapy)
> Schuller: "   "   "   " need to feel I have value.
> Ego need needs satisfied.
> Jesus came to save us from shame (cleansed from sin).[135]

Taken all together, these statements amount to an ethos of "ethical emotionality," encapsulated in the universal "need to feel I have value." This translates into the fundamental iteration of *Neighborhood*: "I like you just the way you are." How these notes connect the import of the program to the sociocultural context in which it emerged bears some discussion. This set of notes offers textual evidence of how Rogers found the artistic modes that connected his Christian-based message to the ongoing redefinition of childhood—a shift due in part to the influence of television in children's lives.

In these notes, Rogers's attempts to reiterate to himself his primary values and mission are striking. He highlights his core understanding of the mission of the pastor—to identify and serve human spiritual needs. He then puts this mission in dialogue with the most powerful and current theories of the human being developed by the new science of psychology. In this way, the document embodies the dialectic he places at the center of *Neighborhood*: two distinct knowledge systems whose conclusions about human behavior, needs, and general psychic health often overlap.

Rogers begins by setting up three key problem-solution action models of approach for success. The first instructs one to "find a need and fill it;" the second to "find a hurt and heal it;" and the third to "find a problem and solve it." He then asserts that success is unselfish; its objective, as in clarifying theological positions or enforcing church doctrine, is to serve the needs of the other rather than those of the self. Unselfish success is the only possible definition of success; it "cannot tolerate alternatives." Here, Rogers digs in his heels; his position is steadfast and unwavering; approaching any ministerial act from a position of selflessness rather than doctrinal authority is his imperative. Success, therefore, only comes when the minister yields to the needs and concerns of the other, instead of asserting doctrine or judgments blindly. Adopting and practicing the Christian virtue of selflessness (caritas and agape) requires the subject to relinquish the initiation of action and control to the other. As a result, the role of the subject becomes centered on an act of listening and responding in the spirit of service as opposed to telling or lecturing.

In this dynamic, the traditional role of the "authority" is transfigured from one who imparts knowledge and is the repository of the meaning of rules and values into one who listens and learns from others and offers response in a dialogue.[136] In contrast, for Freire's dialogical educator, whose approach is founded upon "love, humility, and faith," emotional terms that speak of an ethical emotionality, dialogue becomes "a horizontal relationship of which mutual trust between dialoguers is the logical consequence."[137]

Having established that success can only come from a position of selflessness, Rogers decries those who use the medium of television to "manipulate" the minds of others in order to get them to "vote the way 'we' vote." That act is selfish because is only interested in fulfilling the wishes of the persons initiating the engagement. By contrast, Rogers's approach consistently emphasizes the worth of the other, the receiver of the message. He actively refrained from any actions that he thought could betray the good will he had established with his viewers. For example, in 1984 he testified in support of a Supreme Court decision that allowed Sony to sell home video recording devices by arguing that it would allow television users to become more active in programming their family's television schedule. "Very frankly," he stated then, "I am opposed to people being programmed by others. My whole approach in broadcasting has always been 'You are an important person just the way you are. You can make healthy decisions.' Maybe I am going on too long, but I just feel that anything that allows a person to be more active in the control of his or her life, in a healthy way, is important."[138] Rogers's comment illustrates the high value that he, as a Protestant, places on the individual's freedom.

However, his value of individual freedom and individualism does not reaffirm anything like the laissez-faire doctrine of individualism that preceded him. Instead, Rogers seeks to restore the human-relational individualism of the American Protestant tradition through a reformulation of an "I and Thou" ethic. He is particularly rejecting what C. B. Macpherson has called "possessive individualism." Constantly at work in asserting a transformative philosophy of the individual in which the sovereign "I" of the individual gives way to the "I" of ethical emotionality in an I-Thou relationship, Rogers reasserts this once dominant, now countercultural ethos.

As noted in the introduction to this chapter, Rogers's interest in transforming the ministerial approach into a practice based on an I-Thou model dovetails with the discussions that arose at the Pittsburgh Theological Seminary during the postwar period. When Rogers writes that "those who preach to broken hearts will remain relevant in contemporary life" while "those who wed themselves to the spirit of the times will find themselves widowed" he intervenes into discussions concerning the mission of the church in the current historical moment. Working within the debates between the traditional Pietists and the neo-orthodox reformers in the church, Rogers offers a third way of possibilty. With striking brevity, he addresses the benefits and dangers of the reformists, who, in response to the "cries of human hurt, anger, and need" arising from the crises of urban poverty and race relations went as far as asking why the Pittsburgh Theological Seminary was not becoming "more of a social service agency."[139] Rogers affirms this social gospel branch in praising the timeless relevance of ministering to broken people as emphasized in the gospel. He follows this, however, by warning against the danger of becoming too attached to the messages and spirit of the times. In this regard, he appears to view the potential for confusing the Christian directive to minister to the broken with the secularist, social justice ethos of the 1960s and 1970s. His third way, based on the I-Thou relationship of Christian care, would set a general societal climate of values that in the long run addresses the problem of poverty and isolation in society at large through a social pedagogy that stresses an ethic of care as practice (rather than a set of rules).[140]

Embracing the conviction that "the ultimate human need is anthropocentric" and not theocentric, Rogers addresses the controversy between Pietists or conservatives, who focus on more traditional understandings of Christian practice such as prayer, witness, and theology, and the reformist branch of the church interested in applying the gospel to social work in the community. Pittsburgh Theological Seminary came into existence in 1958 by way of the merging of two Pittsburgh seminaries—Pittsburgh-Xenia Theological Seminary and Western Theological Seminary. From the moment of its inception, PTS dealt with an underlying conflict between Western students, who embraced contemporary theology and were considered more liberal and modern, and Pitt-Xenia students, who were more interested in the "traditional understanding of Christian faith as well as the classical signs of personal piety." Western students often criticized Pitt-Xenia students for practicing their faith in insular, strict, and old-fashioned ways. The emphasis at Pitt-Xenia was placed on the "gospel ministry" whereas Western stressed the "pastorate." These two approaches were joined in the establishment of PTS, which placed heightened value on educating persons "for the work of the Christian ministry."[141]

In this context, Rogers's statement that the "church has abandoned the human being to the psychologists" calls for close analysis. On the one hand, it would seem that Rogers's keen interest in child psychology would hardly qualify him for claiming that the church has "abandoned" persons to psychologists. However, if one takes into consideration Rogers's understanding of his craft and ministry as a healer/healing, departing from the Christian understanding of the care involved in the I-Thou relationship, then his criticism of the church makes sense, especially considering those who claim that the church's main concern is theology and prayer. As William Guy notes in his essay on *Neighborhood* theology, Rogers's emphasis on care for the other contrasts not only with secular media messages of "I can have it all" but also with a theocentric theology that asserts that "I as an individual can and must be saved by establishing a personal relationship with Jesus Christ." Both worldviews, Guy asserts, lack any attention to "other people."[142] On the contrary, his entire enterprise attempts to harness the insights of child development theory into his communication art in order to convey and act out an I-Thou relationship. Rogers's new understanding of Christian ministry calls for an integration of the insights of psychology with the message of the gospel. This criticism of the church identifies the trend, well established by 1984, in which the psychologist has essentially replaced the church as an institution that helps people work through emotional, though not spiritual, wounds.

In these notes, Rogers is critical of particular positions of the church and the television industry. He disagrees with those who think that spreading the gospel translates into "selling Christian theology." For him, evangelization requires the healing of hearts. In regards to psychology, he seems to question whether this practice/discipline is fit to replace the position of the church in society.

In regards to the television industry, he decries the use of the medium as a tool for political manipulation and the commercialism that posits the viewer as a consumer—that is to say, an object of capitalist exploitation.

Rogers's parting with both the theological and the social activist approach is evident in his concept of an anthropocentric approach to human suffering. This third way is further evinced when he writes that "there is nothing magic about faith in God. It stems from very human roots." This theology, which honors the individual's unique worth and emphasizes how he is made in the image of God, is repeated in various linguistic and visual discourses on each program. Rogers concludes his reflection on the human roots of knowing God by arriving at the very crux of the Christian faith. "God knows. God's son came in human form so that we might be able to believe all the more in God's trustworthiness, discipline and care—so that we might believe in God's love!"[143] The anthropocentric approach is thus what enables Rogers's achievement of creating a television program for children that while deeply rooted in the foundational message of love and care in the Gospel is at the same time able to dispense with theological or Christological language and iconography.

A THIRD WAY

By putting to work psychological and ethical insights derived from his experience with children at the Arsenal Family and Children's Center, Rogers figured out how to communicate ways of making meaning in the world. Rogers connects deeply with children at various stages in their development, a skill that he learned studying child development and working with Arsenal children. In the elaboration of his craft, he developed a dialogical communication ethics and practice centered on learning and the

creation of meaning, which he later honed and developed for the
television medium. With its focus on mutuality, learning from one
another, and active I-Thou engagement, this model not only was
difficult to deploy by means of a mass communication technology
like television but in fact seems to stand paradoxically against
the nature of "mass" communication. Rogers, however, proved
prescient in his understanding of television as a paradoxically personal mass medium. He correctly assessed the socially affective
potential of the new technology in ways described by Horton and
Wohl in their theorization of the parasocial dimension of episodic
television programming. Rogers developed an understanding of
television communication practice that identified the medium's
power to affect human perception on a deeply personal and
social level.

Rogers's analysis discovers that people respond to characters
on television in the same affective manner they associate with
members of their immediate peer group or family. He realizes
the importance of developing an ethic of communication that
goes beyond the individual and asserts essential community
values such as charity, the dignity of the human person, caritas,
acceptance, and respect. As Guy notes, "What Mister Rogers is
'preaching' . . . is cooperative, communal life—the covenant community if one prefers, or even the Kingdom of God. His parables
suggest that the answer to our problems of personal dissatisfac-
tion lies in the establishment of a community in which people look
out for each other and are looked out for in return." In this kind of
community, one defined by care of the self and other, one cannot
conveniently "deny others as centers of importance corresponding
to oneself," as the bullies of his childhood were able to do to him.[144]
From this understanding, based on his own experience and New
Testament theology, Rogers grounds his ethic in the image of the
wounded healer, a position he seems to have adopted as a result of

the bullying he experienced as a young boy and one that functions out of a core ethos of mutuality and dialogue.

This communication ethics implies not just individual choices and commitments but community understanding. For Rogers, healing occurred when he came to acknowledge and communicate the pain he experienced in the form of music, an art form universally known for the expression of deep and profound emotions.[145] As the wounded healer, he brings together "invisible essentials," messages that communicate that which is "invisible to the eye" and connect with the viewer's own invisible interiority. Rogers sees the heart as the organ of his vision and offers himself to the viewer as the neighbor who can be trusted with the viewer's inner feelings and emotional needs. Such an ethic of trust involves an I-Thou relationship, out of which Rogers's ethical emotionality develops, producing a third way, an alternative to a variety of cultural and political tensions present within an American society caught up in a revolutionary moment of change within the creation-destruction cycles of advanced capitalism. In this regard, his "attention to the feelings of individuals and to the holiness of each heart's affections," Guy notes, illustrates Rogers's reverence and celebration of life within what Pope John Paul II termed "a culture of death" and Adrienne Rich described as a "death-culture of quantification, abstraction and the will to power which has reached its most refined destructiveness in this century."[146] Undoubtedly, Rogers asserts an anthropocentric affirmation of love and care that emerges from his understanding that "there is a divine personal force at the center of reality" and that this force "has no instruments other than human beings by which or through whom to convey its feelings about those same human beings."[147]

Rogers offers also a third way with regard to the tensions within the Presbyterian church (and Christian churches within the society at large), where modern liberals advocate movement away from Pietist understandings of Christianity in favor of a stronger emphasis on social services. By speaking the gospel to contemporary life, integrating his knowledge of classical theological disciplines with modern disciplines such as psychology and the behavioral sciences, "recognizing the possibility of positive values of diverse opinions" inside and outside the church, being "sensitive to persons where they are at a particular time," and listening to understand people's points of need, Rogers constructs this third way.[148] He honors and puts into practice the seminary's call to develop the "skills needed for ministry in our times." Rogers seeks to build communication bridges between his Protestant beliefs and a 1960s culture that placed increasing value on liberal tenets such as social reform attendant to racial discrimination and urban poverty. The seminary's "Exhibit A" called for a historic development in the training of the pastor to become at once a "teaching elder" and "social activist" in order to honor the "diverse opinions in the church."[149] Such missionary transformation identified "sensitivity" as a key disposition for a pastor in regards to extending communication to diverse groups.[150] Rogers functioned as both a teaching elder in the ways he communicated the fundamental teachings of the gospel and a social activist in the ways he reached out to serve others. He taught his flock a way to understand and constructively manage their feelings in order to foster healthy growth and development. Moreover, Rogers is firm in his understanding of this reform as it intended to ensure that modern knowledge systems such as psychology do not overshadow the primary messages of the gospel. Thus, while he wants to provide his viewers a space of therapy, he does not marry his enterprise to psychology in general and expresses concern that the church has ceded all healing powers in American society to psychology.

Finally, Rogers's communication project offers a third way for adults to negotiate the pressures and tensions of a rapidly changing sociocultural and economic postwar culture. In his *Neighborhood*, Rogers offers an affirmation of the critical bonds of community essential to sustaining human life and a return to the "simple," enduring values and manageable social structures of old. He celebrates the home as a space of bonding and security, and the neighborhood as a place where people interact and work in fellowship and for the common goal of living together peacefully. In 1970 Philip Slater wrote, "One of the first goals of a society is to make its inhabitants feel safe. . . . Yet Americans feel far less safe, both at home and abroad, than they did fifty years ago. Our nuclear arsenal, the guns under pillows, and the multiple lock[s] on city doors betray our fears without easing them."[51] Thus, though his enterprise overtly targets a child audience, Rogers simultaneously seeks to address the suffering and insecure feelings of American adults who are busy adjusting and readjusting to the rapid changes of advanced capitalism while simultaneously instructing their children about how to live in such a dynamic and complex world. With his third way, he offers a space of emotional safety, security, empathy, and mutual understanding. As such, he not only ministers to the emotional needs of adults, he offers them a model of parenting and behaving with children that, in its pedagogical way, provides relief and a sense of control.

Inside
Mister Rogers' Neighborhood

OBJECTS, PLAY, AND
THE CULTURAL DIALECTIC

DURING THE OPENING SONG OF *Neighborhood*, Mister Rogers enters his "television house" smiling and looking into the camera, singing,

> It's a beautiful day in the neighborhood
> A beautiful day in the neighborhood,
> Would you be mine?
> Could you be mine?
>
> It's a neighborly day in this beauty wood,
> A neighborly day for a beauty,
> Would you be mine?
> Could you be mine?

I have always wanted to have a neighbor just like you!
I've always wanted to live in a neighborhood with you
So let's make the most of this beautiful day
Since we're together we might as well say,
Would you be mine?
Could you be mine?
Won't you be my neighbor?
Won't you please,
Won't you please,
Please won't you be my neighbor?[1]

In a matter of four lyrical stanzas, Rogers establishes an immediate, dialogical relationship with the individual viewer by employing a direct, sustained, interpersonal greeting. This greeting is enacted by clear and unmistakable verbal and nonverbal messages that guide the social and emotional act of coming together in relationship. The first four lines of the song establish the foundational I-Thou relationship of mutuality that characterizes the program. Mister Rogers first acknowledges the day, which he describes adoringly as "beautiful," and then he invites the viewer to step into it with him in a rather intimate way: "Would you be mine?" he asks. His invitation is not a statement, such as "Welcome to the program," or "It's good to see you," as is the case with many television programs both old and new in which the host addresses the viewer(s) directly.[2] Rather, Rogers delivers his greeting in the form of a question: "Would you be mine?" he asks.[3]

Whereas "Welcome to the program; it's good to see you," would set up a one-way, sender-receiver communication transaction, in which the sender holds power and authority and the receiver falls into a subject position characterized by passivity and voicelessness, Rogers's greeting, "Would you be mine? Could you be mine?" creates a transactional space for interpersonal exchange between himself and the viewer. He asks the viewer to enter the space with him, and in a most intimate way. With "Would you be mine?" he beckons the viewer to become his own, as in a love relationship. A question we could envision a young man saying to his sweetheart or a mother to her baby, "Would you be mine?" creates a kind of immediate and intimate sense of bonding and togetherness. Further, in this invitational question, Rogers humbles himself to the viewer, asking her if what he proposes is agreeable to her. In this way, Rogers's gesture communicates handing off his speaking privileges to the receiver in order to create a sense of equal dialogical exchange that levels the plane of interaction, along with an I-Thou relationship of mutuality.

In the third stanza, Rogers continues his focus on the viewer, in a kind of playful inversion of the standard relational dynamics of television, often conceived as a one-to-many communication medium. Indeed, this expectation would suggest that Rogers, as the "star" of the show, is supposed to be the focus of the enamored and distant home viewer, not the other way around. "I have always wanted to have a neighbor just like you," he sings, "I've always wanted to live in a neighborhood with you." Thus, the show is incomplete without the viewer's acceptance of the invitation, stressing that mutuality is the foundation on which the rest of the program unfolds.

Rogers begins each program by singing this song as he enters his "television home" through the front door. His face always displays a genuine smile and his voice projects a positive and pleasant tone. He is dressed in plain pants, a button-down shirt with a tie, and a men's suit jacket. While he sings the opening song, he strives to maintain eye contact with the camera/viewer as he removes his jacket, hangs it on a hanger in the closet a few feet away, and puts on a plain-colored cardigan sweater. He then sits down on a bench in his living room and changes out of his work shoes and into a pair of Keds. As the song comes to a close and Rogers finishes tying his shoes, he sings:

Won't you please,
Won't you please,
Please won't you be my neighbor?

After the song concludes, Rogers takes a moment to transition out of this I and Thou welcoming greeting by saying hello to the viewer and by introducing her to an object that he has brought with him. With this move, he replicates the most important event in the infant's path to becoming socially viable by providing the viewer with a transitional object that will serve to foster the move from total dependency on mother into relative dependency via engagement with the world. The child's interest in and manipulation and transformation of the object, in tandem with the development of a secure, trusting attachment relationship with mother, and later dependable adults like Rogers, will serve her healthy and stable development. Rogers deploys this sequence, which begins with relationship establishment/reestablishment and moves toward the examination of and play with an object, in nearly every episode of *Neighborhood*. The objects he brings with him to show the viewer serve as fodder for the show's anthropological conversations about artifacts, their transformative abilities when handled and examined by people, and their relationship to the social world of people and things.

The first year of *Mister Rogers' Neighborhood* represents some of the program's most important work. In its 130 episodes, Rogers constructed a framework for the show—a framework he and his team would sustain for over thirty years. In this chapter, I examine the primary rhetorical and aesthetic choices that Rogers made in creating the first year of the program. Having identified Rogers's dialogic communication method as an important strategy of engagement, I now wish to examine the ways Rogers interweaves this anthropocentric, dialectical ethos with a meticulous study of objects, play, and the creation of social-material culture. A detailed look at programming that ran during the first year reveals that a consistent and ritualized emphasis on investigating the uses of everyday material objects, their social meanings, and their creative potentiality is central to the show's construction. I have chosen for extensive discussion a number of "television visits"— Rogers always referred to his program as a "television visit," not a "show"—that effectively exemplify the overall character of the dialogic mode of inquiry and communication that Rogers uniquely employs. Episode after episode begins with the introduction of an everyday object (such as a scale, a shoe, a stone, or a painting) that is designed to prompt a thoughtful dialogical, social, and bodily investigation of its potential uses, transformative capacity, and various meanings.[4] The object thus becomes the starting point for the creative, enacted, and embodied unfolding of a culture and a people who constitute and occupy a small, manageable world called *Mister Rogers' Neighborhood.*

The program, I argue, constitutes the representation of a culture's materiality that is organized by social principles that promote values of discovery, creativity, transformation, and growth at the levels of the material world, the social world that gives meaning to the material world, and the emotional and moral world of *Neighborhood.* In *Neighborhood,* the material object leads to the social, which includes the aesthetic, ethical, and emotional aspects of human life. This is to say that each object presented always exists and operates within a relational framework—no object exists by itself. From an anthropological perspective, the concept of *Homo faber* is necessary for analyzing Rogers's display of objects that constitute the architecture of the imaginary world that is *Neighborhood.* That is, once Rogers picks up a wig, plays the piano keyboard, makes a cake, receives a letter, opens a door, puts on his shoes, etc., these objects are resemanticized in a complex network of communication. Rogers not only displays the objects themselves but also shows how the object is made and used by human hands or human technology. Its functionality, in human terms, is explored at length and from different angles. For example, in episode 12 of season 1, Rogers pulls several of his different-color cardigans out of the closet and shows them to the viewer. Next, he says, "But first I want to show you a picture of the person who made them." He pulls out an 8-by-10-inch photograph of an elderly woman, and as the camera closes in on her face, he reveals that the woman is his mother. "She knits the sweaters that I wear when we have our television visits," he tells the viewer. Then he focuses closely on a red sweater and its cable-knit stitching, asking the viewer to join him in "looking very carefully at the beautiful work she does with her knitting." The camera closes in as he runs his hand over each different-colored sweater, noting "each stitch she makes with her hands." In less than a minute, Rogers has delved into the materiality of making an object, its connection to human activity, its position in the social milieu, and its aesthetic import.

Rogers deploys objects as vehicles to think about, discuss, and examine the structures of the sociopolitical and material world. He also uses them as venues for exploring and teaching the art of cultural creation, the value of individual action and empowerment, and the pleasurable creative uses of ordinary material objects. Always departing first from the dialogical social relationship he establishes with his viewer, Rogers ritually introduces a third position—an object to play with, manipulate, and dialogically examine together. He first dialogues on various ideas that arise when assessing and thinking about the object. He then homes in on a particular idea and weaves this idea and its derivatives through a dialectic of social action and transaction.

Within the intimate social environment he creates with his viewer, Rogers is primarily interested in artifacts—how people make them, use them, and transform them. He identifies a thing and shows how human activity traverses the thing to make it into an object that has a relation to human beings. In doing so, he ties these objects to their place in the social realm. His use of objects is constituted by activity and the creation and recreation of sociomaterial items by the work of human hands.

Rogers's emphasis on play and object relations, his variations on the object woven together by social activity and relationships, and his use of song to convey feeling and create secure attachment between him and the viewer work in dialectical ways to produce an anthropocentric, safe, yet challenging world in which the child (and adult) viewer is encouraged to engage, cognitively, emotionally, and socially with the questions, ideas, characters, and narratives presented.

ARCHITECTURE OF THE PROGRAM

Let me begin by providing a broad description of the structural elements of each episode by examining one of the first programs from the first season. This example and those that follow will give us a sense of the variety and redundancies of the program content, along with the program's tight structural framework, continuity of characters, recurrence of general themes, persistent structure of feeling, consistent sense of pacing, and revisitation of spaces/places.

Mister Rogers' Neighborhood begins with an instrumental opening of the song "It's A Beautiful Day in the Neighborhood," played solo on celeste as the camera pans over a model neighborhood of buildings, street signs, trees, and houses. After a few seconds, and prompted by a notable musical shift to a solo piano with dense syncopated chords and ascending glissandos, the camera partially zooms in on one particular house, ostensibly Mister Rogers's, and we continue to zoom into the structure until eventually cutting to the inside set, the interior of Rogers's home.[5] The camera pans the living room from right to left. We first see a picture frame, which we later learn plays films and is affectionately anthropomorphized and named "Picture Picture." The frame has the word *Hi* written in large letters on the primary focal area. Underneath it is a small trolley that traverses train tracks in the same direction that the camera pans. Beneath the trolley is a worn plaid couch. The camera follows the trolley, toward the front door of the house, through which Rogers enters, singing, "It's a beautiful day in the neighborhood." Rogers continues in song while changing out of his suit jacket and into a cardigan, which he grabs off a hanger in the nearby coat closet. In the earlier episodes, Rogers enters his television home wearing blue Keds sneakers and thus does not engage in the later transitional ritual of changing from formal shoes into more casual ones. In nearly every episode, after he closes the invitational song, Mister Rogers sits down on the bench and shows the viewer an object that he has brought with him.

In the fourth episode of the first season, Rogers brings with him a blanket and a folding wooden playpen, which he sets on the ground in the living room.[6] He greets the viewer with a simple "Hi" and then discusses the object with him/her. "Do you know what this is?" he asks. "Oh, I bet you played in one of these. Or you have a younger brother or sister who has." Rogers's first use of speech in an episode always emerges in a casual tone and tends to address the utilitarian function of the object, its social meaning or relevance, and sometimes the transformational possibilities of the object. In the case of the crib, he places the blanket into it and says, "Wait until you see who is going to go in it." He then goes to the front door and fetches a little Saint Bernard puppy, picks her up, and returns to the playpen, announcing, "Ladies and gentlemen, I'd like you to meet Lydia Stout."[7] He then turns to the dog and says, "Lydia Stout, I'd like you to meet my friends." Looking down at the playpen with the puppy still in his arms, he asks her if she might like to play in the pen. He pretends to listen to her and then tells the viewer, "Oh, she thinks it looks a little bit like a fence and she's not too sure that she cares too much for fences."

After such initial discussion, Rogers might explore the object's functions with a visiting neighbor, sing a song about the object, or explain how the object is relevant in a current drama in the program's fantasy-play segment called the Neighborhood of Make-Believe (NMB), which the program then leads into. In this episode, Rogers breaks into a song about the complex and sometimes contradictory nature of our relationship to fences.

REFRAIN:
Fences, fences
The world is full of fences
And some I like
And some I don't
Like the kind that keep me out

The kind that keep me out
And the kind that make me pout
They're the kind that have no gate at all
They're the kind that go up much too tall

REFRAIN

The kind that keep me safe I say
Are the kind that keep me [inaudible]
They're the kind that help me drive my car
So I never have to go far from

REFRAIN[8]

In the middle of the song, Rogers places the dog in the pen and the camera zooms in on her as she lies down. Rogers gets down on his knees so that he can pet the dog and continues to sing the song. "How many fences do you know about?" he asks the viewer at the end of the song. "Did you ever hide on the other side of a fence or do you ever just play hide-and-seek?" Without addressing the issues presented in the song, Rogers engages in a game of hide-and-seek with the viewer. Though his song addresses the ways people might not like how fences inhibit their movement, it embraces the ways that they keep people safe. His speech after the song further points to a positive familiarity with the fence and how it can be used to play amusing games. Here, he addresses potentially contradictory feelings about fences from an indirect and nonverbal angle. He uses the fence for play, demonstrating that people have the choice to view the fence either positively or negatively. They can, as he demonstrates, choose to use the fence for pleasurable activities; the fence can have multiple meanings, but we can choose to focus on its positive uses. Playing hide-and-seek with the viewer, he crouches down and sneaks out the front door. After a few seconds go by, he walks through the front door, saying, "See, I came back. I always come back when I say I will," assuring the viewer that he is trustworthy and signaling the game's end.

After discussion of and play with an object takes place, Rogers is often greeted by a visit from a neighbor. In episode 0004, a knock on the front door results in a brief visit by Rogers's mailman, Mr. McFeely (played by David Newell). The Mr. McFeely character became a fixture on the program for its entire thirty-three-year duration. McFeely's delivery provides an important transition from the dialogical environment of Rogers and the viewer (I and Thou) to a social situation that involves a third person from the outside world (the neighborhood). McFeely, dressed in a postal service uniform and conveying his usual urgency through a variety of verbal and nonverbal methods, delivers a box from the puppet King Friday XIII, the sovereign leader of the Neighborhood of

Make-Believe. Thus, McFeely not only inserts himself as outsider into the social reality but, via mention of the package and its sender, puts King Friday's imaginary presence into the mix through the utterance of his name and his relation to the package. In this moment, the package prepares the viewer for the impending segment in the NMB, a theatrical space where puppets and members of Rogers's neighborhood engage with each other in a fantasy drama. Rogers, who both serves as the viewer's adult playmate and represents the viewing child himself, invites the viewer to imagine scenarios that take place in "Make-Believe" just as the child does for imaginary play in his real, everyday life.

After saying goodbye to McFeely—who, Rogers notes, rarely has the time to stay for a visit—Rogers sits down on bench with the package. He tells the viewer that King Friday must be feeling much better than he was yesterday if he is sending presents. Here, Rogers reminds the viewer of where they left off the previous day in the NMB drama. He opens the package and finds an unusual-looking clock, which he takes out and places next to him on the bench. Initially confused by the clock's appearance and nature, Rogers comes to the conclusion that it is a punch clock and explains to the viewer that when some "ladies and men" go to work, they place a punch card under this type of clock and it punches the card with the time that they came and the time that they left.[9] As he demonstrates the device, the camera zooms in on the card and Rogers advances it into the proper slot. Amused by the mechanical punch, he pulls the card out and then shows it to the viewer (the camera zooms in to reveal the printed time). He then punches the card a second time to reinforce the demonstration and begins to examine the workings of the clock by removing its cover.

Rogers often takes objects like these apart to examine their inner workings. In both his discussions about the object and his bodily engagement with it, events that take place in nearly every episode, he performs this kind of an anthropological examination of everyday objects, exposing through their inner workings the social relations that produce commodities. Interested in both form and function, in addition to the object's social use and inner mechanical workings, Rogers counters commodity fetishism. After observing the various knobs and gears in the clock and pointing them out with his hands, he places the top back on and suggests to the viewer that she ask her mother or father if they ever had to use a punch clock in their workplace. Here, Rogers makes the social use of the object immediate and personal by relating it to a member of the viewer's family circle. He does this throughout the program, whether connecting the object to a neighbor, character in the NMB, or the viewer's imagined relations. In doing so, through verbal utterance he extends the realm of his neighborhood to include several places and persons who cannot be seen. Moreover, he creates a much-appreciated sense of continuity between the viewer's social and material world, his domestic space, his neighborhood outside the walls of his television home, and the NMB.

Patting the punch clock with his hand, Rogers says into the camera, "Why don't we thank King Friday for the present, okay?" Then he rises from the bench and heads across the room, where he picks up a tin can telephone next to an old traffic light attached to a column. Sitting down at another bench, he asks "the operator" to connect him with "King Friday the Thirteenth." As he puts the can to his ear, a piano plays a series of loud chords in minor key. The notes serve to communicate the King's speech. Surprised and amused by the loudness of the greeting, Rogers moves the tin can "receiver" away from his ear. He places the can in front of his mouth and says, "King Friday, I want to thank you for that punch clock." A piano plays a few, staccato, dissonant chords while Rogers listens to Friday's response through the tin can. Again placing it in front of his mouth, he says, "Oh, it isn't a present, it's an order. Why is it an order, King Friday?" Rogers learns through this "conversation" that King Friday has set up a system in the NMB wherein everyone must punch in and out as they come and go.[10] This part of the program is, once again, used to build a communication bridge between the world that Rogers and his viewer have been occupying in Rogers's home and the world of the NMB. As noted in the earlier chapters, the place of Rogers's home constitutes the space of "reality"; in contrast, the NMB represents the space of "fantasy" and imaginative play where children work out their psychological and social conflicts. In episode 0004, the NMB segment continues a drama that began at the beginning of the week, in which King Friday has become concerned about the threat of war and continues to mobilize against any possible threat to the NMB—the new visual and social space to which the episode now turns.

In the early episodes of *Neighborhood*, Rogers sometimes uses a telescope to provide a transition from his home to the NMB. In episode 0004, the camera zooms in on Rogers looking through a simple wooden telescope pointed at the camera. He uses his fingers to adjust the focus as the screen becomes blurrier and blurrier, and eventually fades into the NMB. "Do you see Daniel's clock?" Rogers asks the viewer as the visual blurs into a white fog. We then fade into a shot of a tall, round, two-dimensional grandfather clock. Daniel Striped Tiger, a shy, child-like puppet, resides inside it. "There it is," Rogers voice declares as we view the clock. "It looks all right to me." Behind the clock is a stone wall with ivy hanging down it. Two-dimensional trees stand beside each other far off in the background. The camera pans to the left, revealing a punch clock sitting atop a fountain. "Uh-oh," Rogers says as the camera zooms in for a tighter shot, "there's a punch clock sitting right on the fountain." With this declaration, Rogers inserts his own skeptical attitude about Friday's punch clock orders, encouraging the viewer, who has allied himself with the fatherly and trustworthy Rogers, to adopt a position of skepticism as well.

The set of the NMB is composed along a curvy stone wall, alongside which stands Daniel's clock, a stone fountain, a small carousel called the Museum-Go-Round, a substantial oak tree with a wide trunk and big canopy top, a machine with blinking lights, wheels, and gauges that make up a rocking chair factory, a large medieval castle complete with round towers, and a red, white, and blue model of the Eiffel Tower. Each structure represents the home of a puppet character residing in the NMB. Shy and reticent Daniel Striped Tiger occupies the clock; Lady Elaine, an unattractive, red-nosed troublemaker, resides at the Museum-Go-Round; X Owl, a wise and straightforward owl, lives in the oak tree along with a timid and gentle kitten named Henrietta Pussycat; and King Friday, the pompous, paternal, and cordial leader of the neighborhood, lives, as one might expect, in the castle. His cook and border guard, Edgar Cooke, a meager, often worried, subservient servant, also appears to live at the castle. Finally, there is Grandpère, a mustached puppet who resembles Daniel Striped Tiger, though he is dressed in a beret and painter's coat. Grandpère lives, as one also might expect, in the Eiffel Tower. These NMB residents are regularly visited by human characters, who traverse between Rogers's neighborhood and the NMB. These human neighbors role-play as subjects under the leadership of the puppet King Friday. But their role is polysemic—they also appear to serve as trustworthy and in-control adults who, while playing along with the childlike puppets in their community dramas, usually serve as references and guides to help the puppets work through their dramas, using dialogue to guide group conversations toward reasonable compromises and positions. These human characters include Lady Aberlin (Betty Aberlin in Rogers's neighborhood), a young motherly figure who is also King Friday's niece; Carol Saunders, a young African American teacher and musician; François Clemmons, a young African American singer who plays a police officer in Rogers's neighborhood; Chef

Brockett, a portly and jovial chef; Handyman Negri, a handyman, guitarist, and singer; Judy Rubin, the "art lady"; and (John) Reardon, a musician.[11]

In the NMB segment of episode 0004, the camera pans across the set as Rogers's voice narrates a search for other punch clocks. He and the camera discover one at the Museum-Go-Round and at X and Henrietta's tree. "I wonder what they think about it," Rogers says via voiceover. The camera continues on to reveal a punch clock at the factory and then arrives at the castle, where the neighborhood trolley is rolling along the track in the direction of the tunnel that is, in later episodes, used to transition the viewer back to Rogers's living room as musical director Johnny Costa plays on his piano music imitative of the sounds made by a train rolling along tracks.[12] The camera follows the trolley along the side of the castle and into the tunnel as Rogers says, "Well, there's the trolley. We will see what's going on when the trolley comes. Come on, Trolley!"

The scene cuts to Rogers, on his living room couch, telescope in hand, awaiting Trolley's arrival. Rogers asks Trolley if he has to punch in and out as well.[13] Trolley indicates "yes" by shifting forward and back while a few musical notes indicate Trolley's affirmative response. "I thought so," says Rogers. "Well, maybe you can take us right in so that we can hear people talk in the Neighborhood of Make-Believe." At this request, Trolley heads back in the direction he came and the train track music ensues.

Sometimes Rogers will transition out of the NMB in order to touch base with his viewer and help them understand the situation by articulating items he wishes to emphasize. This move also allows for Rogers to reaffirm to the child viewer that he is keeping an eye on the situation, just as a trustworthy adult would make himself available and accessible to a child when she is off on her own in imaginative play. This move also offers the viewer a break so that she can step back and process all or some of the main elements of the situation and storyline. In this case, everyday life in the NMB has been altered due to the insertion of punch clocks that seek to account for residents' movements within the territory. Rogers conducts a kind of interview with Trolley, asking him to provide us a first-person observation of the situation. Rogers's interaction with Trolley also serves to reestablish the connection between Rogers in his living room and the NMB, creating a sense of continuity between the different segments and their respective environments while also clearly demarcating the separate worlds of reality and fantasy play for the child, as emphasized in Rogers's "Philosophy" document.

As we fade back into the NMB, the camera zooms out from a tight shot of the grandfather clock hand to reveal Handyman Negri hammering the punch clock into the larger clock, with Daniel looking on. Daniel expresses confusion about why the object needs to be nailed into his clock-home. Negri says that the reason he is setting up the clock is that King Friday has ordered the action. "King's orders," he tells Daniel.[14] Everyone in the NMB must punch in when he arrives and out when he leaves his residence. Negri and Daniel playfully improvise a song about how funny it is that he has installed a clock on a clock. Next, McFeely arrives on his bike with a package that Negri must sign for. It is another punch clock, the last one that Handyman Negri must install. Negri bids farewell to Daniel and walks toward the castle, where he is greeted by puppet Edgar Cooke, who, dressed as a castle guard, sings/speaks to him in operetta-like stanzas. Negri tells him that he is about to install the final punch clock and quickly bids him farewell. We then follow Negri to the Eiffel Tower, where he is met by Grandpère. Grandpère greets Negri in both French and English. After that, however, he only responds to Negri's cordial questions in French.[15] Negri informs Grandpère that he must install a punch clock at the Eiffel Tower. Confused as to what the object is, Grandpère questions the meaning of the word "punch."

Negri replies with a hand movement of a fist punching the air. "A punch," he says as he punches into the air. "Punch?" Grandpère responds. "Yes," Negri says, holding up the clock before Grandpère. "This is a punch clock."

"And you punch the clock?" Grandpère asks.

"That's right; you punch the clock when you come in and you punch the clock when you go out."

Grandpère confirms in French that he has understood. Then he takes a swing at the clock, nearly knocking it out of Negri's hands. The gesture is playful, but also physically and emotionally violent. Grandpère is clearly rejecting, with palpable irritation, the installation of the clock on his "property." "Piano, easy," Negri says. Grandpère understands that this means that he should punch the clock in the same way but with less force and does so. "You *punch* the clock when you're coming in," he says softly punching the clock face with his fist. "And you *punch* the clock when you're going out," he says punching it again. More comical interactions ensue while Negri explains the function of the card and Grandpère punches the card with his fist. Negri laughs. The scene is playful, whimsical, and humorous. "Oh, I adore the punch clock!" Grandpère says as Negri attempts to install it on the face of the Eiffel Tower. He has, in his misunderstanding of the term, made new meaning of the object. And this new meaning transforms the serious air of concern surrounding the clock installations. Grandpère has, in effect, subverted the social atmosphere that arose as a result of Friday's concerned order.

Finally, Grandpère spots Trolley coming around the bend in front of the castle and insists that Negri show Trolley the object before he affixes it to the Eiffel Tower face. Negri stops Trolley with a greeting, approaches him, and shows him the punch clock up close. "Have you seen the new punch clock?" he asks Trolley. Trolley responds with musical notes that represent his communications. "This is Grandpère's punch clock," Negri tells Trolley.

"Try to punch it, Trolley," calls Grandpère from the tower. "Oh, Trolley doesn't want to punch it," Negri tells Grandpère. "I'm going back to put it up on the Eiffel Tower, okay, Trolley? Bye, Trolley."

With that final goodbye, the camera follows Negri as he moves back toward the tower and chats with Grandpère while installing the clock on the structure. We see Trolley making his way through the tunnel just behind Negri and the camera cuts to a shot of Rogers, sitting on his couch, smiling and holding the telescope that first helped us transition into the NMB.

This return to Rogers's home marks the final segment of the program. It usually involves Rogers summarizing, synthesizing, and/or expanding on the activities in the NMB. Encouraging further thinking on the subject and its meanings, Rogers creates space for his viewers to make connections and ponder different angles both with him and on their own. In the case of episode 0004, Rogers looks into the camera with a sly smile and turns the telescope around with his hands. The celeste plays a variety of dreamlike notes. He is thinking and prompts viewer curiosity about his thoughts with his smiling gaze—as if he is amused but bashful about sharing that which he is thinking. "Well, some people are having a fun time with the king's serious business," he says. He sort of mocks the king's punch clock agenda when delivering the line "king's serious business," aligning himself with the playful acts of Grandpère. He laughs while describing how Grandpère misunderstands the function of the punch clock. He then notes with pleasure how Daniel made up "little rhymes" about the clock and repeats them to the viewer—"the clock on the clock." "You could make up rhymes about anything," he tells the viewer while offering up a few examples. His message is that there are creative and fun ways to deal with the confusion and possible angst that result from changes enacted by authority figures.

At this moment, a doorbell rings and Rogers heads to the back door to greet a multiracial group of young boys, followed by a young African American woman with a classical guitar. He greets the white boy as "Rich," the two black boys as "Titi" and "Kevin," and the woman as "Mrs. Saunders." He shakes each of their hands and asks them to have a seat at his kitchen table. "We've been having punch clock trouble—well, not all trouble, we've been even having some fun with it." Rogers also notes that he was playing some hide-and-seek earlier. Mrs. Saunders tells Rogers that they too have been playing and that they have a song for Mister Rogers. The song is "Where is Thumbkin?" and involves giving names to each finger on the hand while holding them up. Prior to showing the fingers when the song calls for it, participants are to hide their hands behind their backs, which Rogers notes is a little bit like hide-and-seek. They sing the song with the hand actions for a minute or so. Next, they sing a song about birds, "Little Bird, Little Bird," in which they use their hands to mimic the animal with its wings in flight.

> Blue bird, blue bird, fly through my window (3×)
> Buy molasses candy.
> Fly through my window, little turtle dove (3×)
> And buy molasses candy.
> Red bird, red bird, fly through my window (3×)
> And buy molasses candy.
> Yellow bird, yellow bird, fly through my window (3×)
> And buy molasses candy.[16]

The boys look to Rogers to mimic his bird-flying hand gestures, which he makes dynamic by moving them into each boy's space and interacting with their "bird hands." After the song concludes, Mrs. Saunders notes how enjoyable singing together was and Rogers agrees. She announces that they will now have to leave, followed by Rogers's insistence that they must punch out when they depart. At the living room bench, each boy takes a card and inserts it into the punch clock, one by one. Afterward, Rogers leads them to the front door as he says goodbye to each by name as they exit his home.

"Mighty special people," Rogers says into the camera as he makes his way to the playpen in the living room. "Let's see how Lydia is." He pets her in the playpen and asks if she is "about ready to go now." He then tells the viewer that it is time for everyone to go and reassures the viewer that they will see each other tomorrow. Unzipping his cardigan and walking toward the closet, he begins to sing "Tomorrow," accompanied by Costa's piano playing. Rogers sings this song while he changes back into his suit jacket, lifts Lydia out of her playpen, and announces that they now have to punch out. "A card for you and a card for Mister Rogers," he says while punching each card. "Just like King Friday says," he continues with a sigh and a disapproving glance at the viewer. He exits through the front door and we cut to a close-up on the exterior of his model house as it is situated on a street lined with bushes and trees. The camera then pans away, offering the viewer a broader perspective on the neighborhood as the camera zooms out and moves through the community in the opposite direction of the beginning sequence.

The architecture of the program thus revolves around a sequencing that begins at Rogers's home, where both he and the viewer "arrive" and begin their visit with each other around a mutual greeting, followed by a dialogue that emerges from the introduction of an object. Use of and play with the object follow from the discussion and soon the dialogical social situation is transformed by the addition of a neighbor. If a neighbor does not present himself at Rogers's home, then Rogers will go outside his home to visit neighbors in their own homes or workspaces. Next, the viewer is transported via reference to the object and its future appearance in the fantasy world of the NMB, where a drama ensues between the object and the characters, cued by a verbal setting-up of the scene by Rogers. This fantasy world is ostensibly that of Rogers, who imagines people that he knows from his own neighborhood, such as Betty Aberlin and Joe Negri, interacting with puppet characters that he has conceived of in his mind. The viewer is thus subtly encouraged to think of Rogers as an adult interested in play and pretend. In this way, he presents himself as empathic toward the viewer in the sense that he appears to have some understanding, an understanding that many adults do not have, of the things that concern children. And yet he is also clearly a responsible, trustworthy, and dependable adult who can be relied upon to lead the child through a variety of settings.

Sometimes, as in the case of episode 0004, Rogers will interrupt the NMB segment and return the viewer to his living room set, where he inserts commentary on the current happenings in the NMB. If this is the case, such interruption will be rather brief—a minute or two—before he returns the viewer to the situation at hand in the NMB. Finally, the viewer returns once again to Rogers in his living room set, where Rogers concludes the program with more commentary on the NMB that usually includes references to the transitional object that initially bridged the distance between his home and the NMB. During this segment, the episode returns full circle with social and pedagogical transformation having taken place via the object's travels to different social worlds, wherein people ascribed it with meaning. Thus, we can think of the architecture of the program in the form of an A (home), B (NMB), A (home again) sequence, although not always fixed as such. Often, in fact, after the initial greeting in the home and the introduction of an object, Rogers will either show the viewer a film about the origins of the object or travel outside in the neighborhood to a location where more about the object's origins and workings can be learned (such as a shoe store, an auto repair shop, an artisan's workplace, or a luncheonette).

Rogers performs a kind of mimesis of improvisation in

Neighborhood's presentation. The show feels unplanned, as if one is simply spending time with Rogers at his house in the same way one might spend time at the home of a neighbor one morning or afternoon. This contributes to its everyday-life aesthetic and its general charm. In this way, the program feels unpretentious—devoid of the glitz or glamor that electronic media tends to produce—as well as friendly and intimate. The actors do not appear to be delivering exact lines, which adds to the feeling of the program having a kind of natural or organic social flow.

In fact, the program was very planned, as evidenced by the correlational scripts stored at the Fred Rogers Archive. According to producer Hedda Sharapan, from 1967 to 1975 the pattern for *Neighborhood* production took on a reliable trajectory.[17] Rogers wrote all of the scripts over the summer. At the end of September the team would begin production and continue until around May. The schedule followed a four-day-per-week taping pattern, completing some sixty-five programs per year during this eight-year period. "The advantage of children's programming," Sharapan notes in reference to the eventual reairing of episodes, "is that children grow into it and grow out of it. We used to say if a child is seeing the same program six months later or a year later, that child is bringing new things to it and learning new things from it." When the team would receive the scripts at the beginning of each taping period, the production team would sit down with the art crew (props manager Newell and the set designers) and go through the scripts with Rogers to see what props and other set needs the program called for. Rogers would prescribe what he wanted and a week later the team would bring in the props and other set pieces.

The next step involved the creation of field trips, segments in which Picture Picture would visually transport the viewer from Rogers's "television house" to another "real world" place, such as a factory, restaurant, business, or public space. Generally, these segments were narrated by Mister Rogers or Mr. McFeely and, Sharapan says, there would be an established time frame for the completion of this segment. The team would then do the segments that required the construction of an extra set in the studio: a visit to the neighborhood bakery or to the neighborhood music shop, etc. The taping of this segment would take one week because, according to Sharapan, the team had to construct this setup in the studio. This was followed by the taping of the Neighborhood of Make-Believe segment the next week. The studio set would be rebuilt for the taping of this segment and then it would be taken down.

Rogers and his team developed set timing for each segment of the program. For example, Sharapan notes, "there would be the beginning, you had the introduction to Make-Believe, then you had coming out of Make-Believe." Each of these segments had to meet its allotted time limit and Rogers had cue cards, and later a teleprompter, to cue him for his line delivery. However, much of the speech that takes place in Rogers's television house and in and around the "neighborhood" were not highly scripted. "There was no specific dialogue," notes Sharapan. For example, in a now famous episode in which Rogers dialogues with a young boy in a wheelchair named Jeff Erlanger, Sharapan recalls that "Fred said: 'I'll ask you why you need a wheelchair and then maybe we'll sing one of the songs together.'" Looking at a script from a week about play, Sharapan notes that the only scripted lines until Rogers arrives in Make-Believe are: "I brought something to show you but I left it on the porch swing. Do you have any idea what it might be?" The script is structured primarily via a third-person narrative that describes the actions that are to ensue between the characters during each segment. Sharapan notes that Rogers, who was the sole writer of the scripts, revised them several times before arriving at a finished product, because "he knew what he wanted to convey."

Although the segments in Rogers's television house and

surrounding neighborhood were not highly scripted, the NMB was. There, Rogers and other puppeteers worked behind the set pieces, manipulating various puppets. According to Sharapan, who operated a puppet for a time, a puppeteer would sit on a stool behind the set piece. Taped in front of her was the script, next to which was a three- to four-inch television monitor that would allow the puppeteer to see the movements of the puppet she was manipulating. Sharapan notes that one of the primary reasons the NMB segment was highly scripted is that this segment had actors—such as Betty Aberlin, who played Lady Aberlin; Joe Negri, who played Handyman Negri; and Don Brockett, who played Chef Brockett. "But [these actors] weren't child development specialists," Sharapan says, "and Fred wanted to tell a story in a certain way through the puppets and so that needed to be tightly scripted."

In contrast to the highly scripted NMB, the introductory segment of the program, in which Rogers sings his opening musical salutation, was granted more improvisational liberties. Many have noted that when Mister Rogers enters his television house singing, he and the program's musical director, Johnny Costa, perform "It's a Beautiful Day in the Neighborhood" live and anew at the start of every taping. This was unique, as the music in most television programs of the time was not performed live. Costa's musical genius and personal importance to the program was so valued that after he died in 1996, Rogers decided to use Costa's recorded piano music underneath his singing during the "It's a Beautiful Day in the Neighborhood" introductory segment. "It was remarkable how Fred and Johnny connected in the studio," Sharapan notes. "Johnny would just noodle under to give him a key for the song. They were so in sync with each other." Costa was an improvisational jazz pianist, who rarely played *Neighborhood* songs the same way twice, and whose live musical performances throughout the programming communicate a playful spontaneity that further lend to the natural and conversational feel of the program itself.

THE NEIGHBORHOOD, OBJECT USAGE, AND THE WORLD OF REALITY MAKING

One of the most prominent characteristics of *Neighborhood* is the everyday performance of reality making that Rogers practices by connecting the word, the body, the eye, and the object during a thirty-minute enactment. Winnicott asserts that playing, which is inherently object-related and thus inherently dualistic, is the touchstone for a child's emergence into a life of health and vitality.[18] Winnicott's groundbreaking work, which Rogers studied as McFarland's student, appears to inform his treatment of objects on *Neighborhood.*

Only once one learns how an object is made, its possible functions, and how to use it can one establish a mutual relationship with it. That is to say, the object acquires meaning in the human world when the human creates it, transforms it, and thus gives it social, creative, and material value. In this regard, I contend that Rogers's conception and treatment of objects is both anti-glamor and anti-idolatry, to use Jean Baudrillard's terms—both rising phenomena within the emergent postmodern, mass-mediated, cultural moment of the period.[19] According to Baudrillard, the postmodern glamorous object is constituted not by what the human does with the object but rather by the human gaze. Within the glamor paradigm, the object is invested with layers of capital that make it desirable. It is abstracted from its passion. Whether he intends to or not, Rogers's creative and embodied treatment of material objects performs an act of resistance to emerging advertising, glamor-based branding practices that work as part of a new system of commodification central to advanced capitalist American society.

In *Making Sense of Reality,* Tia DeNora notes that the everyday is "the site where experience is made manifest, where it takes shape, where sense is made."[20] Rogers performs this process for his young viewers on *Neighborhood* by keeping at the forefront an advanced understanding of children's deeper psychological needs of healthy attachment, object relations, play, and fantasy. Choosing the space most familiar to the very young child—the home—as his primary set, Rogers engages in everyday reality making drawn from an engagement with objects, tools, sensory and aesthetic media, and his social environment in order to foster a "healthy" acclimation to the world in the young.[21] It is in this quotidian setting that, according to DeNora, "realities are brought into being and into focus in ways that matter—to us."[22] In *Neighborhood*, Rogers creates a representational space composed of a simple, unadorned midcentury home. The simplicity of the set, with its basic pieces of functional 1950s furniture, its early America–inspired, midcentury, Cape Cod, streamlined stylings, complete with knotty pine wall paneling, communicates Rogers's values of anticonsumption, simplicity, austerity, thrift, and moderation. It also points to a colonial revivalism that mythologizes and romanticizes the preindustrial world.[23]

It is here, in this unadorned aesthetic environment, that Rogers meets with his viewer to play, ponder, socialize, connect, and work through problems. The *Neighborhood* set is similar in its stylistic simplicity to several other prominent television programs of the period. Lean sets for domestic spaces were common in early television reaching into the 1970s. So, too, were colonial revival interiors (for example, *The Adventures of Ozzie and Harriet* [1952–1965]; *The Donna Reed Show* [1958–1966]; *Father Knows Best* [1954–1958]; and *Leave It to Beaver* [1957–1963]). Thus, the *Neighborhood* set, while complementing Rogers's general ethos of simplicity and manageability, follows longstanding set conventions. However, although the set mirrors the aesthetics of adult programming of the period more than the aesthetics of children's programming, Rogers deliberately "kiddifies" it with the displays of the traffic light, the trolley, and the train tracks. These moves

FIGURE 1. *Mister Rogers' Neighborhood* television house miniture by Lance Cardinal. The miniture is an artistic re-creation of the set, created entirely from scratch, including funiture, carpet, plants, and so on. http://lancecardinal.blogspot
.com/2014/03/mr-rogers-neighborhood-tv-set-miniature.html

FIGURE 2 (*above*) AND 3 (*right*). *Mister Rogers' Neighborhood* television house miniture by Lance Cardinal. http://lancecardinal.blogspot.com/2014/03/mr-rogers-neighborhood-tv-set-miniature.html

disrupt the conventional domestic visual field expectations while at the same time conveying a dominant aesthetic connotative of adult space. As such, the child is welcomed into the adult space through the display of toy-like artifacts, but the adult aesthetic predominates, communicating to the child that the usual social expectations apply—as opposed to other children's programming, such as *Howdy Doody,* in which children are prompted to behave in an "off-the-wall" fashion prompted by a message that the usual rules do not apply.

In episode 0035, Rogers enters his television home per usual, singing. In his hand is what appears to be a thin, square, wooden cutout. He places this piece of wood on the bench, as he does every object that brings with him at the beginning of each show, and walks to the closet while singing the welcome song. He changes out of his jacket and into a cardigan and returns to the bench while concluding the song. Bringing attention to his sweater, he asks the viewer if he knows of anyone who buttons only a few of the buttons on his sweater, while unbuttoning a button. "I think I'll button three—this one, this one, and this one clear down here," he says as he points at each one. In a casual way, he suggests to the viewer that there is no absolute way to go about buttoning your sweater.

Next, grabbing the square piece of wood from the bench as well as a mesh bag containing wooden blocks and taking them over to a wooden table and chair in the center of the room, he tells the viewer that he has just returned from the neighborhood lumberyard. Sitting down in the chair, he explains that while there, he collected some scraps of wood, along with a "great big piece of wood," each of which he holds up in accordance with his verbal utterance of the respective object. He tells the viewer that he wanted to do some hammering, nailing, and pounding. Setting aside a nail box already lying on the table, he sets his square block of wood onto the table and asks the viewer what tool he needs in order to pound the nails into the wood. As he says, "Pound the nails into the wood," he makes a gesture of pounding nails into an object with his right hand, visually reinforcing the meaning of his utterance with the correlating nonverbal, bodily message like he did earlier when discussing sweater buttons.

As if hearing the viewer answer the question with "hammer," he gets up and walks toward the bench behind him saying, "All right, there's one right back here." Reaching into a drawer by the bench below the train tracks, he pulls out a hammer, utters its name casually, and returns to the chair. There, he sorts through his nail box looking for the right size nail, pointing out the variety in nail sizes out loud. He grabs a big nail, places it in the center of the wood slab, and sets it in the proper position to be hammered, saying, "That's a big daddy nail." "Ready to pound it in?" he says looking into the camera. He then hits the nail four times with the hammer until it is firmly secured into the wood. He looks into the camera with a relaxed smile that communicates satisfaction. He continues by grabbing another, slightly smaller nail from the nail box and hammering it in just beside the larger one. "Mother nail," he declares before pounding it in. "We'll put a whole family of nails in here." Grabbing another, slightly smaller nail, he says, "That's a great big sister," and pounds it right beside the mother nail. Pounding in yet another slightly smaller nail beside the "sister nail," he says, looking at it, "That might be a brother nail." The sequence continues as he pounds in "another brother" and then decides to "do some more hammering just for fun." "Do you ever hammer just for fun?" he asks the viewer. "Who does most of the hammering in your house? Your dad? I know a lot of boys who would like to be just exactly like their dads." From here, Rogers transitions into a song titled "I'd Like to Be Just Like Dad."

What has Rogers done in this beginning sequence? First, he gestures toward the manipulation of an object by commenting on his own act of buttoning his sweater, which he does at the beginning of every episode. Rogers does not offer a fixed directive on how to properly button one's sweater. Instead, emphasizing the agency and freedom of the individual, he notes that some people button just a few buttons and demonstrates this by selecting which buttons he will button for today's visit. In addition, Rogers's short moment of discussing buttoning alludes to the forthcoming session on hammering, nailing, and pounding. Both acts involve the manipulation of components (button; nail) of the object (sweater fabric; wood), which, when connected with another part of the object, express the object's full functionality.

In demonstrating hammering a nail into a piece of wood, Rogers playfully imagines that he is creating a family of nails and identifies one as father, another as mother, and so on according to height. After bringing this absent social reality (members of the family) into his activity, Rogers creates a further social and personal connection among himself, the object-centered action, and the viewer by asking the viewer who, in her family, does the majority of hammering. He then slowly breaks into a song about a child wanting to be just like his father, the parent most likely to engage in the domestic task of hammering nails. As the camera pans around him, Rogers looks into it and sings the gentle but uplifting song "I'd Like to Be Just Like Mom and Dad."

> I'd like to be just like my dad
> He's handsome and he's keen
> He knows just how to drive the car
> And buy the gasoline
> And mommy likes the things he does
> The way he looks and gee!
> I'd like to be just like my dad and have someone like me.[24]

After pounding another nail into the wood slab, Rogers declares that he will now use the scraps, which he lifts onto his lap, to make something. He looks at the three small pieces of wood in his hands, shows them to the viewer, and then asks, "What would you make with three pieces of wood like this?"

Highlighting that such objects for playing can be obtained without charge, Rogers declares, "The man at the lumberyard just gave them to me." He then sets them on top of each other to form a small pyramid. Shifting the blocks around, he shows how placing two in opposite directions and on top of each other can look like an airplane. Gliding the newly formed plane in the air, he makes a whistling noise with his mouth to vocalize the sound of flying.

Pleased with his airplane idea, he decides to make this creation more permanent by nailing the two pieces of wood together. Once again, he glides and spins the object around in the air. "Now," he continues, "let's turn the airplane into a boat." He turns the top piece of wood around so that it now rests parallel to the bottom piece and nails the smaller, third piece of wood to the top, back end of the object. "How's that for a boat?" he asks the viewer, displaying his new creation in his hand. "Would you like to sail into the kitchen?" He rises and "sails" the boat into the kitchen. There, he fills up the sink, asks the viewer if she likes to watch the faucet stream water into the sink, and watches as the water rises while the celeste plays gentle, happy background music. Turning off the water, he gently places the boat in the water, asking, "Is it going to float?" The camera zooms in on the sink. "It does!" he gently exclaims. "It's fun to make believe, isn't it?" he asks. "Speaking of make-believe, let's just float into the other room and see if it's almost time to go into the Neighborhood of Make-Believe."

WINNICOTT, OBJECTS, AND THE LOCATION OF CULTURE

Let me pause here in recounting this episode so that I may address this example of object relations and play in *Neighborhood* through the lens of Donald Woods Winnicott. Winnicott posits that at a particular stage of early development, the infant, who for a while after her birth conceives of herself as part of the mother, must take a symbolic journey "from the experience of her mother's adaptation to her needs" at the time of her total dependence on her, toward a place of relative dependence.[25] She begins to view her mother as not herself and comes to the conclusion that she must exert her own agency. It is through the adoption of an external object, which Winnicott names the "transitional object," that the symbolic journey from total dependency on mother toward relative dependence is made. Though the transitional object represents many of the elements of mother, such as comfort and security, the event also importantly signifies the critical importance of "the infant's ability to *create* what he needs." This creative act is key to the resulting sense of confidence and agency that the child develops. The transitional object "truly belongs to him, because he has created it," writes Jan Abram, a Winnicott scholar.[26]

In the common postwar parlance on parenting, the most prominent example of the transitional object is the "security blanket." The infant asserts naming privileges over the object, assumes rights over it, and "affectionately" cuddles, "excitedly" loves, and mutilates it.[27] Here, cuddling and loving refers to the calm and excited inner states in relation to his mother. Although language acquisition is important during this stage, Winnicott notes the act of naming in regards to agency and the creation of a personal word. Interestingly, he notes that the transitional object does not need to be an actual material object. It can be a word, melody, song, or a mannerism that becomes "vitally important . . . for use at the time of going to sleep, and is a [defense] against anxiety."[28] The creation of this transitional object is the first reparation that the child makes; it is an ego attempt to maintain his continuity of being while mother is away. He substitutes the special object for the mother, or mothering person.[29] Rogers, who wrote about the similarities between the breastfeeding child gazing into the mother's eyes and the child sitting in front of the television gazing into the screen in the 1960s, appears to be exploring the idea of television as transitional object, offering a dyadic adventure into this intermediate, potential space where the child can learn and cognitively practice acts of creation, object relations, and usage that will foster increasing independence and interactivity with the world and others.[30]

According to Winnicott, during this stage of human development the infant struggles internally with the experience of the object-mother, whom he "excitedly" loves, and his "environment-mother," who provides calm and quiet moments. Winnicott reads this use of the object by the infant, via enactment, as a way of relating to these two mothers and trying to bring the two together. The fate of the transitional object in regards to the child is gradual withdrawing of one's feelings of attachment such that it is neither forgotten nor mourned but rather relegated to limbo, where it loses meaning. This withdrawal of one's attachment feeling and loss of meaning occurs because over time transitional phenomena in general "have become spread out over the whole intermediate territory between 'inner psychic reality' and 'the external world as perceived by two persons in common,' that is to say, over the whole cultural field."[31] By this time, the young child is capable of distinguishing between Me and Not-me due to the work he did with the transitional object. Further, he can now live in this third, "intermediate area of experience," a term coined by Winnicott, where he keeps inside and outside apart but still interrelated.[32] In his Winnicott primer, *Attachment, Play, and Authenticity*, Steven Tuber describes Winnicott's third, intermediate area of experience as the overlapping space in a Venn diagram.

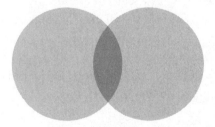

It is in this third, intermediate space that Winnicott locates cultural experience, and where Rogers representationally reinforces this cultural, creative work. Winnicott's paper linking these two concepts (inner reality and the external world) was published in 1967 and is titled "The Location of Cultural Experience." Essentially, Winnicott explains the infant's path toward becoming human in the world in a series of critical moves involving mutuality, object relating, object usage, and the development of cultural practices. He begins with the identification of the dyadic self, inscribed in the infant through the first experience of being—through the mother. From here, a transitional phase that helps the child become less dependent on mother ensues with the creation of the transitional object. Transitional phenomena are birthed out of this experience of being, which, Winnicott posits, becomes the terrain or "location" of cultural experience.

In his 1967 article "The Location of Cultural Experience," Winnicott argues that cultural experience begins with a kind of creative living that first exhibits itself in the act of play.[33] Play occurs in the intermediate space that is created when the child chooses the transitional object—in between Me and Not-me perception. Winnicott creates an arena for this intermediate experience, which he calls "potential space," which Tuber calls "a wonderfully named term in its dynamic about-to-be-yet-not-quite-being quality."[34] Winnicott connects the creation to this space to the act of playing and makes playing a "precursor to the creative living that is manifested in cultural life."[35] According to Tuber, this "puts play at its most exalted status in Winnicott's hierarchy of necessary ingredients for a vital life."[36] He links transitional phenomena to artistic creativity, religious feeling, dreaming, and also to darker phenomena such as fetishism, drug addiction, and stealing. The key to understanding how the transitional object provides the catalyst for the development of culture and creative living is understanding the infant's action in creating it. Tuber explains, "While we as adults see the transitional object as a symbol of mother, from the baby's perspective, it is the *creation* of a symbol for mother that matters. As the baby progresses and can understand or even later put into words the use of a symbol, she has had the transitional object to help tolerate the loss of mother long enough to take on the world and to begin to use it and other symbols to navigate it."[37] Here, in this potential space where engagement with the world manifests and the human becomes a manipulator of objects, the human asserts his creative life force and is able to defend against anxiety in ways that are less dependent on his mother.

Winnicott theorizes that it is in the potential space that play, the primary work of the child, takes place. "The playground is a potential space between the mother and the baby or joining mother and baby," he writes. "The thing about playing is always the precariousness of the interplay of personal psychic reality and the experience of control of actual objects." In the early stages, the mother or mother figure participates in play with the child, helping the child to go through the process of repudiating, reaccepting, and objectively perceiving the object. This process can succeed only if the mother is "prepared to participate and to give back what is handed out." In this way, she allows the baby to experience a kind of "magical" control, which provides a sense of omnipotence. "Confidence in the mother makes an intermediate playground here," writes Winnicott, "where the idea of magic originates." This sense of magic and the pleasure and excitement it creates in the child arises in intimacy. Most important with regard to *Neighborhood*, it arises "in a relationship that is being found to be reliable."[38] From here, the child moves toward a play situation where he is alone yet in the presence of someone. In this stage, the child plays on the basis of a key assumption that the person she loves, in large part due to her reliability, continues to be remembered after being forgotten. The child can hold the memory of this person in his mind and maintain a sense of security and confidence. The person is felt by the child "to reflect back what happens in the playing."[39]

Rogers read Winnicott during his advanced studies with McFarland, and emphasized throughout his life the importance of play and its misapprehension in conventional wisdom. "Play is often talked about as if it were relief from serious learning.

But for children, play is serious learning. Play is really the work of childhood," he is still quoted as saying.[40] On *Neighborhood*, he offers both mutual play and play in which the child viewer is unaccompanied by him. He constantly offers verbal and material connections between himself, other neighbors, the characters in the neighborhood, and the objects of play in order to create this sense of holding, trust, and an expectation of return. In speech, he offers dialogue about the objects in play, creating a sense of reflectivity that the child will, according to Winnicott, use when Rogers is no longer with him.

As the baby grows and becomes a small child, according to Winnicott, he searches for reliance on other trustworthy adults with whom to engage and upon whom to rely for security, inter-activity, and help. Mister Rogers inserts himself into the child's life here. Recall that in his "Philosophy" document, Rogers artic-ulates his role in communication with the child as fitting into a network of home and family relationships that constituted the world of the very young child. The first bullet point under the section "Premises" is titled "*Growing Up and the Importance of Family Relationships.*" It states the following: "Fred Rogers has originated and developed MISTER ROGERS' NEIGHBORHOOD out of his studies and own personal sensitivity to the growing up world of children. He maintains that childhood experiences have poten-tial for being joyful and fearful; the nature of these experiences is greatly determined by the quality of support that the child receives from adults. In the early years, the most dominant influences on a child come from his home or family relationships."[41] From here, he moves to assert himself, as a television on-air personality, into the sphere of the home and family. As such, he understands himself on-air as serving in a trusting and influential adult role in relation to the viewing child. In the second premise, "*Television and tele-vision artists—participants in family relationships,*" the author or authors assert that when Rogers looks into the camera and speaks with the child at the dialogical level, "the child's environment has been extended to include a meaningful relationship with another adult."[42] In this way, the author(s) asserts, Rogers achieves participant status in family relationships. Thus, by offering his program as a transitional object, indeed one that is itself located within the child's (ostensibly) nurturing home environment, Rogers extends himself into the space of kinship.

As the trusted adult, Rogers meets with the child in the space most familiar to her—the home. There are a few layers of "home" that exist in viewing *Neighborhood*. The child is ostensibly in his own home, where the television is situated. Mister Rogers, too, presents himself to the child in the setting of his television house, constructed to look like a modest 1960s home. Finally, for the small child, the home is the space where most living takes place. It is where he and his kin eat, engage socially, rest, and sleep. It is also where the young child engages in the work of childhood—play. Also, at least for most of the day, the very young child occupies this space *with* mother.[43] Thus, the space is inscribed by the activities and relationships that take place and are developed within it. Rogers wishes to present himself in this space of home because the child immediately identifies it as familiar, safe, and endowed with the warmth and closeness of family bonds. So while he overtly positions himself as a kind neighbor and is not technically a part of the family by blood, he functions at the parasocial level and in the larger symbolic cognitive space, perhaps due to his warmth and the home space in which he operates, as a familial figure—substituting as a kind of father surrogate or as the compassionate father figure children desired but maybe did not have. At the same time, he is involved in transitional objectification with the aim of advancing the child's developmental history.

For Winnicott, play involves a kind of "near-withdrawal" state, which Winnicott compares to *concentration* in older children and adults. The child in play cannot be easily interrupted nor can she admit intrusions. This area of playing lies outside the individual—it is not inner psychic reality. Thus, play consists of the child collecting "objects or phenomena from external reality" and using them "in the service of some sample derived from inner or personal reality." In play, the child exudes a bit of "dream potential" and "lives with this sample in a chosen setting of fragments from external reality";[44] he manipulates the external phenomena he chooses in the service of the dream. He invests the chosen phenomena with dream meaning and feeling.

Recall that in episode 0016 Rogers enters his home with a mesh bag full of pieces of wood and a larger, thin wooden slab.[45] He goes on to hammer nails, one by one, into the wooden slab, eventually engaging with the objects in imaginative, symbolic play by assigning each nail a role as a family member according to its size. This leads him into a short song about the feeling of wanting to be like one's mother or father. After the song, Rogers engages with the smaller wood pieces by placing them in different positions in relation to each other. In one position, the pieces of wood resemble a plane—in another, a boat. Pleased with the boat, he nails the pieces together and travels to the kitchen to fill the sink with water to see whether or not it will float. It does. The pacing of the play is slow, and the camera cuts are few, enabling the viewer to develop a sense of *preoccupation* with the on-screen activities. One tends to become somewhat mesmerized, even as an adult, when watching this segment of the program.

Rogers demonstrates a deep understanding of Winnicott's elements of play—the gathering of objects, the sense of preoccupation that develops while engaging in play with the objects, and the use of the object "in the service of some sample derived from inner or personal reality." This latter aspect, I posit, is illustrated by Rogers's desire to merge the nail with the wood, his efforts to imagine the nails as family members, and then the development of this fantasy via a song about the love of a parent and the desire to become like him. This appears to be Rogers's attempt to supplant the father through invitational identification with the child, being recruited in Oedipal desire. The wooden objects are then further utilized to explore conceptions of advanced transportation technologies: planes and boats. Rogers places his newly built boat in a basin in order to model a boat in its natural habitat—floating on water. He spends a moment watching with pleasure as the water runs and fills the sink, and asks the viewer if she enjoys watching water run from the faucets. Rogers consistently creates ties between the everyday objects he adopts for discussion and use on the program with the life and perceived interests of the child viewer.

Rogers's display of care and mutuality throughout the play sequence illustrates yet another one of Winnicott's primary elements of play—trust. "Playing implies trust," he writes, "and belongs to the potential space between (what was at first) baby and mother-figure, with the baby in a state of near-absolute dependence, and the mother-figure's adaptive function taken for granted by the baby."[46] Rogers introduces the hammer and nail and begins to use them in a nonthreatening manner. He offers assurance throughout the project by engaging in play and communication with the viewer in a relaxed, yet focused way. In playing with the objects and tools successfully, relating to the viewer on an interpersonal level by calling to mind her father, singing about his own inner longings to be like his father, and consistently addressing the viewer with a direct and friendly gaze, he builds and maintains a sense of trust.

In the next sequence of the program, Rogers helps the child viewer prepare for a transition to the NMB, the realm of fantasy on *Neighborhood*, by speaking into his pretend tin can phone to an NMB puppet. Over the "phone," Rogers tells the puppet Edgar that he has been hammering nails into wood and learns from Edgar that a famous sculptor named Virgil Cantini is visiting the NMB.[47]

When the "phone call" ends, Rogers announces to the viewer that they will now go and visit the NMB. Further helping the child prepare for the environmental transition, Rogers counts to thirteen. As he and the implied viewer count, the camera slowly zooms into the yellow bulb of the traffic light next to Rogers, which blinks in concert with his counting aloud. Layers of message redundancy are intentionally built into *Neighborhood* in order to provide clarity and consistency for the young child, who is at an age where transitions can easily produce anxiety if not prefaced and prepared for. We then cut to a shadow on a wall of a spinning sculpture of what looks like a human figure dancing. The spinning makes the sculpture look as if the figure is actually dancing, and Costa overlays a dreamlike composition on the celeste providing audio background. It is relaxing to look at and also mesmerizing with the overlaying music. As the camera zooms out, we see the sculpture beside and below its twirling shadow on the wall.

At the castle, King Friday asks Cantini to tell him what he used to make "that beautiful sculpture that goes round and round."[48] Looking over at the sculpture, which we see as well, Cantini responds. He says that he used "nails and steel and bronze, and a hot acetylene torch." As we get a closer look at the twirling statue, we can see that the human figure is made out of short, thin pieces of steel. Friday asks, "Well, how did you make that man?" Cantini explains that he used flat nails, on which he brazed a coat of bronze. "This is man as he is exploring the universe, just like the astronauts who are going off into space," he says.[49] Friday adds that "they certainly are looking and looking and enjoying what they can find." He compliments Cantini on the beauty of the sculpture and the celeste continues to play dreamlike music throughout the dialogue as the camera cuts back and forth between Friday, Cantini, and the twirling sculpture.

The introduction of play with nails and wood (basic forms) in Rogers's home has thus led us into a deeper dreamlike sequence where imaginative puppets engage with real, everyday people in a dialogue about things having to do with the objects in their basic forms. Here, the correlation between the subject matter in the first *Neighborhood* segment is directly linked to the happenings in the NMB. Rogers plays with wood, a hammer, and nails with the child to create new forms out of the originals. His constructive choices involve making fairly basic new items. Hammering the nails into the large wood board is primarily an action of practice—a kind of first step in learning to hammer nails into wood.[50] Next, he engages in more advanced artisanal work by creating a plane and a boat by manipulating a few pieces of wood. Still, he works at the level of the child during this segment. In the NMB, which aims to simulate the child's experience of fantasizing and playing "make-believe," he expands on the creative play that he engaged in in the "home" segment. In the NMB, characters often engage with the same object in both similar and different ways, producing their own creative and social experience with the object(s). In this particular segment, Rogers showcases an adult artist who works at a very advanced level with nails in order to show the depth of possibilities in working with just a few basic material elements. *Look and see what you can do with these objects both as a child and later in life, as a grownup. You can learn to create and craft interesting and complex things with these everyday items.* "There is a direct development from transitional phenomena to playing, and from playing to shared playing, and from this to cultural experiences," Winnicott writes.[51] Rogers interweaves these inter-actions to produce a dialectical movement of cultural engagement and reality making.

Further connecting the child's play with the work of the artisan, Friday asks Cantini if he always enjoyed playing with nails "and things and such" when he was a young boy. Cantini says that he thinks all boys enjoy playing with nails and hammers and hatchets and notes how easy they are to find around the house.[52] He shows

Friday a figurine he crafted of a bull, which he then playfully thrusts at Friday, who hops aside, avoiding the bull's charge. The camera zooms in on Friday and the bull figurine, which Cantini suggests he touch, perhaps in order to "tame" it. Gently, Friday places his mitten-like puppet hand on the bull's horns and asks Cantini if they were made out of nails. "The horns are bent nails," Cantini says, "and the other ones I use just straight." Here, Cantini and Friday demonstrate how, through gentle and respectful play, combined with dialogical examination, people can learn and discover new possibilities for the satisfying work of creating/playing by manipulating objects with one's hands.

The sequence continues to open up as Cantini shows Friday the other animal figurines he has crafted. "I have a whole family of deer in here," he says pointing at a table that showcases several deer-like figurines made out of nails. Friday points to one figurine that he perceives has a mane. Cantini notes that this deer is a "fighting deer" and he places it and another in combat using his hands to buck the deer into each other. This part illustrates another key element of play as articulated by Winnicott—that play involves the body "because of the manipulation of objects" and "because certain types of intense interest are associated with certain aspects of bodily excitement."[53] "They fight with their horns, don't they?" King Friday asks while the camera remains focused on the manipulation of the two deer figurines. "And all those are nails?" he asks. Cantini responds affirmatively, listing the different kinds of nails he used—"sharp nails, some flat nails, some penny nails, an eight-penny nail." The camera moves into an even tighter shot of the deer and of Cantini's large hands as they touch the figurines while he speaks about them and the work he did to create them.

My memories of watching Neighborhood as a child and my experience of watching the program now, as an adult, are dominated by feelings of pleasure that I think relate to two prominent aspects of the program. First, I feel that Mister Rogers actually knows and cares about me at some interpersonal level.[54] I sense that he recognizes me when he looks into the camera and speaks directly to me. It is as if we are engaged in a kind of affective relationship imbued with trust and mutual respect. I enjoy listening to him speak to me in his patient and settled manner. As the program unfolds and he shares his world of objects and neighbors with me, I feel a satisfying sense of connectivity and continuity. I settle into viewing the program as one might when visiting the home of a friend. There is an overlying air of reassurance and warmth that translates from the screen. Second, I derive gratification from the ways he relates, with his body and his speaking voice, to the objects he presents. There is something in the simplicity of the representation—the uncluttered environment, the slow camera movement, the lack of adornment on the items of furniture, persons, and objects in his home and in the NMB—that evokes a feeling of the "organic" and a sense of "the real." There is nothing that is distracting in the communication. In fact, the layers of focus—Rogers's focus on me, on his object, and on his neighbors, along with the camera's limited number of angled shots—create a sense of focus for the viewer. The visual display is clear, direct, and simple, as is the embodied nonverbal and verbal communication. There is no excess of noise, nor sense of clutter. There are no quick cuts from shot to shot. I feel a sense of human bonding, and creative pleasure, similar to the emotions that arise when one feels a part of a dyad or group and engaged in satisfying creative work/play in the warmth of a safe home environment, classroom, or workplace.[55] In episode 0016, these feelings are stimulated almost immediately and sustained by a variety of actions throughout the program: Rogers's simple hammering of nails into wood, his verbal evocation of family members as metaphor for the nails, the vocalization of his song about the deep longing to grow and become like one's parent, the moment he spends watching the sink fill up with running water, his putting the wooden boat in the water, Cantini's big hands holding the nail-deer figurines, his gruff voice.

NEIGHBORHOOD'S SYSTEM OF OBJECTS

When viewing the NMB segment, one does not necessarily imagine people working to create the set, its castle, tree, Museum-Go-Round, etc. with their own hands and shop-like tools. This sense that the object is the work of human hands, a preindustrial object, I would argue, exists at the visceral level of meaning in the mind of the modern viewer. It is the lack of perfection in the building assembly, along with the similarly imperfect quality of the paint job, that communicates this homemade, anthropocentric aesthetic feeling. The furniture and the objects in Rogers's television house suggest a similar sensory field.

In the United States, however, style choices like those made by Rogers on *Neighborhood* carry wider cultural consequences, as they tend to highlight New England as the American "hearth zone" and center of the nation's colonial beginnings from which the rest of the country derived historical and cultural lineage.[56] Of course, this means obscuring the South and slavery, the history of African Americans, the development and conquest of the West, the history of American Indians, the relationship between whites and Mexicans in the Southwest, and large cities like New York and Chicago with their many working-class immigrants, as well as southern and urban opulence. In this regard, it is not surprising that Rogers, whose cultural orientation and affinity for the traditions of mainline Protestantism I have discussed, replicates a colonial revival aesthetic on his program. Indeed, *Neighborhood*'s visual artifactual field signifies mainline Protestant cultural dominance.[57]

Rogers clearly values the feeling of authenticity produced by handmade, lived-in objects, as they nurture this perceived human craving for origins and history. Each of the sweaters Rogers wears on the program was made by his mother. The puppets in the NMB are simple, almost ragged in their appearance; they were handcrafted by people he knew. *Neighborhood* features the transformation of objects as they pass through the hands of people, who either transform them physically or who alter their symbolic meaning through human contact and social mobility.

In many episodes, Rogers ventures out into the community in order to visit the places where objects are made. In one popular segment, he visits a crayon factory and we see all the levels of industrial processing that turn colorized wax into crayons. I read this episode as an effort to humanize the faceless industrial factory and dehumanizing processes of industrial production. We can see Rogers trying to bring visibility to human production in the ways that the crayon factory segment illustrates the intricate mechanization steps in creating boxed crayon products. In it, he attempts to reduce the alienation between the producers of the products and its consumers. Viewers of the program watch the inner workings of machines and are shown the ways that people are involved in the process of ensuring the machine's proper functioning and the creative process of making and packaging the crayons. Rogers seems to see the restoration of transparency in the social production and exchange of products as rewarding, and indeed pleasurable, in the ways that such knowledge reestablishes the visibility of social connection in the product creation and exchange process.

A railroad tank car carries hot wax to the factory. From the tank, the wax is poured into a "kind of big kettle," Rogers narrates as we view these actions taking place on the screen. A powder is poured on the wax to make it hard. After this, the pigment is applied to the mixture in the form of colored flour—in this case, yellow. Next, the mixture is drained into a pouring bucket. We watch as a man lifts the pouring bucket full of the yellow mixture and pours it over a metal sheet with hundreds of holes the circumference of a crayon. The visceral nature of the material actions—the mixing of the liquid, the dyeing of the mixture, the pouring of the mixture onto the metal sheets—is remarkably mesmerizing and pleasurable to view. "The people wait five minutes for the yellow wax to get hard and then they scrape off the top, which they will melt and use again," Rogers describes as we watch someone's arms and hands scrape off the top of the metal sheets. Then we watch the cleared metal plates sprout up yellow crayons in magical unison out of the hundreds of holes. A man then grabs the metal sheet and takes it to another area, where he dumps the crayons out onto a shelf and pushes them into an orderly line. Grabbing a portion of at least a hundred yellow crayons, he delivers them to another area, placing them on yet another pile of yellow crayons. From there, we watch a woman use a small shovel to gather another large group of crayons together and place them onto another machine that orders the crayons into a single-file line and produces a mechanized punching sound. "Can you imagine what this machine is for?" Rogers asks. The camera pans over the crayons making their way through sprockets and pockets and knobs to reveal the crayon labels being wrapped around each crayon. "It's like a Ferris wheel, isn't it?" Rogers says. We then cut to a larger room where many people are seen working at various stations. This, Rogers tells us, is the collating room, where sixteen different colors of crayons are put together. A wonderfully colorful shot in which rows of various crayons are side by side in a machine that assembles them into the proper order to be placed in their cardboard boxes follows. Finally, we see multiple hands working with the boxes on a table, placing them into larger shipping boxes. "And then people take those boxes to the stores," Rogers says, "where other people come to buy them."

In this visit and many others, Rogers offers a lens into the hidden spaces created by the capitalist system. As Grant Noble observes in *Children in Front of the Small Screen*, the industrial city can be fragmentary and discontinuous. In contrast, village life—the social structure that people lived and evolved within up into the dawn of modernity—is a cohesive, integrated whole. "In the 'single' stage village community," Noble writes, "the total social organization is visible, and it is easy to see how social roles are interrelated."[58] Noble posits that "exposing disparate individuals to the same familiar content, which is remarkably repetitive, does in part restore a village type of community." Such observation is interesting in regards to the *Neighborhood* project. Noble posits, following Karl Marx, that the consequences of industrial, modern life are such that he is likely to become alienated, "that is, made to feel an alien or outsider, when he can no longer see himself as part of an organic whole."[59] Rogers, it would seem, seeks to flatten the barriers for seeing all aspects of the society's makeup. Indeed, at nearly every level of *Neighborhood*, we see him engaged in a concentrated effort to present a level of processual continuity of form and content. The factory visits are a way of expanding his interest in helping the viewer see the various processes at work in human life, at the level of the individual, the dialogical, the community, and the wider society.

In the case of episode 0016, Mister Rogers verbally notes the origins of the wooden slabs he brings into the house, stating that he has just come from the lumberyard. Using the hammer and nails in his toolbox, he transforms the slabs into a wooden airplane and a wooden boat. Prior to that, he practices hammering nails into the large board and gives the nails family member titles, adding to their symbolic meaning relating to clan and kinship through the imagination and speech verbalization. The theme of creating and transforming objects continues in the NMB, where we meet Cantini, who makes figurines out of nails. Such examination and object usage on *Neighborhood* demonstrate Rogers's interest in understanding the social and material origins of everyday, noncommodified objects. After learning the object's origins, Rogers works his own hands on the object, inscribing his own mark on the item as if attempting to become a part of the object's lineage.

Similar ideas regarding objects, perception, and pleasure have been discussed more recently by Paul Bloom. Bloom has investigated how pleasure works in the human mind from a social-scientific perspective. His research has yielded a compelling theory that posits that humans assign value to objects based on an object's origins, history, and essence. Bloom has noted that one of the most exciting developments in cognitive science is the idea that humans "have a default assumption that things, people, and events have invisible essences that make them what they are."[60] Essentialism, Bloom notes, has been identified by these cognitive scientists as a significant influence on how we understand and process the material and social world. Developmental and cross-cultural psychologists have posited that this essentialism is in fact instinctual and universal. "We are," he writes, "natural-born essentialists."[61] Bloom suggests in his research that this human characteristic not only influences how we perceive and understand the world but also shapes our experience. Bloom pays special attention to pleasure. "What matters most is not the world as it appears to our senses. Rather, the enjoyment we get from something derives from what we think that thing really is," he argues. In a TED Radio Hour, Bloom tells host Guy Roz that we can get pleasure from appreciating an object's utility, yes, but that knowing where an object came from is also a powerful determinant in our appreciation of an object. Knowing where the object came from, Bloom theorizes, transforms our experience of the object. "For any sort of pleasure," Bloom says, "we are obsessed with origin and history."[62] His theories, arrived at from social-scientific inquiry, correlate quite strikingly with those of

Baudrillard, who observed that "the mere fact that a particular object has belonged to a famous or powerful individual may confer value on it."[63]

Bloom's discussion of essence, origins, and history speaks to Rogers's beloved quote from *The Little Prince*—"It is only with the heart that one can see rightly. What is essential is invisible to the eye." Although Bloom does not approach the matter from the perspective of the heart, he does suggest that "essence" is something that operates underneath and is thus hidden. The scene in *The Little Prince* that ends with the "invisible to the eye" quotation suggests that a thing's essence is perceived as having value as a result of a process in which ties are established. The scene begins when the prince comes across a fox in a field. The prince asks the fox to come and play with him. "I cannot play with you," says the fox. "I am not tamed." The prince does not understand and asks the meaning of the word *tame*. "It is an act too often neglected," the fox responds. "It means to establish ties. . . . To me you are still nothing more than a little boy who is just like a hundred thousand other boys. And I have no need of you. And you, on your part, have no need of me. To you, I am nothing more than a fox like a hundred thousand other foxes. But if you tame me, then we shall need each other. To me, you will be unique in all the world. To you, I shall be unique in all the world."[64]

The prince tells him that he does not have time to tame him because he has friends to make and "a great many things to understand." To this remark, the fox replies, "One only understands the things that one tames." Men have no time to understand things anymore, the fox continues: "They buy things all ready made at the shops. But there is no shop anywhere where one can buy friendship, and so men have no friends anymore." He tells the prince that if he wants a friend, he should tame him. When the prince asks exactly how he should go about taming him, the fox tells the prince that he must be very patient. "First, you will sit down at a little distance from me—like that—in the grass. I shall look at you out of the corner of my eye, and you will say nothing. Words are the source of misunderstandings. But you will sit a little closer to me, every day."[65] The prince agrees to tame him and comes back to visit the fox every day. He makes a point of coming at the same hour after the fox explains to him the importance of rites.[66]

After an unknown period of time, the prince is finished taming the fox. "Ah," says the fox. "I shall cry."[67] The fox's sadness over their goodbye makes the prince upset. In an angry tone, the prince submits that he should never have agreed to tame the fox at all if this was to be the result. "I never wished you any sort of harm; but you wanted me to tame you," he tells the fox. "But now you are going to cry! . . . Then it has done you no good at all," says the prince.[68] The fox disagrees and tells the prince to go and look at the many roses. Prior to their agreement, the prince had told the fox that back at his home planet, he had a beloved rose who awaited his return. "Go and look again at the roses," he tells the prince. "You will understand now that yours is unique in all the world." The prince goes away to look at the roses. "'You are not at all like my rose,' he said. 'As yet you are nothing. No one has tamed you, and you have tamed no one. You are like my fox when I first knew him. He was only a fox, like a hundred thousand other foxes. But I have made him my friend, and now he is unique in all the world."[69] He continues,

> You are beautiful, but you are empty. . . . One could not die for you. To be sure, an ordinary passerby would think that my rose looked just like you—the rose that belongs to me. But in herself alone she is more important than all the hundreds of you other roses: because it is she that I have watered; because it is she that I have put under the glass globe; because it is she that I have sheltered behind the screen; because it is for her that I have killed the

caterpillars . . . ; because it is she that I have listened to, when she grumbled, or boasted, or even sometimes when she said nothing. Because she is *my* rose.[70]

Having realized and verbalized the importance of "establishing ties," the phrase the fox used when trying to define the term *tame* at the beginning of the scene, the Little Prince returns to meet the fox and offers him a goodbye. The fox reciprocates and offers him pieces of wisdom. "And now here is my very simple secret: It is only with the heart that one can see rightly; what is essential is invisible to the eye. It is the time you have wasted for your rose that makes your rose so important."[71] According to the fox, this is a truth that men have forgotten. He urges the prince not to forget, telling him that he is responsible for his rose. "I am responsible for my rose," repeats the little prince so as to remember.

In this critical pedagogical scene from *The Little Prince*, the fox, who models the traditional European trope of the wise animal, teaches the young boy about the importance of establishing ties with an other. This process of "taming," as the fox terms it, requires behaviors, orientations, approaches, and uses of time (wasted time) that the fox says have been lost among contemporary peoples. One is invited to conclude that this critique is Saint-Exupéry's message to moderns, who have, in their adoption of practices of industry, Taylorism, commodity consumption, etc., abandoned the acts of "establishing ties" that he argues, via the character of the fox, make living meaningful and rewarding. In these seemingly invisible acts and gestures relations are established by which a deep sense of value, appreciation, and worth is created. The fox notes that the disposition/practice of patience is critical in the taming process. He describes the gradual process of taming as one characterized by incremental steps toward closeness. First, he says, the prince should sit down at a distance from him and the fox will look at him out of the corner of his eye and the prince will not speak a word. "Words are the source of misunderstanding," he says, emphasizing the importance of embodied gesturing, proxemics, and general nonverbal communication. As the days go on, the prince will sit closer and closer to him. When the prince speaks of the ways he established ties with the rose, he details the concrete acts that constituted this process. He watered the rose; he placed a glass globe around her to protect her from the elements; he sheltered her behind a screen; he killed caterpillars who threatened her; he listened to her. These actions all involve material engagement with an other through bodily and sensory action. They involve speech, sharing space, hearing, giving, receiving, and exercising disciplinary efforts. In short, they involve some semblance of personal, interactional care. The fox contrasts the actions involved in this process of "establishing ties" with the act of buying "things all ready made at the shops." In this sweeping action of buying, no significant act is made that establishes ties between the consumer and seller or the consumer and object. The transaction is empty.

Neighborhood is greatly concerned with this process of "establishing ties" and employs simple, embodied acts of care throughout the program. Each episode involves continuous acts of engagement between people and their peers and people and objects that have come out of the hands of *Homo faber*—they are manmade objects, not machine-made objects. Rogers shares space with his "television friend" and with the neighbors who visit him. He interacts with them through speech—a speech that is careful to express care for the other on a consistent basis. Then, he engages with his "television friend" through acts of play that involve demonstrations of and interactions with manmade objects and their creative power. Together, he and the viewer assess, assemble, and disassemble the object(s) during the program. He questions the origins of the objects and attempts to trace them if possible. Through these acts of embodied engagement value is created and maintained in Rogers's interconnected sociocultural world of *Neighborhood*. It is the value of usage in friendship, rather than purchase and surplus value, that establishes meaningful ties and constitutes a sense of community.

Neighborhood episode 0111 illustrates how Rogers weaves the social and material together on the program. At the beginning of the episode, Rogers arrives with a flashlight. After singing his greeting song, he shows the flashlight to his viewer and demonstrates its functions by flicking the switch on and off. He tells the viewer that he has been thinking about pianos and, with the flashlight, moves to look inside his piano and identify its various parts. He opens the top of his upright piano and shines the light into the interior space. "These are called hammers," he says touching one hammer and pushing it up to touch the string behind it. "And the little hammers hit the strings." He then plays the key of the piano to which the hammer is connected and we watch as the hammer responds to the touch by striking the string. Sitting down at the bench and looking into the camera, he says, "each key has a different hammer," and plays a few notes. He then reaches under the piano and pulls out a long, intricate wooden device that apparently is a model of a piano key. "It's one key and it follows back here, all the different things that happen when you press down this key on the piano. All this moving right in here. And then finally the hammer hits the string." The camera moves along with Rogers's finger as it touches the object and points out its various intricacies. "Look at all these little moving parts," he notes with an air of calm wonderment. The camera stays focused on the mechanical detail around the hammer and we are given time to gaze and examine the object as we wish. Rogers then places his face behind this area, hits the keys a couple of times, and makes a sound of the key hitting the string vocally. "Boop, boop, boop," he sings. "Have you ever wondered how people make real pianos?" he asks the viewer. "I've often wondered that. Why don't we ask Picture Picture to show us?" We then follow Rogers as he walks across the small living room interior to Picture Picture.

In the film that details how pianos are made, we are first provided with a bird's-eye view of the basic framework of the inside of a grand piano. A workman is in the process of building it, but the film is silent. All we hear is the overlying piano playing of Johnny Costa and Rogers's extemporaneous narration. Rogers leaves plenty of spaces free of his narration, allowing for the visual images and Costa's background improvisation to unfold. "First goes in the sounding board and then the iron frame that's the support for the piano goes in. . . . That metal pattern marks where the pegs are for the strings to be put. . . . And out comes the frame again. Do you see it going up with the pulley? The insides of the piano are called the belly of the piano." Rogers describes the actions as they occur in the various edited shots. Close-ups of object and hand interaction are interwoven with shots of the various parts of the object, along with close-ups of the workman's face and body. Soon a new workman enters and begins to work with the piano's strings. "Now this man is stringing the piano. There are different sizes of wire. Do you notice the tape on his fingers? Those aren't bandages. Those are just to protect his fingers. That man is the best stringer that the factory has. . . . And he winds the strings around the tuning pegs. And each one of those strings goes in separately. And when the piano parts are all together, they put in that part of it with all the keys." We see the first workman sit down at the piano and test out a few keys with the strings exposed. The film is silent, so Costa plays notes mimicking the sounds that might be coming out of the piano as the workman hits the keys. "Each one of 'em is tested so carefully," Rogers says.

We watch as the workman removes the wood between the keys and hammers and uses a wooden bar to lift a set of around a dozen up in the air, in unison, and then push them down. "See all those hammers?" Rogers asks. The workman then takes a metal tool and digs into one of the hammers with it. We cut to a close-up of this action while Costa plays one note rapidly and rigorously to imitate the action with sound. "Those are little needles that he is using on the hammers. And that softens the hammers to give them a little softer tone," Rogers says. The workman then pushes the keyboard back in, stands up, grabs his tools, and begins to test each note again. The camera cuts to a close-up of his face as he looks down at what he is doing with an expression of deep concentration. We then slowly zoom out to view the film in the frame of Picture Picture, indicating the end of the viewing. The film soon cuts to an image of a piece of paper with printed and signed names. "And he stamps his name on it, on that slip of paper," Rogers tells us. "And everyone who has worked on that piano has his name stamped on it." Another workman appears and polishes the piano with a rag, an action that Rogers, too, observes verbally. Costa's piano playing, soft, graceful, and soothing, signals the film's close. The shot widens out to reveal Rogers standing next to Picture Picture. "Thank you, Picture Picture," he says. In response, the printed words "You're welcome Mister Rogers" appear on the inside of the frame. "Was that interesting?" Rogers asks as he goes and sits down on his couch. "So many things that people do to make things for us that we don't really realize," he says into the camera. "Pianos are very fancy," he says matter-of-factly. "All of them are fancy on the inside. Many are fancy on the outside. Just like all of us, we're fancy." This prompt leads into a song sung frequently by Rogers on *Neighborhood* titled "Everybody's Fancy."

Rogers's use of the word "fancy" to describe the piano, followed by his subsequent singing of "Everybody's Fancy," further connects people to the creation of the beautiful and complex instrument. The piano offers another visual metaphor for the word *fancy*, a term Rogers attributes to human qualities in his song. The film, with its emphasis on the creative work of the piano craftsmen in putting together the instrument, extends the initial human-object relationship that Rogers established in the living room scene featuring only him and the upright piano. In this scene, we see Rogers dissect the instrument in order to understand how the hammer produces sound by striking a string. After getting a brief taste of discovery with this cursory examination that takes place in the familiar domestic space, we are invited to "travel" to a piano factory, where our gaze is expanded and extended to a more intricate and sophisticated viewing of grand piano assembly and workmanship. We see, and Rogers points out, the tape on the second workman's fingers as he handles and manipulates the strings. In a sense, the workman's interaction with the objects in creating the piano speak to Saint-Exupéry's notion of taming. Time is spent understanding and interacting with, in this case, the objects that are used to build a piano.

The workers take great care with the object, executing their tasks with precision and concentration. At the end of the process, Rogers makes a point of noting, each person who worked on the creation of the piano signs his name on a piece of paper to indicate his contribution to the product. In a sense, they make the object theirs with this final rite. At the close of the film, Rogers notes that often we do not realize how much human effort goes into the making of objects—we take it for granted. This observation further speaks to Rogers's concerns about alienation. Rogers is constantly working to connect products with their human creators and with members of the larger community. His emphasis on craftsmanship and the creative arts has at its core a deep appreciation for the creative drive, the joy that it brings, and the social rewards of sharing one's work with others. Concomitant with the emphasis on the creative runs an emphasis on the production of an object that is just so, over and over again. Like a singer who wishes to sing a song *just right* every time, the artisan derives joy and pride in making the same "perfect" object again and again.

Episode 0111's NMB segment furthers social engagement with the piano-as-object via the visiting artist Van Cliburn, who performs sophisticated, classical piano pieces for King Friday and Sara Saturday.[72] Just as Cantini speaks about how he liked making things with household objects when he was a boy, Cliburn, a young man, describes how he learned to play the piano when he was a young boy. In fact, he and Friday have a rather long conversation recalling Cliburn's development as a pianist, in which the artist frequently returns to the piano to play samples of the pieces that he discusses. "I began to study and to practice," he tells Friday. "And I know I was playing . . . the first Prelude and Fugue of Johann Sebastian Bach and also some of the two- and three-part inventions of Bach." Friday confesses to Cliburn that he never got that far in his practice because, regretfully, he "did not work very hard" at the piano. Soon Sara Saturday arrives holding up a record album of *Tchaikovsky Concerto No. 1, Van Cliburn*. She offers it to him and Cliburn tells her that he feels honored that she has a copy of his performance. Saturday expresses interest in listening to the record in the "receiving room" later and makes a point of verbalizing the title of the record—"Tchaikovsky Concerto Number 1"—for the viewer. Cliburn tells them, proudly but not pompously, that Queen Elizabeth of Belgium was at his concert and how thrilling that was for him.

Asked to play another piece for the two, Cliburn prefaces his next performance with a background story. "In the middle of the nineteenth century, there was a particularly wonderful, wonderful song—in Germany they call it *Lieder*—that Robert Schumann wrote to his new bride, Clara Rief. . . . And this song is called 'Widmung,' rather in English 'Dedication.' And I will play a transcription by Franz Liszt, the famous Hungarian composer. So with your permission and your wish, I would be very happy to play the Liszt transcription of 'Widmung' by Robert Schumann." Rief's father, Cliburn notes, though himself a professor of music, was fairly adamant that his daughter not be involved in music—especially not in composition—because at the time composers were very poor. Indeed, Schumann was quite poor and as such all that he had to give his bride for a wedding present was this song, "Widmung." The three chuckle and Cliburn sits back down at the piano and performs, with his notably large hands and long fingers, a minute or so of the charming, romantic, and at times playful piece.

Cliburn's presentation further extends the human connection to the instrument. While the workers in the factory construct the piano, Cliburn plays music on it. In listening to the concert pianist speak about his interest in the piano as a young boy and watching him play advanced pieces on the instrument, the viewer's human relationship to the object becomes deeper and more dynamic. In the beginning segments we entered a discussion and examination of how people construct a piano. This discussion was limited to Rogers looking into the piano and identifying what select pieces of it do to help create the instrument's sound. He then showed us a more acute perspective of the hammer-string action by pulling this extracted part out for us to view closer. Next, in the film, we saw how those parts were assembled by workmen in the space where such tasks occur—a piano factory. Finally, in the NMB, we see a man using the piano for its intended function—to create music.

The NMB segment begins with Cliburn sitting at the instrument and playing a piece. Just as in the beginning of the living room segment, we see the piano in its whole form. From there, in both segments, attention is turned toward a discussion of how these respective wholes were created. In the case of the living room segment, Rogers examines the inside of the piano (whole) where the hammer strikes the string. In the NMB segment, Friday probes Cliburn (whole) about where and when he started the process of becoming a professional concert pianist. He then, through dialogue, uncovers the story of a young boy who takes an interest in the instrument at the age of four as a result of watching his mother give piano lessons in his house. Cliburn describes hearing a particular song played by one of his mother's students and then trying to replicate the melody on the piano himself after the student's lesson. "You had listened to it," Friday summarizes after hearing Cliburn tell the anecdote, "and then tried to pick it out with your fingers."

Here again, we have an example of parts coming together to create a whole. After he tells the anecdote about his first experience trying to play the piano, Cliburn then goes to the piano to play a part of the piece. He has now mastered the piece—the piece is now whole. He was once an apprentice pianist and he is now a master pianist. When he began to learn the piece, it existed only in parts—a melody played with the right hand and supporting notes played with the left hand. As Cliburn plays, he notes that the first time he attempted to play the melody of the piece, his feet could not yet reach the piano pedals. He had to wait until he could grow to apply this part to the piece.

Here, and throughout the episode, we witness a critical staple of *Neighborhood*—an emphasis on process and practice. As is often the case on the program, established visiting artists are prompted to note how becoming masters of their craft took a good amount of *practice*. Rogers, too, emphasizes the discipline required to become skilled at a craft or art, almost always using the term *practice* to describe such dedication. As we fade back into the living room via a close-up of the flashing traffic light, we are greeted by Mister Rogers, sitting on his couch where we left him before entering the NMB. "Oh, what a treat," he says. "And after a lot and lot of practice, Mr. Cliburn got to be one of the world's famous pianists."

In the interest of maintaining his anthropocentric values throughout his programming, Rogers often employs inquiries into everyday objects in which he shows how such objects can be used in a variety of practical, functional, creative, and imaginative ways.

In episode 0112, Mister Rogers brings in a homemade drum and uses lollipops as sticks to demonstrate drumming. Here, instead of bringing in a shiny, new drum he bought at a store, he uses a homemade drum—one that has been created by someone he knows. Further, the drumsticks are created from lollipops; the sticks have already been used, touched, by another, giving them an air of human connection. In episode 0055, Mister Rogers arrives with a bag of vegetables, which are later transformed from raw to cooked by a neighbor, Chef Brockett. Rogers valuing the tracing, examination, use, and transformation of objects sends an anti-consumerist message to viewers. It is also a message that, while delivered via the television screen, does not inspire television viewing. Rather, Rogers uses the virtual medium to inspire viewers to craft and create things with one's body by using objects and items at hand for most (that is, everyday and somewhat affordable) in the material world. For Rogers, arts and crafts, the act of creating, manipulating, and transforming objects using one's body, is what makes for healthy living.[73]

In a classic first season episode, 0011, Mister Rogers enters with an oatmeal container. He has stripped any commercial images off the container and glued on it a strip of paper that has the word *Oatmeal* written on it. Instead of putting on his cardigan he dons a lab coat and tells the viewer what he has brought with him. "Not a drum," he says, tapping on the top, "but an oatmeal box with some oatmeal in it." He shakes the box for audio effect, to communicate that oats are indeed inside. "Do you ever eat oatmeal?" he asks the viewer. "For breakfast, lunch, or dinner? Oats are very good for you, you know." He further notes that there are lots of things one can make out of oatmeal boxes as well. Then he tells us, with amusement, that he once knew a boy who said "open meal" instead of "oatmeal." "Do you ever wonder how oatmeal was made?" he asks. "You know, first it has to grow. Because it's really oats that grow in the fields." Then he turns to Picture

Picture and asks it to show him and the viewer how oatmeal is made. "Picture Picture on the wall," he says, "would you kindly show us all how those oats get into boxes like this?" The way he asks Picture Picture to illustrate how oatmeal is made is phrased in the sentence construction of a child—"how those oats get into boxes like this." Notably, it does not use the wording, "how *people* assemble oatmeal boxes," a phrasing that producer Hedda Sharapan says he introduced later on in programming. Here, the human element of creation is not included in the utterance, a fact Rogers later noticed and explicitly changed.

Once again, starting with the everyday household item of an oatmeal box, Rogers has made an immediate human connection by handling the object himself and then noting how a boy he knows calls oatmeal "open meal." He then moves on to trace both the food and the object's origins via a film. First we view the plowing and raking of a farm field where a farmer on a tractor plants seeds. As usual, Rogers narrates the process as the film unfolds. He notes the dust that the plowing creates. We watch up close as the seeds shoot up sprouts from the dirt. "Of course, that takes a long time for it to grow," Rogers notes. "But that's the way it grows. Up, into the sunlight." The film then cuts to a number of leaves growing into full maturity together. "There are all the oats together," Rogers continues. We then view a moving image of oats falling out of a metal object and onto what looks like a sifter of some sort. "And after they are brought onto the train and brought to the factory, they're put onto a conveyor belt," he says. "Look what a long ride they have," he says as we watch the oats travel along swiftly on the belt. "Boy, that's a fast ride for those oats!" We then see the oats sifted down into a sliding board and listen to Rogers as he narrates each step. The next image is of the cardboard boxes, which mirror the container that Rogers introduced at the beginning of the program. This shot brings great pleasure as it connects the object made personal by Rogers to its origins in the factory. The boxes "are getting filled with the oat-meal," Rogers narrates over the focused, steady shot of one part of the highly mechanized process. We then watch as each box gets a lid. "Many, many, many, many boxes," Rogers says playfully. "And there are their lids." The film is brought to conclusion by the camera zooming out and revealing its broadcast inside the Picture Picture frame in Rogers's living room. Standing beside it, Rogers holds his oatmeal box up near the frame.

"Thank you very much, Picture Picture," Rogers tells the anthropomorphized frame. Continuing the connection with the last item of display, he notes that the lid on his oatmeal box is on. "But we could take the lid off," he says smiling. "And how about making some in the kitchen?" Answering his own question to the viewer, he says, "Sure," and notes, "We've got our lab coat on. We might as well be creative in the kitchen today." This use of "we" is consistent with all of Rogers's verbal and nonverbal communication efforts to create the sense that he is actively spending dyadic time with the viewer.

We follow him into the kitchen, where he notes that the ingredients we need to make oatmeal are present—oatmeal, water, salt, and a pot. "Who makes the oatmeal most often in your house?" he asks the viewer, making the connection between his on-screen cooking and the viewer's personal family environment. He grabs a plastic measuring cup and the camera zooms in on his hand pouring the oatmeal into the cup. "There, one cup of oatmeal and two cups of water," he says pouring the cup into the pot and heading to the sink to fill the cup with water. "I read that in a cookbook," he giggles as he pours the water into the pan. "It's part of the fun of cooking, you know, pouring water and mak[ing] all kinds of mess, and something comes out of it . . . yup, something good." He fills up another cup of water and, holding the cup a few feet above the pot, pours the water into it while watching with a look of delight. Next, he adds the salt. "It's sort of a 'palm of your hand' portion of salt," he says as he pours a teaspoon into his palm and shows the viewer, emptying it into the pot. Finally, he grabs the matches and lights the stove, saying, "Now something for big people only—matches." He clarifies that he says "big people only" because fire is very dangerous. "But you're getting bigger, every day," he says while he stirs the oatmeal. The camera zooms in on the metal spoon as it moves the oats around in the pot of water. Over this close-up, which, I may add, proves quite pleasurable, he sings:

> You used to creep and crawl real well
> But then you learned to walk real well
> There was a time you'd coo and cry
> But they you learned to talk and my
> You hardly ever cry, you hardly ever crawl at all
> I like the way you're growing up
> It's fun, that's all

> CHORUS:
> You're growing, you're growing
> You're growing in and out
> You're growing, you're growing
> You're growing all about

> Your hands are getting bigger now
> Your arms and legs are stronger now
> You even sense your insides grow
> When mom and dad refuse you
> So you're learning how to wait now
> It's great to hope and wait somehow
> I like the way you're growing up
> It's fun, that's all

> CHORUS

Your friends are getting better now
They're better every day somehow
You used to stay at home to play
But now you even play away
You do important things now
Your friends and you do big things now
I like the way you're growing up
It's fun, that's all

Someday you'll be a grownup too
And have some children grow up too
Then you can love them in and out
And tell them stories all about
The times that you were their size
The times when you found great surprise
In growing up and they will sing
It's fun, that's all

CHORUS[74]

"You sure are growing," he states at the close of the song. Then he sings the song's theme, substituting the lyrics, "We're cooking" as he looks back down at the pot, where he continues to stir the oatmeal.

Every subject visited has an appropriate segue and clear moment of both connection and transition. This technique creates a sense of continuity and lessens anxieties caused by sharp and jarring cuts. We then return to the tight shot of the inside of the pot, where the oatmeal-and-water mixture has transformed from thin to thick. "When the bubbles come all in it, that means it's boiling," Rogers says as bubbles begin to form and pop around the edges of the mixture. "Then you let it boil for about a minute." Rogers continues to stir in silence for a few seconds before we cut to a fuller kitchen shot of him over the stove, stirring. "The oatmeal's almost ready," he says. "But after it boils for a while, then you cover it over, take it away from the fire and cover it over. And then it's ready for your friend." Here, we cut back to the tight close-up of the inside of the pan, where the oatmeal looks thicker and nearly done. "See it bubbling?" he says. "There it goes. You're a good, bubbling oatmeal." Returning back to the wide shot of Rogers in the kitchen, we see him look into the camera and smile. "Open meal," he giggles. He closes the segment by turning off the fire and noting that when one turns on the fire, it must always be turned off at the end of cooking. "Now we can let it sit and go to the Neighborhood of Make-Believe," he says.

Heading back into the living room, Rogers sits down on the chair below Picture Picture and below the train track. He pulls a small notepad from his pocket along with a pencil as Trolley pulls up beside him with a whistle. "You know, I was just thinking about something as I was making that," Rogers says. "You know, I've got a friend who works real well with clay, and his name is Jamie." Rogers offers that maybe Jamie could come over later, since cooking the oatmeal reminded him of playing with clay. Here, another connection is made between persons, objects, and their creative interactions and manipulations. Rogers writes his request for Jamie's visit on his notepad and asks Trolley if he would deliver his message. He vocalizes his note while writing it: "Please come and bring some play clay . . . Mister Rogers." To clarify the stops, Rogers asks Trolley to take us into the NMB while he is looking for Jamie.

In the NMB, Trolley drops us off at the castle, where a mime, named Mime Walker, stands in conversation with King Friday.[75] As the two watch Trolley pass by, Friday turns to Mime Walker and says, "Yes, that's our neighborhood Trolley." The statement serves as another transition into the new scene with the vocalization of Trolley's entrance and departure. "Suppose, Mime Walker, you show me how you might be someone who is riding on a trolley," Friday directs Walker. The scene unfolds as a series of miming requests and demonstrations by Friday and Walker, respectively. Walker, who wears white tights, ballet slippers, a striped long-sleeve shirt, and white makeup, in classic mime costume, takes his time in each demonstration. For the first request, he mimes depositing a coin into an imagined coin slot, walks to the back of the imagined trolley, reaches up to clasp the imagined hand rail, and then glides his feet along to imitate the trolley's movement. After hearing Friday's second request, that Mime Walker demonstrate a man flying a kite, he reaches both hands out before him to draw in an imagined string. Pretending to battle with the force of the kite as it is carried along in the air by the wind, his torso and hips bend backward as he digs his feet into the floor and lets the wind pull his arms and torso over and back to its original position. Costa plays dreamlike music on the celeste as Walker follows the kite around in a figure eight motion. Mime Walker's short, yet diligent and sustained miming scenes feel like bodily meditations on simple human action. They have the effect of inspiring feelings of awe, relaxation, and wonder. They invite the viewer to absorb the subtleties in the man's movement, expressions, and sequence. "I feel so strongly that deep and simple is far more essential than shallow and complex," Rogers once told filmmaker Benjamin Wagner.[76] Here, with Mime Walker, *Neighborhood* offers yet another representation of human-object interactions that are easily accessible, relatable, and doable in the world. In this case, the object does not even exist in material form. It is, rather, imagined, yet still played with on a cognitive and bodily level.

Mime Walker continues his playful performance for Friday by miming bird watching, a hobby that the NMB character Lady Elaine has embraced. Friday relates this information to Walker as he concludes their engagement and Walker, interested in Lady Elaine's new hobby, proceeds to visit her, Henrietta Pussycat, and

X the Owl. Over at the tree that X and Henrietta share, Mime Walker entertains Henrietta's request that he mime a cat by pretending to preen himself and drink milk from a bowl. He then pretends, at the instruction and prompting of X, that he is a goldfinch taking a bath. It is a delightfully pleasurable scene in which he involves his whole body, moving his arms and legs about to splash water atop an imaginary giant birdbath. After he "flies away" from the bath, Henrietta and X engage in a discussion of the ways that birds and cats bathe and how they differ. Again, verbal connections are always made in order to fully acknowledge and properly realize an action, meditation, and/or drama that ensues. As Henrietta sings "Goldfinch, goldfinch, what do you look like?" we cut back to Rogers sitting in the chair just exactly where he left us before we entered the NMB. He picks up where Henrietta left off in the song, "Goldfinch, goldfinch, what do you look like?" The music carries us through from one world to another such that Rogers comes in with no audio break. "Goldfinch, goldfinch, what do you look like? You're yellow with a black wing and a black hat," he concludes. "Sure, Lady Elaine will see a goldfinch soon," he assures us, adding one final verbal layer to the closing of the NMB episode.

The final segment begins with a knock at the front door, to which Rogers responds by getting out of his chair and verbally wondering if it is Jamie, the friend who likes to play with clay he referred to at the close of the oatmeal-making scene. "I wonder if he got our note," Rogers says as he opens the door and says hello to Jamie. "Hi, I got your note," Jamie says. Again, repetitive emphasis is used often with verbal affirmations that bring clarity. Rogers notes out loud that Jamie has brought his clay with him and finds a laboratory coat for the boy in the closet. Jamie, who is Rogers's real son, puts on the coat and the two amble over to the kitchen table, where they sit down together with Jamie's plastic container of clay.

"Oh, you've got all sorts of colors here," Rogers says as he looks inside Jamie's container. "Yeah, I brought this one along," Jamie says, grabbing two pieces of rolled-up clay. "I was making something and I thought I'd bring it along." Rogers asks Jamie what he was starting to make and Jamie tells him that he was making a baseball diamond. He places the two rolled-up pieces on the table and pats them down on the table, forming two sides of the diamond. Rogers asks him if he would provide him with some clay for him to play with and Jamie gives him some yellow clay. "Baseball diamond, huh? Well, how'd you think that up?" Rogers asks Jamie. Jamie tells him that he went to a baseball game and smiles bashfully. "Did you enjoy it?" Rogers asks him. "Yup," Jamie responds. Rogers tells Jamie that he remembers how when Jamie was younger, he used to pound the clay together "like so," demonstrating with the clay in his hands. "And now look at you, making baseball diamonds," he says. "You are really growing." The camera zooms in on Jamie's hands working the placement of the clay on the table. He presses a piece in the middle of the diamond he has made into the table. "What's that in the middle?" Rogers asks. "The pitcher's mound," Jamie replies. "The pitcher's mound," Rogers repeats declaratively. He then points out each base with his fingers—first base, second base, third base, and home. Above the baseball diamond, we see Jamie's hands working a piece of darker clay. "Now what are you doing?" Rogers asks. "Making a pitcher and a batter," Jamie says. "Good—a pitcher and a batter," Rogers says as Jamie places the pitcher (an upright piece of clay) on the mound. He continues to work with the batter as Costa's gentle piano adds a sense of calm and pleasantry to the scene. "Is that the batter?" Rogers asks. "It's going to be," Jamie replies while finishing molding it with his hands and placing it on home plate.

Jamie's scene is slowly coming together and transforming from flattened pieces of clay into a baseball diamond, complete with a pitcher and a batter, who stand upright at their proper respective locations. Jamie is maybe seven years old. His depictions of pitcher and batter are nothing special—they are pieces of clay that have been molded to resemble, ever so faintly, figures of human beings with necks, heads, and bodies. Yet somehow, in the process of being placed on a baseball diamond and verbally named, the objects have become something more than what they once were. They now symbolize a cultural expression—a baseball game. And although Jamie's craftsmanship is quite basic, one derives a sense of beauty and pleasure in watching the "sculpture" come together as he molds the pieces on the table.

For the first finishing symbolic touch, Jamie adds a long piece of clay to the batter's top half. It is the bat. Then, placing a little ball of clay just past the second base area, he says, "A ball landed right there." Laughing with Jamie, Rogers says, "A ball landed there," and he points his finger next to the ball. Rogers then shows Jamie what he has made and asks what Jamie thinks it might be. "A birdbath?" Jamie asks. "A birdbath," Rogers confirms, and then asks Jamie if he can borrow a bit of dark clay from him to place at the edge of the bath. It represents a bird. Adding further connection to events in the NMB, Rogers tells Jamie that the next time he has Mime Walker over, he will ask him to mime some baseball actions. He mimes hitting a ball with an imaginary bat in his hands. Jamie brings the attention back to his baseball display by adding more clay pieces that he says will represent the right fielder and the left fielder. The two then clean up their creations together, placing the clay back into Jamie's container. Rogers tells Jamie that he will drop him at home on his way to work. They walk into the living room singing "Tomorrow" together.

> Tomorrow, tomorrow
> We'll start the day tomorrow with a song or two
> Tomorrow, tomorrow

We'll start the day tomorrow with a smile for you
'Til then I hope you're feeling happy
'Til then I hope your day is snappy
Tomorrow, tomorrow
It soon will be tomorrow
And be our day
We will say a very happy tomorrow to you.[77]

"Thanks for coming to visit me," Rogers says as walks toward the front door in his suit jacket next to Jamie. "See you tomorrow, bye bye," he waves as he exits.

As I have noted, Rogers learned early in his life that performing creative acts—in his case, playing the piano—could help alleviate the anxiety he felt as a result of isolation and social exclusion. Abram underscores that for Winnicott and Rogers no special talent is needed for creative living. Because creativity originates from a sense of existing, "creativity is the doing that arises out of being."[78] As Rogers shows throughout his program, creative acts can be engaged in via an endless variety of actions that involve the most accessible of phenomena—the body, the objects at one's disposal, social engagement, and the natural world. Songs can be sung that already exist, or one can invent one's own song. Regular, everyday objects can be used in their own utilitarian way or manipulated to create new uses. *Neighborhood*'s emphasis is on anthropocentrism and the power of the human being to make use of what he has to live creatively through cultural discovery.

Neighborhood episodes from the first season of the program are anchored in the material, social, and imaginary existence and possibilities of artisanal and everyday objects. The episodes introduce the viewer to a world made by man, in which objects are a site for human interaction and creative transformation. When nature comes into this purview, it is also presented as an object of contemplation and knowledge. When, for example, oatmeal is presented, it is rendered as an object that has a story. This story links it to its point of origin—natural and/or manmade. The story or stories show how the object is related organically or functionally to people. The Picture Picture film details the cultivation, harvest, packaging, and transport of the oats and Rogers transforms the packaged oats into oatmeal through the act of cooking. These relations imbue the objects with a story that conveys to the viewer a world of relationships.

Objects are thus presented in their different manifestations and their many possibilities. As such, in each show, the object is introduced not only as an instrument of play but perhaps more importantly as a site of discovery and understanding for the (child) viewer. Each object therefore holds the possibility for creative transformation, several possibilities of which are imagined, discussed, and enacted on the program.

The indispensable and defining presence of an object in each episode constitutes an anthropology of objects. The above analysis constitutes a meta-anthropological study of Rogers's anthropology of objects. "Look at all these moving parts," Rogers says while viewing the intricate workings of the piano.[79] While Clifford Geertz constructs his "thick description" through written notes on a page, Rogers transposes his anthropological observations through the medium of television. As such, he has the privilege of utilizing oral and visual observation, communication forms that Walter Ong identified as primary and thus closer to the realm of human life, to perform his anthropological pedagogy.[80] Using these communication tools essential to the television medium (secondary orality), Rogers mounts an inquiry into the object. He then finds an informant (usually a neighbor or visiting artisan/artist) to dialogue with about the object and its creative possibilities. This move works to assist the viewer in learning not only about the object but its place in the social world. In its enactment of this search for an object's origins and relationship to human history, *Neighborhood*, as demonstrated by its national, intergenerational popularity, its thirty-four-year run on public television, and its plethora of viewer mail, was found by viewers to be deeply pleasurable.

Rogers weaves his analysis of objects starting with an introductory segment in which he introduces the object directly to his viewer. "Look what I brought in today," he begins. He often then brings another person into the scene or introduces a film about the object in order to discuss its origin, the ways that it is made, and how it works. Next, he transitions the object into the NMB, where a second anthropology of the object ensues. Here, the object is inserted into a world of desire and control and constitutes a point of origin for many of the dramas that characterize the realm of King Friday.

In relation to this anthropology of objects, which I have found to be constitutive of the program, one could argue that *Neighborhood* seeks to restore the visibility of the essential relations and workings of a society. In many respects, we can see how Rogers seeks to replicate a village life environment for his viewers through the artisanal quality of objects, the continuity of social relationships, the stability of spaces and places, and a strong sense of origins and general fluidity. Rogers, in his quest for locating an object's origins, connecting it to the social present, and transforming it by the work of his own human hands, produces a program that countervails one of modernity's greatest forces of alienation—the inauthentic production of industrial objects. From Winnicott's perspective, this process is indeed the work of life (play for the child) and the location of culture. In play, the action that occurs in the *potential space* between the individual and the environment (originally the object), cultural experience unfolds with what Winnicott calls "creative living." According to Winnicott, potential space is created "only *in relation to a feeling of confidence* on the part of the baby, that is, confidence related to the dependability of the mother-figure or environmental elements." Thus, Rogers's program, through its emphasis on trust and mutuality, object relations, and social and spatial continuity, appears intent on helping the young individual viewer learn to venture into the *potential space* where she may safely explore and manipulate the world and thus become a healthy social and cultural being.

"Won't You Be My Neighbor?"

INTERGENERATIONAL DIALOGICS IN
NEIGHBORHOOD VIEWER MAIL

IN A 1969 LETTER WRITTEN to Fred Rogers, a mother discusses how her young son, Peter, a *Neighborhood* viewer, pretends to be the program's host by donning a bathrobe and walking about the house singing his favorite *Neighborhood* song, "You've Got to Do It." She thanks Rogers and expresses her wish that other shows would "have the inventive [*sic*] to bring the same type of program into [our] home instead of four hours of cartoons and those terrible Three Stooges." In another 1969 letter, a mother praises Rogers's "quality of instruction," his "excellent approach to all aspects of a child's life," and the puppets' "real-life experiences." "Whenever Daddy gets home early," she continues, "he joins us [in viewing *Neighborhood*]. Often we talk about people on your show for days afterward," she writes.

From the opening of each *Neighborhood* program, Rogers presents an invitation to conversation with his viewers. The letters he received demonstrate the efficacy of this invitational tone in the respectful and conversational manner in which they address "Mister Rogers." Such correspondence reaffirms Rogers's attempts to elicit the implicit dialogical dynamics of communication, and demonstrates Mikhail Bakhtin's sense of a dialogic situation in which "the word in living conversation is directly, blatantly, oriented toward a future answer-word," often characterized as "answerability."[1] *Neighborhood* employs a dialogical communication ethic wherein viewers of the program feel compelled to respond to the call of the program's primary figure or host, "Mister Rogers," through what was, at the time, the dominant communication medium: letter writing. In this chapter I examine viewer letters written to Fred Rogers during the 1970s and 1980s, using the perspective of four scholars of dialogic communication ethics—Mikhail Bakhtin, Roger Burggraeve, Paulo Freire, and Martin Buber—in order to show how Rogers's dialogical rhetorical stance, techniques, and strategies resonated with viewers.

Rogers invites his viewers to spend time with him at his "television house." He refers to each program not by the industry term *episode* but rather as a "television visit," implying an interactive meeting between him and his viewer in real time. As such, Rogers reframes his program as an experience of sharing existence, an event that calls us into dialogue, "not only with other human beings, but also with the natural and cultural configurations we lump together as 'the human world.'"[2] As Michael Holquist writes in his work on Bakhtin and dialogism, "the world addresses us and we are alive and human to the degree that we are answerable, i.e. to the degree that we can respond to addressivity."[3] If dialogue is an essential component of existence, as Bakhtin posits, what does it mean for Rogers to ground his television program in a dialogical communication ethos? And what relevance does this dialogical analysis hold for today's children's media and its producers?

Burggraeve's conceptualization of ethical emotionality, which he defines as "passion through and for the other" or "heteronomous affection," "by the vulnerable face of the other" provides a rich theoretical framework for analyzing *Neighborhood* viewer letters and lends an important Christian ethical communication framework to these dynamic texts.[4] Burggraeve's concept of ethical emotionality dovetails with Bakhtin's dialogical theorization of the conversational moment—a moment that "provokes an answer, anticipates it and structures itself in the answer's direction."[5] Freire's dialogic-relations method of learning, rooted in an understanding of dialogue as "an existential necessity," further elucidates the humanizing and transformative nature of dialogue as witnessed in the viewer letters.[6] As an educator of Latin America's poor and proponent of liberation theology, Freire's scholarship confirms the existential nature of dialogical ethics and social pedagogy within the spheres of education and ethics. Finally, Buber's phenomenological understanding of dialogue as a process in which people come to being in relation to each other offers us additional critical depth in assessing the processes taking place in the "between" space of the conversational interactions.

In the 1930s, and 1940s, prominent industry agents and communication scholars viewed twentieth-century mass communication technologies of radio, film, and television through the lens of the linear transmission model of communication, in which a sender creates a message that travels uninterrupted to millions of intended receivers. Rogers was before his time in his analysis of television as part and parcel of a transactional communication process. In contrast to the transmission model, in which communication is viewed as something one person does to another, the transactional model suggests that communication is not only a collaborative process (something that we create together) but also "an experience that affects us" such that we are changed.[7] The transactional view further suggests that each communicator is at once a sender and receiver, emphasizing the all-encompassing nature of communication as a symbolic production of reality: James Carey's ritual view of communication as a "sacred ceremony that draws persons together in fellowship and commonality," which is "linked to terms such as 'sharing,' 'participation,' 'association,' 'fellowship,' and 'the possession of a common faith,'" offers a particularly enlightening lens through which to view *Neighborhood*.[8] Hans Gadamer, as discussed by Anderson, Baxter, and Cissna, also shared this nuanced understanding of communication. Anderson et.al. synthesize Gadamer's view as follows: "Meanings were not *reproduced* by 'receivers' but *produced* collaboratively and dialogically by communicators who are simultaneously and prototypically speakers and listeners."[9]

Meticulous in his creation of a dialogical communication environment in which calls to reflection, imagination, and understanding take place within a highly ritualized visual and oral communication reality, Rogers, a student of child development and psychology, aimed to create a safe space in which a variety of issues could be discussed on a dialogical level through the new mass communication medium of television. Rogers's viewers do not simply *view Neighborhood*. Rather, they actively *participate* in the program as a result of its dialogical nature. The letters they wrote to Rogers provide evidence that viewers of the program, through their daily, ritualized participation in *Neighborhood*'s symbolically produced televisual reality, developed a relationship with Rogers in which they felt compelled to personally and formally respond to his dialogical prompts and think through issues and ideas together.

By 1975 there had developed a consensus that the power of television was usurping the traditional pedagogical roles of other institutions, an observation that Rogers had made some fifteen to twenty years earlier. In his groundbreaking book *Tube of Plenty: The Evolution of American Television*, Erik Barnouw argues that television has bypassed the traditional roles of parent, teacher, priest, grandparent, etc., in its power to transmit values to children. In the same year, Grant Noble suggested that "the mass media show the adolescent what to do to be a recognisably visible teenager, how to dress and dance and how to treat his parents.'"[10] More recently, Dorothy and Jerome Singer, in their *Handbook of Children and the Media*, identify the popular media as educators and socializers of growing children. This perspective, now recognized as a given in both academia and American society at large, is one that Rogers recognized in the 1950s. Recall that in "Children's TV: What Can the Church Can Do about It?," Rogers wrote that since the television set is bought and placed in the home by parents, "it's as if the parents were bringing—and condoning—what their children see on the set." Barnouw appears to share Rogers's view of television's growing authority when he asserts that the medium has quickly become "the dominant shared experience in the modern world."[11] In "Children's TV," Rogers questions whether "our children (and the children whom the church has never been able to reach) [are] being fed a slick, stimulated sound-tracked trash 1,000 hours a year while our schools try to teach the opposite with posters, crayons, and paste in one-tenth the time?"[12] If television had, by the mid-1970s, become *the* dominant shared experience of modern life, as a host of intellectuals assert and as Rogers foresaw and repudiated, what can we learn from Rogers's ethically and psychologically grounded, dialogical, mass communication practices?

Addressing an audience at Yale University in 1972, Rogers decried the values of those concerned with the business of the television at the expense of the quality of content produced. With a particular concern for the ways that television viewing affects human development, and especially child development, Rogers stated that "within the family—and television *is* within the family—we need to communicate the worth of the simple, the necessity of being honest—and the uniqueness as well as the relationship of all human beings."[13] As I discussed in chapter 1, Rogers and child development specialist Margaret McFarland felt strongly that television programming was destined to become part of the family communication dynamic of the home. Rogers saw *Neighborhood* as embedded in the family communication culture of every home and aptly named his production company Family Communications, Inc.[14] More than thirty years later, Singer and Singer ask the question, "What does it mean for children's development to be growing up in a milieu in which popular reading literature and especially electronic sources of input compete daily with what children can learn from parents, family, or teachers—the 'live' people around them?"[15] This question has been debated since the mid-1950s, when television had become a fixture of American family life.

Most of the research on television and children has centered upon concerns about the "healthy" development of children in relation to the medium. Indeed, the "healthy" development of children was Rogers's primary motivator and ultimate concern, as he stated in his testimony before the Senate in 1969: "I've worked in the field of child development for six years now, trying to understand the inner needs of children . . . and I feel that if we in public television can only make it clear that feelings are mentionable and manageable, we will have done a great service for mental health."[16]

My inquiry into *Neighborhood* viewer letters and the dialogical nature of the correspondence addresses the phenomenon from the perspective of communication theories on dialogue and communication ethics in order to delve deeper into the complexities of Mister Rogers's resounding parasocial relationship with viewers.[17] My method of analysis is interpretive hermeneutics, an approach I find particularly appropriate for dealing with the complexities of discursive expression. Ronald C. Arnett, Janie M. Harden Fritz, and Leeanne M. Bell have identified the process of dialogue as first principle in postmodern communication ethics. Their work on communication ethics and dialogue advances the idea that in a postmodern, global world, characterized in many ways by difference, dialogue becomes a fundamental ethical good and one that must be employed in everyday life. Arnett cites Melissa Cook on how "views of the good respond differently to particular concerns in given historical moments" as useful to his assessment of the dialogical ethical imperative in postmodernity.[18] "The postmodern moment," writes Arnett, "is an opportunity for those wanting to learn from difference".[19] Further, in response to Robert Bellah and Robert Putnam's work detailing the growing isolation and alienation experienced in postmodern American society, Arnett expresses deep concern for the very notion of ethics and human survival. In these developments, encapsulated in Philip Slater's 1970 book title *The Pursuit of Loneliness*, Arnett identifies a very serious "error of the moment," which he characterizes as "the temptation of assuming that we can function without regard for the other."[20]

In their 2004 edited survey on the subject, *Dialogue: Theorizing Difference in Communication Studies*, Rob Anderson, Leslie Baxter, and Kenneth A. Cissna identify the dialogical theories of Buber, Gadamer, Habermas, and Bakhtin as touchstone works for communication scholars focused on dialogue and its theoretical variations. The conceptual turn toward dialogue provides us with a rich and fertile perspective from which to analyze and theorize about mass media texts such as *Neighborhood*, which is rooted in an interpersonal communication ethic aimed at transcending the emotional and broader psychological space between screen actors and viewers. Though I focus primarily on analyzing the viewer letter correspondence of the program from a dialogical communication perspective, this chapter builds communication bridges between a variety of subfields, including interpersonal communication, childhood culture, television studies, mass communication, and communication ethics.[21]

Viewer letters were crucial to Rogers's sense of dialoguing with his audience, and he responded to each one. That his company retained all correspondence received during *Neighborhood*'s thirty-three years of programming testifies to the unusual importance they hold for Rogers's communication project at large. At the Fred Rogers Archives, at Saint Vincent College in Latrobe, Pennsylvania, I read and sorted through hundreds of letters written between the years 1968 and 1983. I selected letters for analysis according to rhetorical patterns of affective expression and communication exchange in content and/or style: the sample of letters analyzed in this chapter are representative of a multitude of viewer letters characterized by affect display, self-disclosure, self-discovery, and an ethos of gratitude. The abundant viewer letters written to Rogers during this period reveal a remarkable consistency in their collective thematic quality and constitute a field of study about the dialogical relationship between the program's host, the historical Fred Rogers, and *Neighborhood*'s audience. Most viewers appear to write to express an emotional and affective identification with Rogers, as well as to convey a sincere appreciation for how the show sparks both their curiosities and their family conversations, as was Rogers's intention. Rogers deploys television as a dialogical medium in which the *active* understanding of the audience is as important as the messages communicated, and his "audience" responds to his invitational rhetoric in kind.

Also remarkable about this collection of letters is the intergenerational and gendered diversity among the viewers that include mothers, children, teenagers, seniors, and fathers. The letters I have selected for analysis are representative of the larger body of intergenerational letters that feature expressions of affect, interpersonal relationship, self-disclosure, and dialogical learning at their center. It goes without saying that the great bulk of the letters written to Rogers were authored by children who had not yet learned to write and apparently requested that their parent express their sentiments on the page. These messages often expressed greetings, love, and a comment or question about a favorite character or program segment. Sometimes they wished to share their personal stories from everyday life with Rogers and ask him about aspects of his life. More often than not, these toddler communications were simply drawings they created for their friend Mister Rogers.

The letters that teens and young adults wrote to "Mister Rogers" are often tinged with a hue of childhood lament and a desire to reconnect. Young adults often express a feeling of embarrassment for writing to their "television friend" from childhood, yet continue to exclaim their deep affection for Rogers and for the meaningful role he played, and in some cases still plays, in their lives. Sometimes the teens seek Rogers's advice or an answer to a question with which they are struggling.

The emotional flow that emerges in these lettered expressions is notable in its relationship to the dialogical quality of address. Most of the writers appear to place themselves almost immediately in intimate conversation and relationship with Rogers and, self-reflexively, with themselves. They take us with them on an emotional journey in which they first expose vulnerable feelings of embarrassment and/or shame, and then shift toward a tone of self-acceptance and reassurance, as if reminding themselves that in conversation with Rogers they are in a safe and secure space that is welcoming and free of judgment. Reassured of the existence of this safe space, they tend to proclaim their appreciation of Rogers's presence in their young lives.

RECOGNIZING, REUNITING, AND RECONCILING—DIALOGUING WITH YOUNG MEN

In his February 11, 1982, letter to "Mr. Rogers," Brooklynite Glenn Greenwald writes that "seven years ago, I used to watch you every day on channel 13 [New York's WNET] and would sing along with you as you welcomed me into your neighborhood."[22] He tells Rogers that he will turn thirteen years old in a few months and that he recently stumbled upon the program. Glenn reveals that while catching the final five minutes of the program he found himself wondering if Rogers remembered him. "You seemed to be looking right at me," he writes, "and your last words were 'I like you just the way you are.'" Glenn recognizes this line from watching the program as a child and recalls that Rogers always said these words while leaving his house and ending the program. "It really took me back," he continues, saying, "I am a graduate of your show and I am not sorry that I am."

Clearly connecting with his inner child through the friendly figure of Mister Rogers, Glenn's letter expresses both affection for his former self and also, at the end of the letter, a hint of shame for expressing those affections. As a thirteen-year-old boy, he likely feels that the sensitive and vulnerable young child who adoringly watched *Neighborhood* is no longer a part of his more experienced and grown-up teenage male self. And yet, in the statement "I am a graduate of your show and I am not sorry that I am" he first expresses pride and then quickly moves to reject any shame others might want to assign to this statement of association with Rogers and his program.

Most interesting for this inquiry is Glenn's confession that while revisiting the show several years after watching it routinely as a five-year-old, he finds himself wondering if Rogers recognizes him. As if engaged in a reunion with a significant person in his childhood life, Glenn relates to Rogers interpersonally. Rogers expressed his interest in television not within the realm of "mass communications" but rather in the interpersonal communication that it allows. In a recorded dialogue between Rogers and McFarland, his professional mentor and a primary consultant for the program, she tells him that "the real difference between your program and most television for children is that it is less a show for children and more of real communication with them." This is the reason, she says, that when the children meet Mister Rogers in person at various events "they run up to you and throw their arms around your legs and call you 'my Mister Rogers' and anticipate that you will recognize them as they recognize you."[23] McFarland's observation reveals not only that Rogers feels familiar to these viewers such that they feel comfortable physically embracing him but also how "real" and established his relationship with them must be prior to experiencing a person-to-person meeting.

Writing in May of 1981, Greg Williams begins his six-page letter to Rogers with a caveat: "Dear Mister Rogers, I don't usually write fan letters but I feel like I owe you one."[24] He then informs Rogers that he is an English education major at the University of Illinois and about to enter the teaching field. "Through the years," he writes, "I have managed to stay a devoted viewer." Greg is now twenty-one years old and presumes that he currently views *Neighborhood* in order to learn from Rogers's teaching methods as well as "the relationships [Rogers] developed with each television friend." Notably, Greg uses Rogers's language, "television friend," as opposed to the more generic "viewer," demonstrating the longevity and dedication of his "relationship" with the program and with Mister Rogers.

Greg informs Rogers that he wants to teach at the secondary level and asks him if the methods for working with younger children are similar. "I can only hope for as much sincerity and patience and love as you have for children," he writes. "And besides learning from you, I still enjoy your program. There is nothing better for uptight nerves due to a hectic pace or difficult class than spending a half hour in your neighborhood." Here, in Greg's reflection on watching the program as a college student, he engages in an analytical examination of his motives for adult viewing. For one, he notes, it offers him a space of relief from the fast pace of young adult student life and its challenges. Then, branching out of his self-examination, he turns toward the leisure practices and coping strategies of his peers. "Feeling good, being happy," he writes in reference to the program's values, "is so much better than all these kids who only find peace in drugs or alcohol. . . . It is really sad. I am constantly around that problem here on campus and I can only wish that they will somehow discover the beauty of nature or in another human being. That is where true happiness lies." In writing his letter to Rogers, Greg discovers the benefits of his viewing of *Neighborhood* and intuits that the program has a therapeutic value that can be extended to groups of people. Although he does not label it as such, Greg finds the viewing process calming and nurturing—a healthy release from the stresses of his college workload and culture. *Neighborhood*, he writes, inspires "good feelings" and a "happiness of being" within him. As Greg realizes the rewards of watching a thirty-minute episode of *Neighborhood*, he shifts his gaze from self to peer, expressing sadness and concern that others engage with drugs and alcohol in a similar yet misguided attempt to find relief.[25] Greg moves from evaluating his own visit to the neighborhood to concern regarding his "neighbors" in the University of Illinois college community. His relatively quick move from self to other underscores a cognitive shift motivated by the ethical imperative to think about his experience in relation to others.

Greg begins a new paragraph to note that, as the son of a United Methodist minister, he was "raised in a good religious environment." He reveals that he recently renewed his faith and "strengthened [his] commitment to God" while admitting that he had become distracted by schoolwork and personal matters. "I guess it is a hazard of being in a university environment," he writes. "Again, your simplicity and freshness pulled me through a few of those rough times." Here, Greg's letter moves deeper into personal spaces of struggle and vulnerability. He refers to the culture of college life as "hazardous," though in this section it is not the perils of drug and alcohol use that pose a threat but rather work and personal endeavors that have taken up too much of his attention. Interestingly, he credits Rogers with providing moments of "simplicity" and "freshness" that helped him carry on the struggle. This alludes to Rogers's understanding of the need to provide a space free of the bombardment of life's demands in order to allow people to return to a "simple" spiritual center that nourishes. The constant dispersal characteristic of modern life brings about a sense of confusion, which Greg finds safe haven from in Rogers's program. In *Neighborhood*, there is a sense of harmony and simplicity that provides relief from Greg's pressures and also from the destructive behavior of his peers.

Moving from the broader picture into more specific personal detail, Greg continues, "I'd like to especially thank you for your week devoted to divorce." He reveals that his parents divorced two years prior and that the programs "helped [him] to reflect on that difficult time." As the oldest of three siblings, Greg noticed that his sisters were feeling "the same things the little girl and Prince Tuesday were feeling—guilt, frustration, confusion." He writes that as a result of the experience of watching the weeklong *Neighborhood* arc on divorce, the relationships between him, his mother, and sisters have "grown stronger." Further, after a period of feeling very angry with his father, the two have "renewed" their relationship. "It will probably never be quite the same but we are communicating at least," he writes. With poised maturity, Greg holds both the grief he feels over the loss of his former relationship with his father and a hopeful emotion tied to developing a new communication space between father and son.

This segment of the letter shows Greg sharing with Rogers (and himself) the emotional processing that he has done, crediting *Neighborhood* with helping him and his family work through the deep social ruptures of divorce and the painful emotional consequences of this familial breakdown. His prose is a testimony to the success of the program in helping viewers to identify, explore, and manage their feelings as a result of dialogue and theatrical narrative. Greg credits a conversation on divorce between NMB puppets with helping him and his sisters put a name on the emotions they were struggling with. As readers, we can assume that when Greg notes that the programs strengthened his bonds with his mother and sisters, these family members watched the programs together and discussed them afterward. Television programming thus extends and circulates ideas into the family communication environment; the dialogical aspects of *Neighborhood* prompted and assisted the family in "reflecting" (to use Greg's word) on the complex and difficult relational and emotional realities that arise from divorce.

In his 1984 article "On the Dialogic Aspects of Mass Communication," Horace M. Newcomb employs Bakhtin's linguistic communication theory and the struggle for meaning in mediated texts. He offers a reading of "Discourse in the Novel" that can be used to study the dialogical aspects of other forms of communication, specifically electronic, mass communication. Newcomb notes that Bakhtin's argument for the dialogic aspects of the novel is rooted in a recognition and examination of the myriad languages embedded in any given social language. The term Bakhtin uses to encapsulate this phenomenon is *heteroglossia*. "Within this communication polyglot we know as society," Newcomb writes, "every utterance that goes out from speaker to listener, from writer to reader, from creators to audience, is bound into a system of multiple meanings."[26] Within expressive artistic forms such as a novel or a television program there exists an added layer of complexity because such utterances are attached to the realities of the character, or the narrator who speaks. "Every such representation is an 'image of a language,' and thus the image of an entire way of life, an ideological system required to interact with other systems in social dialogue." As such, all of these voices are "woven into the dialogue that forms the work as a process."

Newcomb notes that the purpose of the analyst or critic is thus not merely to unravel the text but to recognize that all forms of communication are inherently dialogical in nature.[27] Though the author of the text may aim to establish a "hegemony of intention," that attempt will never result in total success because in addition to the interaction of languages and words to form a new totality there remains the process of reception. Each viewer brings with him a similar complex structure of meaning making to his reception of the program: "Each listener, each reader, each viewer brings a similar sort of complexity to the reception of communication, brings a range of contexts in which the 'word' is received and made part of the receiver's world."[28] Recall the story in chapter 2 of Rogers's janitor friend Jeff, who describes learning about the death of JFK Jr. on television by making connections to his own family. Rogers tells this story to show his keen awareness of the fact that viewers bring their own understandings of the world (heteroglossia) and experiential meaning-making practices to the act of program reception, creating a dialogical process of transactional communication. "Clearly, it is this 'social atmosphere of the word' that is at work in the reception of mass-mediated content," writes Newcomb.[29] Compare Rogers's conception of the act of communication with Bakhtin, who relates the message to a ray of light, a ray-word that enters "an atmosphere filled with alien words, value judgments and accents through which the ray passes on its way toward the object; the social atmosphere of the word, the atmosphere that surrounds the object, makes the facets of the image sparkle."[30]

Greg goes on to tell Rogers about his own artistic interests and pursuits, which include song writing, poetry, short story writing, and community theater. He is curious about Rogers's current production of shows and inquires about taking part in the creation of one. He shares that his favorite film directors are Alfred Hitchcock and Woody Allen and that he enjoys making Super 8 sound movies in the style of his choice directors. He writes that "probably the most rewarding experience I've had was being a day camp counselor at Snow Mountain Ranch, a YMCA family camp in the Colorado Rockies." He credits this experience, working with youth from ages three to eighteen, with inspiring him to work during the coming summer at a camp in Champaign.

"I really didn't plan on telling you this much about myself or asking about a job," Greg concludes. "But I would very much like to have you keep me in mind." He asks Rogers for any advice he has to offer on methods of disciplining, and closes by thanking him for "all the pleasure and guidance you have brought me for the past thirteen years. It *is* nice to know that I am special and you are too."

Greg began his letter by telling Rogers that writing "fan letters" is not an act he usually engages in, but that he feels that he "owes" Rogers one. Despite this language of obligation, Greg also strives to make various gestures of friendship and interpersonal connection throughout the letter. It is likely that Greg's feeling of obligation to reach out to Rogers personally arises from the fact that he feels that Rogers has offered his friendship to him over the course of many years. "I have literally grown up with your program," Greg continues, conveying the significant temporal consistency of his exposure to the show. Indeed, he writes of "running home from school each day to watch you," revealing the everyday presence of Rogers in his young life. This anecdote points to the unique nature of *Neighborhood*'s parasocial functioning considering its everyday showing and thirty-three-year lifespan. The consistency of this "visitation" points toward the inevitable development of a relationship between the viewer and the program's host, especially considering the unfluctuating dialogical and interpersonal style of the primary actor.

If Greg has been engaged in coproductive meaning making with Rogers on a regular basis for a number of years (Greg cites thirteen), then it is no wonder that his first "real" communicative response to Rogers begins with an expressed feeling of obligation (think of Bakhtin's notion of "answerability") to write to him. Moreover, it is no wonder, although it comes as somewhat of a surprise to Greg, that he shares so much of himself with Rogers—"I really didn't plan on telling you this much about myself." Such phenomena reveal that processes of friendship formation appear to be present in Greg's communiqué and speak to Rogers's characterization of each viewer as a "television friend."

Consider the phrase *television friend* in light of the various gestures at play in Greg's letter. Rogers does not refer to his viewers as "friends" alone. Although a gesture toward an affective and personal relationship, friendship, is made here, it is significantly altered and delimited by the qualifier *television*. Indeed, the phrase *television friend* indicates both Rogers's efforts to transcend the mass medium's limitations and simultaneously acknowledge them. Greg, who after years of relating to Rogers through the process of viewing, clearly intends to break down the fourth wall barrier between himself and someone whom he has grown close to and yet has never communicated with outside of his own inner dialogical thinking. Thus, writing to Rogers appears to be an attempt to experience the mutual personal involvement that occurs between real friends. While Greg expresses his appreciation for the care and attention he has felt from Rogers over the years—a care that has "built up on a basis of trust, knowledge, and intimacy" constitutive of friendship—his letter strives to make him known to Rogers in an act of reciprocity. In fact, the more he reaches out to share himself with Rogers through the written word, the deeper he moves into his vulnerable emotional spaces. Greg's willingness—one might even say unabashed eagerness—to share his inner thoughts and feelings with Rogers is illustrative of the "realness" of their imagined friendship. Greg writes to Rogers, therefore, to rectify the one-sided reality of their "relationship," acknowledging its parasocial characteristics and striving to move beyond its virtuality.

The ease with which Greg approaches Rogers not so much as a father figure but as a mentor-like friend, is remarkable and yet not at all uncommon in *Neighborhood* viewer letters. The theme of reconnecting with an old friend pervades correspondence from young adults in particular, as they seek to engage in acts of friendship development that they were unable to enact via real communication as child viewers. The rhetorical dynamics in these letters, as they relate to the phenomena of human friendship, can be more minutely analyzed in light of Mara B. Adelman's six dimensions of human friendship development. Basic to the development in personal is an increase in *"intimacy and emotional attachment."*[31] Greg clearly feels that this sense of intimacy and attachment is already present between him and Rogers. The strong sense of safety, closeness, and secure attachment he feels toward Rogers is what allows him to open up and share his own personal vulnerabilities with him. As we have discussed, Rogers intended from the inception of his program to reach viewers at the personal, relational level.

Greg's memory of running home from school to experience Rogers's "television visit" indicates a longing to visit with Rogers on a regular basis. This illustrates the developing interdependence of the relationship, identified by Adelman, Malcolm R. Parks, and Terrance L. Albrecht as the third dimension of friendship, and its meaningful impact on Greg. In regard to the second dimension, *"the breadth or variety of interaction increases,"* Adelman and her coauthors note that as a friendship develops, the individuals "come together to interact about a variety of concerns as well as intimate concerns." Greg's recollection of the ways that *Neighborhood*'s discussions on divorce helped him process that of his parents speaks to both the second and third dimensions of friendship, as does his interest in sharing his teaching and artistic aspirations with Rogers. Indeed, both intimate and nonintimate concerns are discussed. Adelman, Parks, and Albrecht also highlight that as participants become closer, the situational context of the bond becomes less significant. In letter writing, viewers indeed engage in an act that removes the regular relational context, that of watching Mister Rogers on television, from the dialogue. If "close relationships can serve as sources of social support in a greater range of settings than can 'weaker,' less developed relationships," it would seem that the act of writing to Rogers carries with it a feeling, on behalf of the viewer, of relational closeness.[32]

While we can deduce from Greg's description of running home from school to "visit" with Rogers that he may have experienced the unfolding of this dimension of friendship in his *Neighborhood* experience, we also know that the feeling is not reciprocated by Fred Rogers, at least not on any sort of individual or personal level. As I have noted, it is likely that Rogers learned and honed his interpersonal communication skills with young children during his time working at Arsenal. Still, unlike the viewer, Rogers cannot form a similar parasocial friendship with his viewers because he does not have any secondary (or primary, for that matter) oral experiences of them. As such, the interdependence formed by viewers with Rogers is, in large part, one-sided. The correspondence thus seeks to create a greater and a more appropriate balance in the "relationship."

Adelman's fifth dimension of relationship development is "increasing communication code specialization." This description invites a variety of questions regarding whether and how this phenomenon might occur on *Neighborhood*, or on any other television program, for that matter. Indeed, *Mister Rogers' Neighborhood* is characterized by a discursive cultural system Rogers creates. The viewer enters this world and, over time, engages in a process of decoding and learning the social and symbol systems of this world. He is, in fact, invited to participate in it as a kind of pseudo-member of the neighborhood. The letters indicate viewers' desire to respond to the communication culture that they already feel a part of due to watching the show. So even though Rogers and his team are the sole creators of the communication code specialization, the regular viewer becomes a participant in this process and thus feels a sense of mutuality with the program host. For example, Greg closes his letter, "It *is* nice to know that I am special and you are too." Here, Greg demonstrates the communication code specialization that is constitutive of the bond he feels he has with Rogers. His use of this line, which Rogers repeats at the opening and closing of every episode, functions like a wink. It points to the special, dialogical communication code that the two of them share—the memory of the everyday greeting and goodbye that Rogers offers to Greg each time they "meet."

Because of the repeated exposure of consistent characters, environments in which they reside, and plot problematics on television, the increased predictability offered by television shows has been identified as a primary reason why parasocial relationships tend to develop. Indeed, in 1975, Noble argued that this increased predictability explains viewer involvement in television programs. Noble, who strives to understand what fundamental needs television helps moderns meet, contends that "regularly appearing characters comprise something of a screen community."[33] In television viewing, Noble argues, the viewer is able to "connect" and "interact" with others in ways that feel similar to social life in the premodern village community, where the individual interacted on "a single stage with the extended kin group."[34] That is to say, the episodic viewing of a television program, as observed by Horton and Wohl, results in viewers sensing the program characters as members of their peer or community group. The television characters' personalities and behaviors become predictable, and thus provide viewers with a sense of comfort that comes with the kind of "decreased cognitive uncertainty" that Adelman, Parks, and Albrecht posit as the sixth dimension of friendship development. "Uncertainty reduction involves creating the sense that one knows how to act toward the other, knows how the other is likely to act toward the self, and understands why the other acts the way he or she does," they write.[35]

In modern societies, these kinds of predictable social relationships are fewer and farther between due to the fragmentation of life. In village life, the extended family provides a continuous space for interaction among people who know each other. As a result of the same faces appearing frequently "in" the home space, "the viewer feels he knows these people well enough, for example, to say 'hello' to them in the street."[36] Certainly Greg's letter illustrates a sense of familiarity with Rogers and the characters on *Neighborhood* that involves a sense of cognitive certainty regarding who he is dealing with in correspondence.

Finally, Adelman and her coauthors cite "increasing network contact and overlap" as a fundamental component in relationship development. At first glance this characteristic may seem the least applicable to the parasocial relationship that emerges between Rogers and the viewer. "Our personal relationships," write Adelman, Parks, and Albrecht, "are also social objects existing within the broader context created by our surrounding social networks."[37] The authors cite the perception on the part of the relationship participants that their friends and family support their relationship, communicate with members of the others' networks, and are generally pleased with the other's friends and family. How can such a process occur in a televisually based parasocial relationship, one might ask? Yet Rogers identified these complex social workings in relationship to television in his coauthored piece, written with Linda J. Philbrick, for the *Pittsburgh Area Preschool Association Publication*. In it, he notes the apparent parental sanction that the child is likely to read into television programming simply due to the fact that it is the parents who have purchased the device and placed it in the living room of the home. He writes about the nonverbal messages that adults send to children during television and movie viewing in which they often do not wince while viewing unethical behavior taking place on the screen. Such apparent unconcern may confuse children, he writes.

Indeed, Greg makes a point of telling Rogers how his family's viewing of the episodes on divorce helped its members make sense of their experiences of that process. In doing so, Greg illustrates an example of the kind of incorporation that Rogers expected would occur with *Neighborhood* viewers. In his "Philosophy" document Rogers wrote, regarding the show's second premise, "Television and television artists—participants in family relationships": "When Mister Rogers looks into the camera saying, 'You are a very special person. I like *you* just the way you are,' he makes an impression on the child viewer. The child's environment has been extended to include a meaningful relationship with another adult. In this way, Mister Rogers becomes a 'participant' in family relationships; the child first 'accepts' Mister Rogers into the family and then seeks support for the acceptance from the immediate family." Greg's letter demonstrates this characteristic of network contact and overlap not only in the way that he extends his relationship with Rogers to touch the outer network of his immediate family but also with his college peers, when he expresses a longing to share those habits and values that Rogers has taught him to embrace with those in his extended university environment who have turned to drug and alcohol use. Finally, he wishes to consult with Rogers on how to teach young children, seeking once again to connect Rogers to yet another important network of people in his life.

ON BECOMING MORE HUMAN—DIALOGUING WITH A YOUNG WOMAN

On March 4, 1975, seventeen-year-old Julie Cruise of Saint Louis, Missouri, penned a letter to Mister Rogers noting her avid viewership of *Neighborhood*. Although some of her peers find it "weird," she writes, she "immensely" enjoys the program. She confesses that she did not "always feel this way" and notes that even recently, when watching the program at her six-year-old nephew's insistence, she could "barely endure each half hour."[38] Julie found the Neighborhood of Make-Believe segment "particularly annoying" but viewed because she "generally had nothing better to do." Then, in a reflective turn, she writes that while holistically she did not enjoy the show itself, "there was something in the attitude of the performers" and especially Rogers's approach that did appeal to her. "You actually seemed to care about the viewer. There was a type of communication there that I had never experienced before—particularly from the television. I was impressed." Julie found herself tuning into *Neighborhood* after her nephew departed for the summer when she sat down to view another PBS program, *Villa Alegre*, which helped her with her Spanish skills. She tuned in when Rogers was saying his goodbyes to his television audience, singing, "And you'll have things you'll want to talk about. / I will too." Julie writes, "That lyric meant a lot to me because I believed that unless I had something revolutionary or brilliant to talk about, it wasn't worth speaking." She goes on to say, "You seemed to say that it is all right to tell people what I think, brilliant or insignificant." Thus, she gradually found herself tuning in earlier in order to watch the full program in its entirety.

Julie continues, reaching into her interior spaces when writing about Rogers's messaging regarding feelings. She writes how she hears Rogers tell his viewers "again and again" of the importance of expressing their feelings. "Whether it be anger, happiness, fear, or worry," she writes, "they must come out." Julie states that she knows from experience that his message is "true" because she grew up in an environment wherein feelings were viewed as "bad things" and a "sign of weakness." After holding on to this perception for years, she observes that she has become "not a person who doesn't express feelings, but one who doesn't have them. . . . I have become dehumanized to an amazing degree," she writes, noting how beneficial Rogers's program has been to her of late as she has been experiencing good feelings from watching his show. "I have hope and almost believe now that I can change and become a caring person," she writes. She closes by thanking Rogers for caring about people and for sharing himself and his ideas with people like her, who need support. "God bless you," she writes, and ends with a postscript that states, "I can even enjoy the Neighborhood of Make-Believe now."

Julie's reconnection with and reassessment of *Neighborhood* establishes another theme often found in letters from young adults—the need for healing and its discovery through a return to viewing Rogers and *Neighborhood*. Julie first finds *Neighborhood* silly and "annoying" when she revisits it at the age of seventeen with her six-year-old nephew. Later, in the absence of her nephew, she finds herself turning toward the program when she realizes Rogers's deeper messages of care below the surface of the show's everyday activities.[39] Such expressions of care, along with Rogers's encouragement of feeling expression, touches Julie on a deeper level, such that she has a self-realizing moment wherein she recognizes how years of stifling feelings have transformed her into an unfeeling, "dehumanized" person. Seeing herself in a new light, as a result of her interior dialoguing with Rogers, she expresses how Rogers has healed her, and his expressions of care for her have inspired positive emotions. The internalization of Rogers's caring expressions has given Julie hope and empowered her to believe that she can now change from being an unfeeling person to a caring one.

It would appear that Julie, in her letter, has come to some self-realization about the ways she has self-censored in both thought and speech. As Paulo Freire writes on dialogue and freedom: "Dialogue is the encounter between men, mediated by the world, in order to name the world. Hence, dialogue cannot occur between those who want to name the world and those who do not wish this naming—between those who deny others the right to speak their word and those whose right to speak has been denied them. Those who have been denied their primordial right to speak their word must first reclaim this right and prevent the continuation of this dehumanizing aggression."[40] Finding such self-censorship oppressive and stifling, Julie remarkably employs the same term Freire uses to describe the oppression of indigenous communities in Latin America—*dehumanizing.* Julie credits her continual viewing of Rogers's program, and more specifically the care she feels he emotes to her throughout the show, with placing her on the path to a liberating self-realization process regarding the expression of her feelings and thoughts. From the perspective of Freire, Julie's letter, in which she proclaims her transformation and newfound voice, is a self-affirming exclamation of her rediscovered humanity through her perceived relationship with Rogers and *Neighborhood.* It could also be considered her formal dialogical response to a conversation she has been having with Rogers internally since she began rewatching his program. Freire writes, "If it is in speaking their word that people, by naming the world, transform it, dialogue imposes itself as the way by which they achieve significance as human beings. Dialogue is thus an existential necessity."[41] In characterizing her inability to vocalize her feelings as *dehumanizing* and her awakening to feeling and vocal expression as *good,* Julie, a young American, validates and universalizes Freire's argument regarding the "existential necessity" of dialogue.

Consider a 2013 discussion on the Fox News channel's *Fox and Friends* in which on-air commentators decry the implications of Rogers's primary message to children as characterized by the phrase *You are special.* In the segment, Fox News personalities criticize Rogers's message for creating a generation of young

adults who carry with them a problematic "sense of entitlement."
The importance of this phrase to the piece was emphasized visually by its placement on the screen, below an image of Rogers.
Lead on-air personality Steve Doocy begins the segment by noting
that experts are currently arguing that millennials who grew up
watching *Neighborhood* were told by Rogers that they were special just for being themselves (read: for doing nothing). Doocy then
quips that Rogers did not say, "If you want to be special, you're
going to have to work hard."[42]

The *Fox and Friends* critique speaks, on a number of levels,
to the misreading of Rogers's guiding principles and aims. For
one, the hosts, speaking on a network known for its ideologically
conservative perspective, read messages of liberal childrearing
practices characterized by indulgence and pandering into Rogers's
media text. Their rhetorical work has the effect of distancing Rogers's pedagogy from values of hard work and discipline, which are
reinscribed as values exclusive to conservative ideology and colored with an air of traditional American masculinity characterized
by toughness, emotional restraint, and grit. On-air commentator
Elisabeth Hasselbeck flippantly calls Rogers "an evil, evil man" at
the beginning of the segment, supposedly for fostering this "sense
of entitlement" in his viewers. If these ideologically conservative
commentators knew that Rogers's message to children was partly
rooted in a Christian theology based on Christ's love for each and
every human being regardless of sect, class, race, and individual
deeds, perhaps they might have considered celebrating, rather
than condemning him.

Regardless of the value judgments at work in this example, the
more relevant takeaway for our discussion is that scholars and citizens alike must be mindful and thorough when researching and
analyzing empirical texts and agents in order to understand them
in their proper context and in all their complexity. Because Rogers
strove to meet the rhetorical constraints of public broadcasting

by operating within a strict secular discourse, he left room for others to derive their own assumptions and narratives about the framework he was bringing to his television encounter. The *Fox and Friends* example points to the broader problem of the way secularism and pluralism have developed in the United States. From its early manifestations in the first half of the twentieth century, calls for pluralism have almost uniformly resulted in the privatization of religion and religious expression rather than the public, plural articulation of a variety of religions.

In "A Holistic Values Education: Emotionality, Rationality and Meaning," Roger Burggraeve discusses the importance of a "relational and emotionally involved God" in the Christian tradition, noting that Jesus, who always speaks of God in a well-defined way by linking Him to the idea of kingship and lordship, announces not a high and mighty image of God but rather "a God who comes near and who precisely discards His 'tremendous majesty' and binds Himself with 'the poor, the weeping, the hungry, the crushed' (cf. the Beatitudes)."[43] In this conception of the divine, God is not, as he had been conceived of prior to this point, described in terms of an alienating theoretical or metaphysical category, Burggraeve writes. Rather, "God is always Someone, a You, a 'person,' which is understood as merciful and loving. He is touched by what concerns and happens to people. This implies that God is also sensitive and moved, and this in His deepest being. We can also call this the 'sensitivity' of God insofar as He is no abstract-philosophical, or necessary principle of explanation, but a living Someone who in His 'heart,' unto 'the marrow of His bones,' is moved by what people go through in their history." This involvement of God, writes Burggraeve, is understood "*emotionally.*" God "suffers and feels pain in His belly by the suffering of people. He is affected by what happens."[44] He is thus, as Burggraeve writes, dynamic, not static. Such understanding of the Christian God here is critical to Rogers's project in light of the fact that he credits his ability to transform his pain into care for himself and for an other (as pointed out earlier) when he realized, after suffering from peer abuse, that God cared about his suffering. Indeed, this discovery of God's care is the key that enables him to reach viewers on a personal and healing basis, like he does here with viewer Julie Cruise.

Burggraeve's discussion is rooted in an understanding of "emotionality as an experience of belongingness in security and participation, whereby both the confrontation with what is 'reasonable' and ethically responsible, as well as the integration in a sustaining perspective of meaning is embedded and made possible."[45] Burggraeve's definition of "emotionality" excludes many emotional phenomena due to its basis in an ethical appeal. Because it is an experience of belongingness, it inherently excludes violence, bigotry, fear, shame, and other negative or dark primary emotions. Employing Winnicott's terms, Burggraeve proclaims that emotional embedment creates the necessary "potential space" for education by creating a "milieu" of "safety, ambience, security, conviviality, and familiarity" in order to provide young people with a sense of home in themselves and in relation to one another.[46]

Rogers begins his response letter to Julie by creating the kind of safe, affirming, convivial milieu described by Winnicott through words of appreciation, praise, and welcome. "Your beautiful, sensitive letter was a real gift," he writes. "I was deeply moved by your description of how your own discovery of your feelings developed as a part of your relationship with our program."[47] This heightened understanding of the relational role his program plays for viewers is a consistent theme in his early writings on television. In his Yale speech, Rogers notes that because television has become a fixture in every American home, the attitudes expressed on it naturally "become involved in family communications" and as such, viewing it "must be considered as having its roots at the core of human development."[48] He understands the affective power of the television medium to reach people directly and fashions his program in an intentional dialogical relationship with the viewer and within the domestic milieu of the family. By employing Burggraeve's "emotional embedment," he seems to create Winnicott's "necessary potential space" for education. Julie's letter demonstrates the success of Rogers's efforts in her detailing its transformational healing process.

In his reply to Julie, Rogers writes how he imagines that Julie's growing ability to communicate her feelings to others and "feel their response" must give her great pleasure.[49] Sharing in her experience, he then notes that he feels pleasure in hearing that she has grown in this way. Recognizing the depth of her interior process in such growth, he states that the insight she must have had into herself in order to express her transformation "could only have evolved after an intense inner struggle." "Growing isn't easy at any age," he confesses. He tells her how he deeply admires the openness and honesty with which she shared her feelings about herself and *Neighborhood* with him. Careful to credit her with the success of her self-realization and transformation, he writes, "I am very aware that you were already striving to become more open to your feelings, and that the program was only a part of your own desire to reach out to others. But I'm so glad to feel that I was a part of it. You are a special person. I like the way you're growing and I like you, exactly as you are." Here, Rogers not only credits Julie but minimizes his program's exigent role in Julie's transformation. While Julie writes to praise Rogers for the positive personal effects *Neighborhood* has had on her, Rogers humbly credits her with an already present effort to liberate her feelings and their expression while placing his program's agency in the process as a secondary force.

Rogers's minimization of the role of *Neighborhood* here is aligned with Freire's idea that a liberating education must consist in acts of cognition rather than in the transferral of information.

Freire critiques the standard model of Western education in which information is "deposited" into the minds of students by teachers and names this process the "banking model of education." Such an approach to educating is not in fact educational at all, he writes. On the contrary, it is oppressive in its exercising of domination and control by obviating thinking and operating at the level of narrative.[50] Such praxis results in the alienation of both teacher and student. "Authentic liberation—the process of humanization—is not another deposit to be made in men," he writes.[51] In contrast, "liberation is a praxis," he continues, "the action and reflection of men and women upon their world in order to transform it."

For Freire, the ideal method to employ in this liberation praxis is what he calls "dialogical relations."[52] "Through dialogue, the teacher-of-the-students and the students-of-the-teacher cease to exist and a new term emerges: teacher-student with students-teachers. The teacher is no longer merely the-one-who-teaches, but one who is himself taught in dialogue with the students, who in turn while being taught also teach. They become jointly responsible for a process in which all grow." Several aspects of Freire's "dialogical relations" method appear in the correspondence between Rogers and Julie. First, Julie writes that she perceives in Rogers's television presentation an expression of care. His communication of affect, which she perceives as sincere, creates receptivity within Julie and compels her to continue to view the program. Next, she begins to internalize one of Rogers's daily messages: the song lyrics that highlight the dialogical relationship Rogers has or wants to have with his viewer—"And you'll have things you want to talk about. / I will too." Her internalization of Rogers's lyric prompting her to listen makes it a tool for analyzing her own inner dynamics.

Rogers's rhetoric throughout the show, because it is grounded in dialogical practice, calls for the viewers to listen not only to his speech but to the inner responses to his prompts they are experiencing. This repeated invitation gradually begins to cognitively penetrate Julie's understanding of self and environment. She realizes that Rogers's encouraging his viewers to speak and share with him are in stark contrast to the messages she has received and internalized for most of her life. Prompted by this dialogical exchange, combined with Rogers's affectionate affirmation of his care for the viewer, Julie sets out on a journey of self-realization and healing that is directly tied to speech communication, thus fulfilling Freire's aspiration for a liberating education that stresses engagement in productive listening and speech. Then, in reading Julie's long letter, Rogers, too, learns from his viewer. In the dialogical process, Freire writes, teacher and student "become jointly responsible for a process in which all grow." The authority figure of teacher (Rogers) is "on the side of freedom, not against it," as Freire puts it. "Here, no one teaches another, nor is anyone self-taught." Rather, "people teach each other, mediated by the world."[53] While Freire envisions a space of exchange where the teacher and students are materially present, Rogers offers his television program as the ground (world) where a communication exchange takes place.

In addition to the pedagogical dialogic, Rogers embraced an understanding of Jesus as advocate, fusing these two images of Christ. This idea of Jesus as advocate was articulated to Rogers by his seminal professor and mentor at Pittsburgh Theological Seminary, William Orr. In a handwritten draft of his "Invisible to the Eye" speech, Rogers celebrates Orr's theological understandings and pedagogy. He describes a Sunday morning at church, singing "A Mighty Fortress Is Our God" and wondering about the meaning of one particular verse:

> The Prince of Darkness grim
> We tremble not for him
> His rage we can endure
> For lo! His doom is sure
> Our little word shall fell him.

Rogers asked Orr about the meaning of "Our little word shall
fell him." "What is that one little word that will fell the Prince of
Darkness?" he asks. After a few seconds of thought, Orr replies,
"Forgive . . . Father forgive them, for they know not what they do."
He continues, "You know, Fred, there's only one thing that evil
cannot stand and that is forgiveness." In his speech, Rogers notes
that this was "the kind of lesson that you remember forever." This
line and the ones that follow are crossed out of the speech draft.
Yet its content is most pertinent to our discussion here. Rogers
continues by detailing the fundamental differences between the
Prince of Darkness and Jesus according to his conversations with
Orr. "Evil," Orr told Rogers, "is the ACCUSER." "Evil wants you to
feel as negative as possible about who you are so you will look at
your neighbor through your negative eyes and see your neighbor
in a negative way. That's why evil would use any means available
constantly to secure you so you would think of creation as BAD."
In contrast, Orr describes Jesus as "our ADVOCATE." "[Jesus] wants
us to feel as positive as possible about who we are so we will look
at our neighbor through our positive eyes and see our neighbor in
a positive way. That's why Jesus would use any means available
constantly to be our advocate so we would think of creation as
GOOD."[54] It is this role of advocate that Rogers seeks to embrace
and perform. On *Neighborhood*, he encourages his viewers to
love themselves, to embrace their curiosity and wonder, and to
understand that they have the power to manage their feelings in
positive and nonharmful ways. In his response letter to Julie, he
advocates for her self-discovery and praises her healthy transformation. He tells her that he is proud of her and the ways she has
grown. Indeed, Julie describes her experience of Rogers's mutual
affirmation as freeing and liberating. Growing up, she has been
told that speaking, expressing herself, her emotions, was something bad and unwanted by others. She embraced this and found
herself "becoming dehumanized." Rogers's support breaks her of

this negative hold on her sense of self. She feels him advocating on her behalf, encouraging her to speak her thoughts and love herself exactly as she is. The message, which Julie heard over and over, results in a radical transformation toward a positive self-image and speaking confidence.

SHARING EXISTENCE—DIALOGUING WITH A GRIEVING MOTHER

In the autumn of 1974, mother of three Sally Rector wrote to "Mister Rogers" to inform him of the death of her five-year-old son, Tommy. Rector begins her letter stating that she is, at the moment, "listening to your wonderful voice," which reminds her of the joy Rogers brought to her son.[55] Next, she informs him that the boy died at 6:45 a.m. on August 19, just a few days after Tommy received a letter and pictures from Rogers. "He was very happy about your caring—as were we all," she writes. Noting her impression of children's general innocence and acceptance, she tells Rogers that her other two children—twins, Donny and Marty—took the news "very well." She was relieved by their reaction to Tommy's death but writes that "after having seen my son die, I am full of bitterness, that hopefully, will fade with time." She wishes that Rogers could explain to Donny and Marty why she gets so angry about "Tommy being gone," as she feels that she does not understand her own feelings enough to explain them to the boys. Sally wishes to share a thank-you letter Tommy wrote to him but states that she simply cannot part with it and will thus attempt to emulate it in his own "five-year-old penmanship." In her emulation, she writes, "Dear Mr. Rogers thank you for the record I like it very much. I.V. doesnt hurt just a little bit when they put it in. Love Tommy." She adds, "I miss his beauty and wish so many people could have met him." Sally concludes by expressing hope that Rogers will continue to "generate all that love and care" she saw in Tommy and in others.

Sally's letter, together with her posthumous emulation of her son's letter, constitutes the point of loving encounter that Freire finds indispensable in the true dialogic relationship. The dialogic encounter, for Freire, is not a place wherein two people speak to one another but rather a place where two people share a moment of affective movement. Freire contends that "dialogue cannot exist . . . in the absence of a profound love for the world and for people. . . . Love is at the same time the foundation of dialogue and dialogue itself. It is thus necessarily the task of responsible Subjects and cannot exist in a relation of domination. . . . Because love is an act of courage, not of fear, love is a commitment to others. . . . And this commitment, because it is loving, is dialogical."[56] Further, he writes that dialogue cannot exist without humility, a disposition he deems the opposite of both arrogance and self-sufficiency. "Someone who cannot acknowledge himself to be as mortal as everyone else still has a long way to go before he can reach the point of encounter."[57]

Sally's letter reveals the dialogical nature of her relationship to Rogers in the rhetorical spirit of love, humility, and faith with which she writes. She presents herself, in all her humility, grief, and confusion, to Rogers in her most vulnerable state. The act requires not only courage but a deep faith that Rogers will respond to her gesture with love and understanding. Along with love and humility, Freire identifies faith in humanity as the third and final component of dialogue. Such faith can be found in Rector's letter, which displays her struggling with the forces of anger, grief, and despair that she is experiencing and that cloud her love for her two other children. For example, after she hand-copies Tommy's letter and expresses her admiration for his lost beauty, Sally communicates her faith in Rogers to "continue to generate all that love and care" that she saw in Tommy and others. "Faith in people is an *a priori* requirement for dialogue; the 'dialogical man' believes in others even before he meets them face to face," writes Freire.[58]

Sally's letter thus attests to the fact that *Neighborhood* functions as a space for dialogical interaction and not simply as theatrical entertainment. *Neighborhood* occurs in both virtual and real time, for in its movement of the emotions and invitation to interact with Mister Rogers as a "real" person, the distance between the viewer and Rogers's "character" is breached in ways unique to the television programing of his time.

In his response, Rogers opens by telling Sally how he wishes that she "could have been here" when he and his colleagues "shared [her] grief in losing Tommy."[59] Notice what Rogers does here in the opening of his letter. He describes a group of real people, himself included, who gathered together to share the news of Tommy's death. The rhetoric of the letter's opening creates an immediate communication circle that includes, in addition to both him and Sally, a group of friendly others—an empathic community that shares in Sally's grief. With this statement, Rogers creates a larger "we" between himself and Sally while still maintaining the intimate dialogical nature of their personal communiqué. The image that comes to my mind when reading this sentence is that of Rogers, standing among his staff, reading Sally's letter, while his colleagues express sadness and empathy for Sally and her family's loss. The scene evokes a eulogy and funeral, wherein people connected in love or friendship to a recently deceased person gather together to say goodbyes and honor that person's life. This social ritual is constituted by both the gathering of bodies and a public speech. In the shared process of listening to a recollection of the deceased and the lives he left behind, a reality of solidarity is created. In effect, Rogers provides for Sally a kind of funeral for Tommy attended by the creators of his favorite television program. Such an event also yields a sense of "suffering with" central to Christian theology and to the role of the minister. Just as Jesus Christ places himself within the suffering of those who seek his healing ministry, the priest or minister takes on this role as a servant of Christ. In *The Wounded Healer*, Henri Nouwen contends that the minister must be willing to go beyond his strictly professional role and become open as a fellow human being with similar wounds and suffering. The minister must first recognize the sufferings of his own time and then make that recognition the starting point of his service.[60]

As in other cases, Rogers affirms not just the positive feelings of his interlocutor but also "negative" feelings such as anger and grief. "Of course you have bitter and angry feelings about your loss," he writes. "How strange it would be if you didn't." Rogers attempts to reframe Sally's feelings when he tells her that "otherwise, you would have never done us the honor of sharing yourself with us. . . . [S]o much of Tommy's beauty must have come from you." Here, he reminds Sally of the fullness of her own humanity. He does not negate or lay negative judgment on the difficult feelings she is experiencing but rather acknowledges them as valid and then moves on to focus on her appreciation of Tommy's beauty. Then, assigning value to the observation Tommy made in his letter—"Tommy's note about the IV is very helpful to me"—Rogers informs Sally that he will use Tommy's statement in a series of shoots for hospitalized children currently in production. "I am constantly learning from children," he writes.

This last line demonstrates the importance of the dialogical relations method of education, in which both teacher and student learn from each other. Freire writes that "education must begin with the solution of the teacher-student contradiction, by reconciling the poles of the contradiction so that both are simultaneously teachers and students."[61] Rogers's humility (another of Freire's fundamental requirements for dialogue) resounds as he reverses the normative and assumed knowledge transfer *from* teacher *to* student and places the capacity to illuminate the world with the student/child. This move further serves to place both Sally and her son Tommy on equal footing with Rogers in their shared humanity. Each has authentic knowledge and experience to share with the other and that dialogical exchange results in true learning for all participants.

Finally, Rogers shifts his attention to Sally's remaining children, Donny and Marty. He tells Sally how fortunate they are to have her as a mother. He also, albeit without going into much detail, informs her that her impression of their reception of Tommy's death may not be as painless as she perceives. "Their fantasies about Tommy's death could be very frightening," he writes, sharing with her his knowledge of child psychology in a straightforward manner. He concludes by telling Sally that his thoughts and prayers, and those of his production team, are with her. "Again, my thanks for allowing us to be part of your wonderful family. Most sincerely, Fred Rogers." The final sentences conclude in the same familial way that he opened the letter, emphasizing his (and his staff's) kinship with Sally and her family. However, it is not simply a relationship that Rogers creates with this statement. It is an imaginary formation of a familial group, created through the written word. Again expressing humility, he thanks her for "allowing" him (and his staff) to be a "part" of her *family*. Here, Rogers again inverts the assumed relations between himself and Sally by expressing his gratitude to her for accepting *him* into her intimate, familial world. In doing so, he disembowels the consumer paradigm of other television programs in which the viewer is understood as an anonymous consumer of both programming and the products advertised on it.

PARENTS RESPOND TO AND CRITIQUE *NEIGHBORHOOD*

The letters we have examined thus far are demonstrative of the dynamic, deeply intimate, parasocial relationships that viewers developed with Rogers. However, not all letters to Rogers carry with them that aura of penetrating connectedness and emotional attachment. Letters exist in the archive written by parents and other elders that seek to dialogue with Rogers within a discourse of observation and critique. These letters offer us a perspective on the ways in which parents observed their children communicating with Rogers. Like Rector, their concerns are focused on the ways that Rogers's program has affected their child and family life. Although they do not seek to connect with Rogers on a deeper, emotional level, their letters illustrate the broader interpersonal dialogical system at work between Rogers and viewers—one in which an I-Thou orientation is embraced and employed (in contrast with the "I-It" attitude where the partner is treated more like an object than an individual).

Unlike the previous letter writers who communicate through handwritten penmanship, Alan Headbloom of Ann Arbor, Michigan, writes to Rogers on a typewriter. He admits that he has only been aware of Rogers for the past six months, but proclaims that it has been a pleasure to have *Neighborhood* "in [his] house."[62] Headbloom notes that he and his wife have steered their children away from television at large either because of the "poor quality of the programs" or because of the "insipid or harmful values taught by much of the children's programming." He and his wife recently "pulled the plug" on *Sesame Street* after determining that the show had "little value for [their] child." Then Headbloom moves to commend Rogers for his program. "Let me mention why you are such a regular part of our week," he writes. First, Headbloom notes Rogers's "easy manner of delivery," complimenting him on the ways he speaks to the viewer "*cheerfully but deliberately.*" Headbloom expresses gratitude for *Neighborhood*'s absence of a "whiz-bang pace, full of added graphics or sound effects." He says that this allows children to clearly follow what Rogers says and notes his appreciation for Rogers's effective communication strategy of introducing new topics and ideas in a simple manner and then reinforcing them over an entire program or week. Headbloom notes that this provides the child viewer with "plenty of time to digest and assimilate." He likes how Rogers "speaks *to* the children just as in real conversation," underlining the word "to," emphasizing the interpersonal nature of Rogers's communication method. "Unlike other programs, our daughter [Katy] responds to you singing along, nodding her head, or answering your questions," Headbloom continues. "You involve her," he concludes.

Headbloom's analysis of the reasons why he appreciates *Neighborhood* recognizes Rogers's dialogic communication style. He emphasizes the way that Rogers clears a space for meaningful communication between himself and the viewer by speaking in a slow, conversational manner that allows the viewer "plenty of time to digest and assimilate." Headbloom finds the intentional creation of this critical "between" space in stark contrast with the aesthetic content of the usual children's programming, which he describes as fast-paced and noisy. According to Headbloom, there is room in Rogers's delivery for the viewer to follow along in a realistic way due to the lack of distractions in the presentation. In contrast, other programs' "whiz-bang pace," combined with busy graphics and sounds, impedes real communication in the ways that it confuses, divides, and disturbs the senses.

Buber argued that dialogic communication could only emerge from a situation in which persons treated each other as "Thou." If this stance toward the other in conversation is not established by either party, he suggested, the exchange would result in monologic communication, an I-It dynamic. In the I-It situation, persons view the other as object rather than as an individual. According to Richard Johannesen, monologic communication is characterized by a tendency to "command, coerce, manipulate, conquer, dazzle, deceive, or exploit."[63] Headbloom notes the presence of these characteristics of monologic communication in describing commercial children's television programs. Unlike dialogic communication, which "upholds and respects the freedom of [communication partners] in the transaction," monologue seeks to control the other. When Headbloom notes how his daughter responds to Rogers by singing along to his songs, nodding her head, or answering the questions he poses to her throughout the program, he further illustrates the dialogical process at work. Katy must sense the ways Rogers values her, not as an object to be used but as a unique person worthy of acknowledgment and respect.

Headbloom next praises Rogers for the discursive content of his programs, writing that *Neighborhood* "topics are relevant to developing youngsters" and that Rogers talks about concerns and problems that are "very real to them." Headbloom notes that he and his wife "identified" with Rogers's program on witches, in which Rogers invites onto the program Margaret Hamilton, the actor who played the Wicked Witch in *The Wizard of Oz*. During the program, Rogers talks with Hamilton, who appears in everyday clothing, on playing her role.[64] While some themes carry through the entire program, Headbloom writes, "others are presented as underlying values," like courtesy, helpfulness, self-pride, and belonging. "I feel that these concepts are so important to our children," he concludes. Throughout his letter, Headbloom maintains a discourse that contrasts the lessons and messages in Rogers's program, which he appreciates, with those of commercial television, which he clearly disfavors.

In the final paragraph, Headbloom tells Rogers that, "most importantly," he and his wife like Rogers because they feel that he is a "very sincere person." He lauds Rogers for speaking openly about feelings and for speaking in the "kind and understanding manner of a friend." This observation about Rogers's ability to speak openly about his feelings points toward the intrapersonal dialogical dynamic that is part of Rogers's own interpersonal style. In an effort to highlight the self-dimensions of dialogue that are brought to a relationship by the individuals involved, T.

D. Thomlison discusses the central characteristics of intrapersonal communication. One of these primary characteristics is
self-awareness, a quality that involves a conscious recognition of
one's feelings and an ability to "live them" in the present.[65] Feelings are "a real part of our experiencing and sensing the world."[66]
As such, they provide us with important information about how
we are internally reacting to our surroundings. Recall how Rogers
decided not to follow his elders' advice to ignore the feelings he felt
after being bullied because doing so suppressed the authenticity
of his experience. Instead, he felt the emotions and expressed
them through the creative and dialogical (both intrapersonal and
interpersonal) act of piano playing. Rogers gave the feelings voice.
This act of self-expression, Thomlison writes, follows the act of
becoming self-aware in the intrapersonal dialogical dynamic.
"Our self-disclosure is characterized by clearness, comprehen-
siveness, sensitiveness, and sincerity. There is expression of
what we *are* at that moment," he writes.[67] This openness to one's
internal state, which Rogers practices daily on his program,
includes a congruence between one's feelings and expressions
that is authentic and comforting to the other, as it has been to
Headbloom.

Weeks before writing the letter, Headbloom notes, Katy asked
him and his wife if they could invite Rogers over for supper, indicating, according to Headbloom, how close she feels to Rogers.
"I sense you really love your t.v. children and have a great deal
of concern for their healthy personal and social development."
Headbloom notes that Rogers has served as a positive example to
him, providing him with "good insights into parenting and relating
to children." He proclaims that in some households it may be the
case that Rogers is the sole positive adult role model that children
view, a thought that he finds both gratifying and terrifying at the
same time. "I am sure you are aware of the job you are doing," he
concludes.

To close, Headbloom offers his explicit thanks to Rogers. Interestingly, he reveals how he feels that Rogers "visits his home" via the television program. "Thank you for coming into our house and working the magic you do. You are truly a fine person. May you have many more years to touch children in your special way." While the bulk of Headbloom's letter details his empirical observations, they are infused with feelings of sincere appreciation for the good things Rogers has bestowed on his child and family at large. Headbloom's letter, like the others we have examined thus far, illustrates the strong mirroring effect that occurs between viewer letter writers and Rogers. These writers often praise Rogers for the very characteristics that they display toward him in their own discursive expressions. This mirroring effect illustrates the mutuality at play in Rogers's communication with viewers. Thomlison writes that the twentieth-century scholars credited for first addressing in depth the human need for effective interpersonal relationships in modern life and its relationship to human communication (Buber, Ashley Montagu, Carl Rogers, Erich Fromm, and Jean-Paul Sartre) all make references to "an open, sincere form of interpersonal communication called dialogue."[68] Thomlison characterizes dialogue as a one-to-one interaction in which participants do not feel any need to employ a facade or a need to conceal oneself. This kind of communication is opposed to coercion and exploitation and other dishonest forms of human interaction that are employed to manipulate persons. In contrast, "dialogue includes trust, openness, spontaneity, caring, sensitivity, sincerity, and empathy," Thomlison writes. Headbloom senses that this ethic of honesty and care undergirds *Neighborhood* and, as a result of feeling this ethos at work in his own reception of the show, he answers Rogers's call for dialogue through letter writing. In an act of reciprocity that mirrors the sincerity and mutuality that he recognizes in Rogers, Headbloom writes his letter of appreciation.

In early December of 1981, Kathy Glaser typed a letter of thanks to Fred Rogers in the spirit of the "holiday season." She writes on behalf of herself and her four-year-old daughter, Amira, because they hold Rogers in "special" regard. "We want to thank you for the gift of your television program—and the wonderful messages you communicate," she continues. Glaser commends Rogers on the "quality" programming he provides for Amira and especially for the ways that he pays special attention to process. "Your focus on processes of learning, thinking, feeling, and imagining have been a very constructive and important part of Amira's development. Particularly in a world that is preoccupied with instantaneous products and superficial fragments of experience, your focus on process has helped me teach Amira about the importance of life long relationships with both people and ideas." Glaser's keen observations about the ways Rogers values process on *Neighborhood* points to the underlying philosophy that informed dialogical communication ethics, especially in regard to its emphasis on lived experience. Thomlison points to the existentialist philosophy of the nineteenth and twentieth centuries, more specifically "religious existentialism," as foundational in creating the categories of thought upon which the modern understanding of dialogue is built.[69]

We are always evolving, becoming, or emerging, the existentialists contended. This position diverged from the traditional narratives that sought to explain human behavior and existence from the perspective of fundamental ideas that were thought to have emerged from *reasoning*, and not from "lived experience." The traditional Enlightenment metanarrative of human existence, which explained our behaviors and existence as following standard patterns and guidelines, was, therefore, rejected by the existentialists, who embraced experiencing as a means of understanding and as a way of evolving our own meanings and views. This experiential perspective broke free of the dominant paradigm of scientific measurement and mechanization that became dominant in the mid- to late nineteenth century.

As Glaser keenly observed, Rogers places value in learning through the process of living and experiencing the self and the world (which includes both the material world and others). Interestingly, she contrasts this "way of knowing" not with the rhetoric of scientific measurement and rote learning as did the early existentialists but rather with the emerging characteristics and values of her own postmodern moment, characterized by increasing fragmentation, instant gratification, superficiality, and conspicuous consumption. Rogers's focus on process, she implies, is at odds with a culture that is "preoccupied with instantaneous products and superficial fragments of experience." In contrast with these emerging characteristic of late capitalism, Rogers, Glaser observes, attends to a more humanistic ethos of meaning making by way of an emphasis on *process* and becoming. Rogers's attention to the process of learning through experience, whether it be about the self (one's feelings), a material object (an electric car), an other (neighbor François Clemmons), or an act of creation (how people make crayons), turns away from the lens of commodification and toward the existential subject and his free interactions with the world around him. This focus, she insightfully asserts, teaches her child about the "importance of life long relationships with both people and ideas."

Thomlison credits this "humanistic-existential approach to communication" as altering the way we perceive the communication process itself, as "it becomes a process of experiencing our physical, interpersonal, and self-identity worlds in the present tense, as well as a process of moving toward becoming all that we have the potential of being."[70] How interesting that in her analysis, Glaser draws parallels between Rogers's focus on process and a pedagogy that stresses the importance of relationships with both people and ideas. Glaser tells Rogers that as an educator who "prizes thinking and focusing on a task," she highly values the way that Rogers concentrates on a particular concept throughout one program and develops it in an idea or narrative over the duration of several days. She credits him with helping to "dissuade children from the unhealthy belief that commercial television often fosters in children—that there are quick, easy and simple solutions all of life's problems."[71] In her description of the ways commercial children's television deceives viewers by way of programming that repeatedly displays both quick fixes for problems and instantaneous production, Glaser points to the proclivities of monologue.

Rogers, recall, explicitly critiqued commercial children's television for teaching children that problems can be solved in unrealistic ways and at unrealistic speeds. In "Children's Television: What the Church Can Do about It," he wrote that "a steady diet of the weak always magically winning and the villains always being the big ones, of people getting flattened out one second and then popping into shape the next, of conniving and teasing and hurting and belittling and stopping tears with elaborate gifts (of everything imaginable that those of us who have worked (and played) closely with children feel they should have <u>less</u> of in their experiences rather than more) is a steady diet of this what we would choose to feed our children?" In this description of the interactions that occur between screen personalities, there appears to be a lack of any real acknowledgment of the other as well as a discarding of the space where processing occurs. When a cartoon character is flattened out, he quickly pops back into place without going through any process of recovery that would, notably, require the dedicated help of an other. Characters who are hurt via the act of teasing and belittling are made to feel better not via a dialogical process of reconciliation and apology but through the act of receiving a new, material good. No attention or acknowledgment is paid to processing. Hurtful actions occur, characters quickly recover and move on to the next thing.

In Buber's terms, we could characterize these interactions that Rogers describes as neglecting the essential space of the "between." For Buber, life is made meaningful by existential communication—a process in which two people become more than the sum of two individuals through dialogue. As paraphrased by Stewart and D'Angelo, Buber posits that "the fundamental fact of human existence is person with person. The unique thing about the human world is that something is continually happening between one person and another, something that never happens in the animal or plant world. . . . Humans are made human by that happening. . . . That special event begins by one human turning to another, seeing him or her as this particular other being, and offering to communicate with the other in a mutual way, building from the individual world each person experiences to a world they share together."[72] Meaning is derived through the communication transaction, Thomlison notes, not by the individuals who compose it. Further, this "between" is created only when human beings turn toward one another and offer to communicate "in a mutual way." Only in this mutual sharing of selves can each participant move from the individual paradigm to a paradigm that both share together.

Toward the end of her letter, Glaser tells Rogers of a story that her friend recently relayed to her. The friend works in children's programming at PBS and described a lunch she had in San Francisco with Rogers and other television industry colleagues. At the lunch, she described how children in the restaurant recognized Rogers and approached him at his table. "Grace told us . . . of how you stopped eating and held long, thoughtful conversations with each child," Glaser writes. She writes that when her daughter heard of this story, she suggested inviting Rogers over for a meal at their home. Glaser describes telling her daughter that while it was unlikely that Rogers would be able to visit them, they could certainly let him know that if he were ever in the Washington, DC, area that they would love to "drive up" and to take him to lunch. Here, Glaser responds to her daughter in a way that extends the dialogical ethos between the three of them as opposed to closing the conditions of possibility.

Glaser, whose analysis of the pedagogical and social values presented on *Neighborhood* is keen and sophisticated, demonstrates well the fluidity of conversation and mutuality that has been operating between her and Rogers via her televisual encounters with the program. In Karl Jaspers's view of existential communication, "the single Self communicates *with* the other single Self by communicating to it an incentive *to* selfhood. The evocative power of this appeal from Self to Self creates *in* the world a community of inwardly grounded Selves."[73] This kind of communication facilitates the movement of one self "authentically entering" a relation with an other—an encounter that emerges from individual freedom. It creates, according to Thomlison, "a community of dyads or interpersonal relationships."[74] The quality of authentic communication in Glaser's letter speaks to the ways that Rogers presents himself (to her) on his program. Individuals must be candidly engaged in a mutual attempt to develop common ground in order for "the mutual, reciprocal, dialogic exchange to grow." Glaser, and, of course, the other letter writers, must sense from Rogers a genuine attempt to develop, through existential communication, this common ground between "I and Thou." Jaspers describes this process as follows: "In existential communication I feel responsible not only for myself but also for the other, as if he were I and I were he. I feel the beginning of existential communication only when the other meets me in the same way. . . . If the other does not become himself in his action, neither do I. Neither the submission nor the domination of the other permits me to become myself. Only in mutual recognition do both of us become ourselves."[75] Glaser recognizes in Rogers's communication ethos the feeling that he cares for her and her daughter. Of course, we can point to the obvious rhetorical display of Rogers's existential communication in his opening song, in which he asks the viewer to be his neighbor and the redundancy of his line "You are special," but, as we have discussed, this rhetoric of mutuality and care unfolds continuously throughout each episode in various rhetorical forms.

Glaser concludes her letter by telling Rogers how much she and her daughter value and appreciate the "warmth, caring, and understanding" that he "brings into [their] home." She thanks him for the many gifts he gives them every day and wishes him a holiday season filled with "love, renewed energy, and many delightful surprises."

LETTERS FROM PROFESSIONALS

Other adults write to Rogers from professional perspectives, illustrating the ways they found the program of use for various pedagogical pursuits. Gary P. Gormin, a lawyer in Clearwater, Florida, typed a letter to Family Communication, Inc. in December of 1981. In direct and concise prose, he requests five copies of Rogers's "Talking with Families about Divorce" booklets, which he read about in his local newspaper, the *St. Petersburg Times*, in a November 29 article. Gormin writes that he plans to make the booklets available to his clients.[76] Anne P. Copeland, a professor in the Department of Psychology at Boston University, sent Rogers a brief request for the same pamphlet. She notes that she is an "old Pittsburgher" who grew up watching Josie Carey's *Children's Corner*. Like Gormin, she read an article in her local paper, the *Boston Globe*, in which Rogers discusses divorce.[77]

Mary Beth Hagaman, a child psychiatrist living in Melville, New York, writes to tell Rogers how a program gave her "hope and enthusiasm" about television.[78] As a director of a children's hospital, she has felt "a great need to help families 'parent'" and at her institution she has helped develop classes for parents of "over-active or autistic" or emotionally disturbed children. "There are so many things to communicate to parents as well as to children," she writes, noting that she would enjoy having the opportunity to talk with Rogers about it some time. Hagaman shares with Rogers that she wishes to return to Pittsburgh in the near future and create an "Institute on Life Craft," which she describes as a loosely structured idea for an organization that models an "extended family." "This institute," she writes, could "help people explore and experience the joy of raising children" by focusing on helping "high-risk families" and helping "promote maternal bonding and infant stimulation." "I could go on and on," she writes as she closes the letter by reiterating her interest in children and western Pennsylvania. Again, she repeats the idea that perhaps she and Rogers could meet some time to discuss their mutual interests. "Many thanks for an awakening of the positive powers of t.v.," she concludes.

On a notepad that reads "Union Free School District No. 2, Uniondale, L.I.," Wilma Caldwell, S.N.T., penned a brief memo to Rogers requesting two hundred copies of publications that she intends to use for the instruction of her health classes.[79] In the "To:" field, Wilma has written "Family Communications." In the header between "Union Free School District" and "Health Office Memo" she has written "Northern Parkway School." Her letter, which is a straightforward request for materials, lists the publications she wishes to receive. They are:

1. Having an Operation
2. Wearing a Cast
3. Dentist
4. Beginning School
5. Separation & Divorce

She closes simply with where to address the publications.

On February 27, 1975, Dottie Jeffries, director of the Early Childhood Education Center in Denver, Colorado, wrote to Rogers proclaiming that she watches the program daily with her children. The address places this education center at the Mount Olive Lutheran Church. "We agree so much with your philosophy," she writes.[80] Jeffries asks Rogers for information from Family Communications, Inc. that he feels she could use. She declares that she has a master's degree in child guidance and a "Minor in Religion." She works with the parents of ninety-six children who "are very interested in values, music appreciation, family film discussions, etc."

While these letters are not deeply infused with ethical emotionality, they illustrate Rogers's pedagogical efficacy and the diversity of dialogical communication he inspired. These professionals write to Rogers with an interest in utilizing the educational content that they think is present on *Neighborhood*. Like the other letter writers, these professionals view Rogers as a person with whom they can converse directly through the medium of letters. Each writer finds particular educational value in the televisual content that Rogers produces. A few seek to obtain the tangible printed materials that discuss the subjects of interest to them that Rogers presented on the screen.

RESPECTFUL DISAGREEMENT

Not all the letters that Rogers were received were favorable toward his program. While some viewers wrote to suggest programming topics and approaches, others engaged in strong criticism of the ways in which Rogers discussed various issues. I would like to close the chapter with a discussion of these letters as they illustrate further dynamism and diversity among the viewer mail library. Moreover, they demonstrate how viewers who disagreed with a particular program's discourse felt that engaging with Rogers via letters was both within their power and a proper response.

Writing on February 27, 1981, Frances Cunnane, a mother of three children from Westchester, Pennsylvania, begins her letter to "Mr. Rogers" with a compliment. "Your regular programs are unquestionably the best children's programs on TV," she writes. "You have always treated children with dignity and you have respected the different backgrounds from which they come." However, Cunnane continues, "your series on divorce, I believe, departed from that tradition." Cunnane writes that she does not believe that a children's television program should deal with an issue that is both a social problem and a "moral, religious, spiritual, and deeply personal family problem." In a rhetorical move that places her in solidarity with Rogers, she notes her recognition of the rising divorce rate in American society and then that "some parents may not deal with it the way you or I believe they should." Here, Cunnane tries to align her sense of morality with Rogers. She communicates her solidarity with him by stating that she understands his desire to "educate" those parents who are in need of instruction on how best to deal with divorce. "Nevertheless," she writes,

> parents have the natural and exclusive right to deal with it as they deem fit whether or not you or I disagree with their method. . . . There are some areas of child-rearing where I disagree with the values of my neighbors, for example, but I do not have the right even when my children are in their temporary care to inculcate the children with our own family's religious values. In my religion, "discussing your feelings" with outsiders about personal family failings or problems is a serious breach of charity. In the ethical order, it undermines family loyalty and the parent-child relationship.

Cunnane notes that bringing up issues regarding divorce on *Neighborhood* can have the negative effect of producing unnecessary anxiety for children for whom divorce is not an issue. For example, Cunnane's children never thought of the possibility of going down the drain in the bathtub until Rogers addressed this common anxiety on his program. Only after they viewed Rogers's discussion of this imagined fear on *Neighborhood* did her children begin to become frightened while taking a bath. "There are things which are better treated only if and when they arise on a child-parent basis," she concludes.

Cunnane's detailed and emphatic letter of critique demonstrates how she perceives herself as a stakeholder in *Neighborhood* and in dialogue with the program's host. It is because she understands her position as viewer *not* as a passive receiver but rather as an active participant in a cultural dialogue that she feels comfortable and, indeed, prompted to offer her perspective and impressions to Rogers. "We teach our children that problems between people arise when people grow away from God. Psychiatrists, psychologists, and counselors in general can only treat human problems very superficially. It is my hope that you will leave matters like this to parents in the future and return to your usually excellent material." It is difficult to understand where exactly Cunnane has placed Rogers in this final paragraph of her letter. One might deduce that because Rogers refrains from employing any religious language on his program, Cunnane has placed him in the category of modern, secular professionals who she believes can only "treat" human problems at the superficial level. And indeed, Rogers's discourse on divorce addresses the topic from a secular, psychological perspective and not overtly from a religious one.

Cunnane makes clear that she does not think Rogers's intervention into a family matter as private and personal as divorce should be the topic of discussion on a children's television program. Indeed, she is making an ethical appeal based on the cultural and religious understanding that there are personal matters that should be left entirely to the realm of private, family life. She sees Rogers as overstepping his "appropriate" reach as a television producer by discussing such matters in what she likely considers the public space of broadcasting. Cunnane's complaint demonstrates the collapsing of the public and private realms that television is rapidly bringing about. She clearly feels that Rogers has overstepped his bounds as a television personality by addressing a subject that was traditionally reserved for discussion only within the very private space of the family. Yet, as Rogers observed at the beginning of his venture into the medium, the television's placement in the home space will result (and has) in public communication entering the family culture in a highly personal way. It has also resulted in the creation of programming produced with a sense of the intimacy of the domestic viewing space in mind. Indeed, it is no surprise that Rogers used his forum to address the troubling rise in divorce rates during the period, since his interest as a pastor and child development specialist was to assist families in their struggles through the powerful tool of television communication.

Cunnane notes that Rogers's address on divorce violates her religious mores. In her letter, she begins from the premise that divorce is a "family failing." Thus, to discuss it in public would involve shaming those who have been involved in it. She views the absence of discussions of the subject in the public sphere as a charity to those who have gone through it. The public discussion of divorce, she writes, is "a serious breach of charity" because it ostensibly lays out people's dirty laundry for public voyeurism. Cunnane's letter illustrates the relative novelty of Rogers's philosophy and psychology's teachings on the expression of open talk about feelings and issues that were formerly taboo. Her concerns are representative of the still dominant mores of an old Protestant American culture in which matters relating to the personal and emotional aspects of individuals and families remain in the realm of the private. To her, Rogers's decision to discuss them on television is not only a "breach of charity" to those who have dealt with divorce but also a breach of the normative consensus about what is appropriate for discussion in public and what is reserved for the private sphere. Her letter demonstrates the cultural struggles surrounding the novel approaches to children and family life, such as the open discussion of feelings, that Rogers (informed by McFarland, Benjamin Spock, and Erik Erikson) engaged with on his television program.

Rogers also received complaints from those on the other side of the political spectrum. One such letter was written by Linda Levgnino on June 23, 1975. Levgnino begins her letter with a direct criticism of a *Neighborhood* song. "Dear Mr. Rogers, I want you to know how terribly disappointing it is to listen to the song 'What do you do?'" she writes.[81] Levgnino's complaint regards a line in the song in which Rogers sings, "For a girl to be someday a lady / And a boy can be someday a man." "You confound lady/gentleman and man/woman," she explains. Expressing her own modern perspective on this language, she continues, "I don't think girls want to grow up to be ladies anymore than boys want to grow up to be gentlemen." To further her point, she notes that she wishes for her daughters to become women. "Ladies sit with their legs together; women live," she declares. In addition, she notes her strong dislike for the way the song's tonal inflection favors the boy as primary and places the girl as a kind of secondary afterthought. "My second objection is to the incidental character of the girl's line as compared to the triumphant emphasis of the boy's line." She says this makes her "feel sick" and suggests that Rogers try singing, "For a boy can be some day a gentleman / And a girl can be some day a woman!" instead.

Levgnino closes her brief but poignant letter by telling Rogers, "Otherwise, I love you to pieces." She also shares with him her wish that he produce a show, book, or records for "grownups," noting that "we really need you." Her signature reads, "Love, Linda," and includes a postscript that details how "terrific" it was for her family to see him in person at KCET, southern and central California's community radio station.

While Cunnane calls for Rogers to refrain from addressing "private matters" on his television program, Levgnino advocates for adjustment and correction. Both seek to influence Rogers's production via letter writing and address their concerns from their own cultural and political perspectives. Both appear to be equally outraged by particular choices made by Rogers and both feel a strong affinity for his program in general. Thus, they seek to influence him via a dialogical communication ethic that involves constructive criticism. They both note how much they like him and his program but find value in voicing to him the areas which they find disturbing.

I was able to locate a response to Levgnino's letter from producer Hedda Sharapan, which further emphasizes the dialogical stance that *Neighborhood* assumed at all levels of programming and public relations. Nearly a month after Levgnino wrote to *Neighborhood*, Sharapan typed and sent her a response. In it, she thanks Levgnino for her comments, noting that "as growing people, we need to be open to remarks such as you wrote."[82] Sharapan reveals that Levgnino was not alone in her critique of the gender politics embedded in the song "What Do You Do with the Mad That You Feel." In fact, she writes, after receiving a similar letter the year previous, "Fred Rogers changed that song to end with . . . 'A girl can be someday a woman, and a boy can be someday a man.'" She notes that while they have not been able to dub over past programs that reair from time to time, the song's lyrics have been revised in this regard. Further, she writes, the staff are currently engaged in a "re-evaulation project" in which they are going over past series to create a library of "2-year showings." "One of our concerns," writes Sharapan, "is the sexist remarks that were made on early programs in the late 1960s but are inappropriate today." Here, Sharapan acknowledges the direct link between the current reevaluation and Levgnino's criticism, but also ties the current actions of *Neighborhood* to a self-identified recognition of the need to revise and adjust in accordance with the newer social norms, which they clearly accept. "It was good to know what our group's visit to KCET meant to your family," she concludes. "Your thoughtful comments will always be welcome."

Sharapan communicates authenticity in her response. She provides accurate detail about the ways Levgnino's complaint has been addressed and acknowledges her comments as valuable and legitimate. Indeed, she emphasizes at the beginning of the letter how dialogue between viewers and producers—more specifically letters of observation and critique from viewers—helps producers grow. Here, she strategically identifies herself and *Neighborhood* producers as "growing people," eliminating the professional terminology that places her in a different category from Levgnino and instead unites them in solidarity at the level of human beings. Still, her letter is direct, honest, and straightforward, communicating the essential dialogical qualities of authenticity, inclusion, presence, confirmation, and mutual equality.

DIALOGIC COMMUNICATION ETHICS AND THE GOOD

In identifying difference as the defining characteristic of postmodernity, wherein competing understandings of the truth make up the dominant discursive lens from which we view the world, Arnett, Fritz, and Bell posit that the postmodern moment, rooted in the reality of difference and pluralism, requires "a public map-

ping of a sense of the good."[83] In examining philosophical and
other mission-focused documents written by Rogers during the
foundational years of the program's creation and execution, it is
clear that Rogers, in witnessing the troubling social and political
tumult of the 1960s, identified a crisis of values—a crisis of the
society's sense of the good and how to foster it.

In July 29, 1969, Rogers testified before a session chaired by
Congressman William S. Moorhead titled "Opportunity for Creative Work Needed in Our Country's Educational System." In his
remarks, he spoke of the reasons why, in his view, the youth of
the country were revolting, turning away from virtue and creativity and toward "alleys and cellars and nudity and pot." Rogers
identified the progression in the school system from preschool's
encouragement of creative engagement to an overwhelming
amount of noncreative work in elementary, middle, and high
school. "It is my conviction that the Youth who are in revolt are
being revolted by our failure to know who they really are," he said.
"They are tired of being enrolled, assigned, programmed, graded
and molded from without. They are weary of the passive-verbs of
education and they want to work at their own developmental level
of becoming who they really are."[84] Rogers then paints the picture
of a nursery school child, building highways and skyscrapers with
wooden blocks, who twelve years later learns that everything he
cared about in school wherein he feels that he was creating was
somewhere along the way labeled "extracurricular." "The child's
own growth tasks, his own inner ways of coping with his environment, as well as his feelings, were all labeled as unimportant and
the business of memorizing somebody else's book and doing what
he's told became the only way to PASS."[85]

He then speaks about the value he places on children's creativity in his "television visit[s]." The object of these visits, he states, is
to "remind children that each one of them is unique and that each

one has something special to bring to any relationship." After such value is communicated, he notes that he is only now able to teach social and cognitive lessons, emphasizing the primary importance of his articulation of the child's unique worth. "The child's real triumphs are reflected in his abilities to cope with his own feelings to make the most of his own unique endowment and those are the triumphs that I applaud. It is a person's creativity which allows him to make something of himself. It is this natural human creativity for which I have such deep respect. It is this creativity which must be fostered far beyond the five-year-olds."[86] Here we can see how Rogers's philosophy emerges from an assessment of the crises of his time, a task emphasized as essential for the role of minister by Nouwen, Rogers's contemporary and friend. From this analysis of the systemic, institutional problems affecting the young people of his time, Rogers puts forth his prescription for repair and reform. He always begins his communication transaction with the viewer by reminding the viewer of her unique worth. Only after this has been established can Rogers "teach social and cognitive lessons," inasmuch as having worth requires the recognition of the other.

While one might be tempted to draw parallel connections between Fred Rogers's approach to dialogue and the humanistic, psychological dialogue of Carl Rogers, I would argue that Fred Rogers's approach more accurately falls within Buber's phenomenological dialogue. This distinction is an important one because it speaks once again to the reasons why presuppositions or narrative commitments matter in regards to communication and interpretation. Carl Rogers's understanding of dialogue holds the psyche at the center of its departure. In contrast, the "between" is at the center of Buber's dialogical understanding, which approaches dialogue from a phenomenological view. Indeed, Carl Rogers uses language similar to Fred Rogers in asserting that, through dialogue, one is able to "get in touch" with one's "real self."

But, as Arnett clarifies, Carl Rogers's "emphasis on 'internal locus of control' results in communicative meaning being possessed inside the person." Buber rejects this notion, as does, it would seem, Fred Rogers, who builds learning, growth, and self-discovery around the dialogical imperatives of the social, and, more specifically, the other and the "between." "A dialogic perspective rejects the psychologistic assertion that a human being is a set of owned potentials that construct the abstract notion of a 'real self'; instead individuals must be sensitive to what is called for by the situation."[87] It is thus the space of "the between," as identified by Buber, where the dialogical occurs and unfolds. From this perspective, "the psychological, that which happens within the souls of each, is only the secret accompaniment to the dialogue." That is to say that the meaning of any dialogue is found in neither of the two dialogical partners or each of them combined together but rather in and within their interchange.[88]

While the psychological emphasizes becoming oneself by developing one's own potentials, Rogers's approach operates within Buber and Maurice Friedman's situational framework, in which a person may have to abandon her potential in order to "honestly answer an invited dialogue from another." This is the case with Julie Cruise, who must, if only a little bit at first, abandon her perspective in order to accommodate the rhetorical situation. It is in this process of meeting Mister Rogers and putting aside her prejudices that she finds meaning in "the between" where she slowly experiences self-transformation. "Being means responding without letting the potential help or harm to oneself limit one's answer," writes Arnett. "An individual's response must be called for by the situation and by his or her role, not the potentialism of humanistic communication."[89] When the focus is on that which occurs in the "between," Buber notes, there should sometimes exist a struggle between what one feels and that which one says or does. Indeed, Cruise often experiences this tension, yet she returns to the dialogue because she finds, in the "between," a personal shift towards something good.

Because Carl Rogers views the human as innately good, from his perspective dialogue is encouraged to unleash the psyche in the hopes of drawing out organismic desires and inner reflections. Fred Rogers does not engage in such a practice. Rather, he creates a space for dialogue, critical thinking, and learning to take place within the space of a dialogical "between" that is guided by both ethical conversation and creative play. He does not forget his role as teacher in his relationship with the viewer, to promote both dialogue and creative thought and activity. "Such an understanding of intentionality implies the acceptance of a nonsubject/object world view," writes Arnett, " in which the meaning of a communication happening emerges 'between' persons, not in each person's internal perceptions or through environmental control."[90] This position puts ethics before being as first philosophy, as articulated by Emmanuel Levinas, who posits an ethics of being for the other before oneself.[91] For Levinas, the "I" finds identity in response to the other, as does Cruise. It is thus of particular importance for understanding Fred Rogers as he works from an ethical "I and Thou" premise within a culture of supreme individualism.

Following Levinas's ethical framework, albeit unintentionally, Fred Rogers speaks to a "culture of narcissism" through the countering act of dialogical invitation, which he honed and practiced during his studies in pastoral counseling at Pittsburgh Theological Seminary and in the child development laboratory setting of the Arsenal Family and Children's Center.[92] Rogers actively creates a space of coconstruction, in which both he and his dialogical partner learn from one another in the space "between." Moreover, that which is created in the "between" space on *Neighborhood* continues its communication path of becoming in the acts of letter writing.

Thus, by consistently establishing and reestablishing a dialogical conversation between himself and viewers, and through repetition of similar messages that express value for the unique worth of his viewer, Rogers is able to reach the viewer's inner child, regardless of age, and pull them into the "between" space with him. Careful to maintain a rhetoric of care, respect, safety, and appreciation, he creates this place of sharing and ethical exchange wherein he and his viewer cognitively communicate with each other from the spiritual space of interiority, wherein the deeper, most authentic feelings and primordial ethical sense of I and Thou reside. Because Rogers tends to reach viewers on this deeper dialogical level of communication on *Neighborhood*, many identify in Rogers an interlocutor and treat him as such by writing letters to him.

As noted earlier, Rogers named his production company "Family Communications," emphasizing how he viewed mass communications from the perspective of intergenerational and interpersonal human communication working within the domestic social unit of the family. The recognition of this intentional positionality harkens back to the anecdote with which I began this chapter, a letter written by a mother who describes her son walking around the house singing the *Neighborhood* song, "You've Got to Do It." When her husband returns from work early, she notes, he joins in viewing the program, and they talk about it for days afterward. This story exemplifies Rogers's initial hope for the show as he was charged to minister to children and families through television. Although in our contemporary social, mass communication environment television coviewing is no longer the norm, recent social-scientific studies have shown, as we might expect considering our current discussion, that this practice can have beneficial learning effects on children.[93]

A critical examination of Rogers's correspondence with his viewers shows how Rogers effectively deployed a profound understanding of the dialogic method of communication and education. This analysis shows the efficacy of Rogers's deployment of his vision for the program as it offers tangible proof that he connected with his viewers along these channels of ethical emotionality, healing, dialogic and interpersonal communication practices, and pedagogy.

Conclusion

POPULAR UNDERSTANDINGS OF FRED ROGERS tend to paint his project with a monochrome brush of Christian "kindness" and "progressivism." In this work, I hope to have revealed the nuance and complexity of Rogers's thought, the dialogical integration of his various influences, and the intentionality and care with which he strove to create a program that would speak to the affective, cultural, and educational needs of both young children and people of all ages during a period of social, political, and cultural upheaval and technological change in the United States. Over the course of more than thirty years on the Public Broadcasting Service, Rogers's communication efforts succeeded in reaching generations of Americans at interpersonal and affective levels within a heightened parasocial plain. Rogers and his behind-the-scenes collaborator Margaret McFarland presciently recognized in television the parasocial possibilities for making the critical embodied social-emotional communication connections that human beings need to function and cope with life's struggles.

Breakthroughs in neurological research over the past twenty years are only now beginning to reveal and confirm scientifically the critical socioemotional practices and dialogical ways of relating that Rogers, McFarland, Erik Erikson, John Bowlby, and others were discovering and employing beginning in the mid-twentieth century. For example, the clinical research of Jim Coan has revealed that social proximity, peer bonding, and soothing behaviors facilitate the development of nonanxious temperament and inhibit the release of stress hormones.[1] Rogers experienced the converse of this firsthand as a boy: social subordination, rejection, and isolation are powerful sources of stress that threaten both psychological and physical health.

In this regard, Rogers ritually established in *Neighborhood* the critical orientation of "ethical emotionality" necessary, as posited by Roger Burggraeve, for a holistic and moral education. In beginning every encounter by establishing a place of "emotional safety" for the viewer through embodied and enacted visual and verbal rhetorics of care and connection, Rogers anticipates Stephen Porges's very recent neurophysiological findings on how the feeling of safety is a fundamental requirement for optimizing human potential, bolstering at the neuroscientific level Burggraeve's theory of "ethical emotionality" and Ronald Arnett, Leeanne Bell, and Janie Harden Fritz's argument for "dialogical learning as first principle in communication ethics."[2] According to Porges, "the neurophysiological processes associated with feeling safe are a prerequisite not only for social behavior but also for accessing both the higher brain structures that enable humans to be creative and generative and the lower brain structures involved in regulating health, growth, and restoration."[3] Recall that Rogers's "Encouraging Creativity" speech drew upon the writings of Erikson to expand on this idea and to bolster his own thesis that a major goal of education must be "to help students discover an awareness of their own unique selves in order to increase their feelings of personal worth, responsibility, and freedom."[4] Here, Rogers articulates in language his ritual enactment of "emotional safety," to use Porges's term, ties it directly to the learning process, and connects it to the broader community by noting its implications for national health and societal success.

When I first embarked on this project, I intentionally, though perhaps somewhat naively, conceptualized it in the broadest of ways. I planned to examine and analyze the program from the three primary aspects of the television event—conception, production, and reception. I aimed to investigate the rhetorical and cultural meanings of *Neighborhood* from the intersections of American and religious studies—a broad undertaking, to say the least. And indeed it was. The more I began to research Rogers's writings on television and his life experience, the foundational works in television studies, critical concepts in attachment theory and child development, the programs themselves, and the correspondence from viewers, the more the reasons behind Rogers's success as a televisual communicator, educator, and in many ways, as a kind of minister became clear and remarkably profound. At times I felt as though my efforts to delimit the project's scope and direction were a fool's errand.

Once I opened the door to better grasp one facet of *Neighborhood* (Rogers's prescient comprehension of the parasocial experience, for example), another perspective of understanding would reveal an inherent and significant connection—for example, Ong's understanding of oral and embodied communication and its relationship to what he calls "secondary orality"—the relatively new oral culture created by electronic mass communication technologies. What I found in the inherent consequences of conceptualizing the project in such a broad scope was the reality of Buber's claim that "all real living is meeting" and the complex verity of Bakhtin's discovery that "life is dialogical by its very nature."[5] Indeed, my own anthropological examination into Rogers's rhetorics, through in-depth, dialectical inquiries into the various experiences that shaped Rogers's values and thinking, has produced yet another vast layer of dialogical knowledge about the intersections of television, education, and the imperatives of healthy social-emotional relationships and practices.

I have tried to show how Rogers's communication project came into being, the ways he negotiated his media project within the postwar cultural landscape, the means by which he integrated new forms of knowledge and understanding about human development into his overarching ministerial goals, and the diligent and meticulous ways that he honed and manipulated the televisual medium to connect relationally with a vast number of Americans at the social-emotional level. Rogers successfully translated sophisticated child development theory and knowledge on best behavioral, cultural, and social practices to a mass public by way of mass media representations of oral cultural practices characterized by embodied communication acts. Moreover, in an effort to tackle the communication process of the program from all critical perspectives, I have shown the success of Rogers's dialogical methods of engagement through a detailed and thorough exploration and analysis of viewer mail that speaks not only to the parasocial nature of episodic television itself but, more importantly for this project, to the ways that dialogical enactment undergirded by social-emotional bonding techniques can result in meaningful learning, engagement, and processing. The letters demonstrate how Rogers established deep dialogical levels of communication and emotional connections with viewers, who identify him as an interlocutor and treat him as such in their lettered address; likewise, they show how Rogers's knowledge of attachment and the importance of establishing social-emotional bonds with people in general, but children specifically, translated through the television medium to produce heightened parasocial interaction that was both immediately resonant and long-lasting.

From the production end of *Neighborhood*, McFarland repeatedly said that "attitudes are caught, not taught."[6] From the reception end of the program, a woman viewer embarking on her master's thesis confided in Amy Hollingsworth, "It's uncanny how [Rogers's] simple messages of acceptance and encouragement helped me to write and be productive. I would almost hold my breath while Fred sang his songs, for so often they soothed some tender place in my heart."[7]

First and foremost, Rogers's ethos of ethical emotionality and his keen deployment of it at the parasocial levels of televisual communication, as evinced by the decades-long run of the program and by the overwhelmingly positive viewer response, was remarkably successful in achieving his stated goal of providing "a great service for mental health."[8] Now that new neurological research evidencing the holistic health imperatives of embodied practices of affective social-emotional behaviors has affirmed the understandings of child development that earlier researchers such as Erikson, Bowlby, McFarland, and Rogers honed and deployed, children's television practitioners and other leaders in the televisual arts and sciences can take bold action in incorporating and integrating these enacted practices of creating and sustaining "emotional safety" into all types of programming. Further, dialogical participants in television viewing and other digital media now have at their disposal, thanks to the informational abundance that digital culture affords, a wealth of knowledge about the importance of healthy social-emotional engagement and can make choices about their electronic media consumption accordingly.

This study on *Mister Rogers' Neighborhood* will, I hope, further spread the word about ethical emotionality, the power of the parasocial, and the practical steps people can take toward improving their lives through adopting and fostering of healthy social-emotional behaviors in various social situations. Another hope I have is that these findings shift the conversations about Rogers in mainstream media away from the kind of one-dimensional rhetoric often used to characterize his message, such as "kind," "saintly," and "wise," and toward more substantive pieces that connect Rogers's communication techniques with the new neurological research on attachment, social-emotional bonding, and the critical importance of fostering feelings of emotional safety. In these and many other ways, I have intended to provide a space for continued questioning of the role of television and its unique place in our busied, mobile, virtual, and fragmented lives, especially as it relates to the formation of the young. I trust that this book, sparked by the ethical turn in the humanities, not only breaks new ground on studies of *Neighborhood* but establishes avenues for new inquiries into television studies, communication studies at large, and especially communication ethics.

Notes

INTRODUCTION

1. Fred Rogers, "Invisible to the Eye," speech, Memphis Theological Seminary, Memphis, Tennessee, May 10, 1997, Fred Rogers Archive, Latrobe, PA.

2. Rogers, "Invisible to the Eye."

3. Hollingsworth, *Simple Faith of Mister Rogers*, xxii.

4. Donald Horton and Richard Wohl coined the term "para-social relationship" in 1956. It describes the intimate, "face-to-face relationship" that they argue comes to exist between the mass media spectator and performer(s). This perception is, however, illusory and solely takes place within the mind of the viewer, who feels as if he/she is involved in real interaction with the performer. Horton and Wohl, "Mass Communication and Para-social Interaction," 215–29.

5. Bakhtin, "Discourse in the Novel," 672.

6. Vande Berg, Wenner, and Gronbeck, "Semiotic/Structural Criticism," 69.

7. Condit, "Rhetorical Limits of Polysemy," 103–22.

8. Leah R. Vande Berg, Lawrence A. Wenner, and Bruce E. Gronbeck, "Semiotic/Structural Criticism," in Vande Berg, Wenner, and Gronbeck, eds., *Critical Approaches to Television*, 2nd ed. 69.

9. Vande Berg, Wenner, and Gronbeck, "Semiotic/Structural Criticism," 69.

10. Lyrics used courtesy of the Fred Rogers Company.

11. Burggraeve, "Holistic Values Education," 1.

12. Burggraeve, "Holistic Values Education," 1.

13. Burggraeve, "Holistic Values Education," 17.

14. Hollingsworth, *Simple Faith of Mister Rogers*, 34–35.

15. Buber, *I and Thou*, 11. Buber posits a primary relationship (I-Thou) that is "characterized by openness, reciprocity, and a deep sense of personal involvement." Kenneth Seekin, "Martin Buber," in *Cambridge Dictionary of Philosophy*, 104.

16. Fred Rogers Company, "About Us," accessed July 1, 2013, http://www .fredrogers.org/about/.

17. Rogers's theology emphasizes the message of Christ, the reformer, who brings forth a God that cares for his creation and is accessible and in touch with mankind.

18. Hollingsworth, *Simple Faith of Mister Rogers*, 34.

19. Rogers, "Invisible to the Eye."

20. Arnett, Fritz, and Bell, *Communication Ethics Literacy*, 4.

21. See Packard, *Hidden Persuaders*.

22. One of the earliest (1930s) media theories that sought to understand the effects film and television had on the population was called the "hypodermic-needle model" (or "magic bullet theory"). It suggested that the media "shoot" their messages directly into passive viewers. By the 1950s, television criticism "constructed the audiences as persons of little cultivation or motivation, passively consuming whatever TV presented, and depicted the industry as crass commercializers." Richard Butsch, *The Citizen Audience: Crowds, Publics, and Individuals* (New York: Routledge: 2008), 104–5.

23. See Spigel, *Make Room for TV*, 99–135. See also Meyrowitz, *No Sense of Place*. While it is true that entertainment was a prominent feature in the American home prior to this point in the form of print materials, pianos and other musical instruments, and family singalongs, the type of fully embodied communication that constitutes cinema and television had not been introduced to the domestic environment until this point.

24. Spigel, *Make Room for TV*, 1.

25. While one could argue that radios are also imbued with this symbolic meaning, I would argue, citing Meyrowitz, *No Sense of Place*, that the fully embodied communication nature of television penetrates the viewer's perception at a different level of intimacy.

26. Horton and Wohl, "Mass Communication and Para-social Interaction," 215–29.

27. Horton and Wohl, "Mass Communication and Para-social Interaction," 215.

28. Freire, *Pedagogy of the Oppressed*; Ong, *Orality and Literacy*; Horton and Wohl, "Mass Communication and Para-social Interaction," 215–29.

CHAPTER 1. SITUATING ROGERS'S VISION

1. Rogers and Philbrick, "Television and the Viewing Child," 1. Indeed, concern regarding the media as creating and inciting children's fears and emotional disturbances has been present in American media discourses since the arrival of film in the early twentieth century. The most famous, in regards to the history of the mass media, are the Payne Fund Studies of 1928–1933. Articles and press releases from the fall of 1932 touted the studies' findings that purportedly discovered "deleterious effects of the movies on children" (95). In 1933, Herbert Blumer, author of *Movies and Conduct*, noted that 93 percent of children he spoke with reported being frightened or horrified by a film.

2. Rogers and Philbrick, "Television and the Viewing Child," 1.

3. In his 1984 notes Rogers understands the term *anthropocentric* as an ethical thrust that places the healing of human wounds as central. I will use this term in the same sense that Rogers ascribes to it.

4. Noble, *Children in Front of the Small Screen*, 7.

5. Meyrowitz, *No Sense of Place*, 96.

6. Meyrowitz, *No Sense of Place*, 99.

7. For more discussion of television and family culture/communication, especially as it relates to the communication device's emotional, cognitive, and spatial importance in postmodern everyday life, see Silverstone, *Television and Everyday Life*.

8. Fred Rogers, "Yale," Television Professionals Look at Children's Programs, New Haven, CT, October 16, 1972, box #EU3, Fred Rogers Archive, Latrobe, PA. See also "Simpler Shows for Television Urged by 'Mr. Rogers' at Yale," *Bridgeport Telegram*, October 17, 1972, 13.

9. See Spigel, *Make Room for Television*, 36–72. Note that my approach is cultural and not behavioral, like that of some family communication scholars. Family communication scholars "focus the messages and discourses by which members define, develop, and enact families and on the specific communication processes by which family is performed across different family types and contexts." Of critical importance to scholars of family communication is the "recognition that families are discourse dependent." (Braithwaite, Galvin, Chiles, and Liu, "Family Communication.") Fred Rogers saw himself inserting ideas and prompting discussion about a variety of phenomena within the family sphere of communication and social interaction. Rogers named his production company Family Communications. He was especially interested in having conversations with viewers about the nature of the family, family dynamics, family conflicts, parenting, and other everyday concerns related to the family. He viewed the family as the most important and critical educational and social institution in the child's life.

10. Historically, the invention of modern childhood emerged simultaneously

with the invention of the modern family. As noted by Philippe Ariès, the "event" that created the modern family was the invention and gradual extension of formal schooling. Ariès, *Centuries of Childhood*, 412. Publishing *The Disappearance of Childhood* in 1982, prolific sociology and communication scholar Neil Postman also ties the invention of the modern family with the emergence of writing and print culture, and more specifically with democratized access to education. He writes that "the social requirement that children be formally educated for long periods led to a reorientation of parents' relationships to their children" as "expectations and responsibilities became more serious and enriched as parents evolved into guardians, custodians, protectors, nurturers, punishers, arbiters of taste and rectitude." Postman, *Disappearance of Childhood*, 44.

11. Writing in 2002, some forty-five years after *Mister Rogers' Neighborhood* debuted on public television, child advocate James Steyer described television as "the other parent." Steyer, *Other Parent*, 5.

12. Rogers, "Philosophy," folder "Videodiscs," box EU88, Fred Rogers Archives.

13. Ong, *Orality and Literacy*, 74.

14. Ong, *Orality and Literacy*, 74.

15. Schwartz, *More Work for Mother*, 23.

16. Spigel, *Make Room for TV*, 23.

17. Schwartz, *More Work for Mother*, 45.

18. Schwartz notes that "those who lived in urban areas probably had shifted from the production to the consumption of most goods earlier than those who lived in rural districts, and those who were economically comfortable before those who were economically deprived." *More Work for Mother*, 78.

19. Strasser, *Never Done*, 242–43.

20. See Strasser, *Never Done*, 243. Also notable in regards to the various pedagogies of the new economy is the phenomenon of home economists, who schooled women in shopping planning and techniques.

21. Spigel, *Make Room for Television*, 50.

22. "Built for the Future. Admiral 20" TV. World's Most Powerful TV. Ready for UHF Stations," Duke University Libraries, Digital Collections, http://library.duke.edu/digitalcollections/adaccess_TV0010/.

23. "Greatest Television Achievement in Years. New Form Factor in Magnavox Design Gives You 27-Inch TV Screen in Compact Cabinet Scaled to Grace the Average-Size Room," Duke University Libraries, Digital Collections, http://library.duke.edu/digitalcollections/adaccess_TV0018/.

24. Gould, "Elvis Presley," 131–32.

25. Spigel, *Make Room for Television*, 51.

26. Spigel, *Make Room for Television*, 51.

27. See Jowett, Jarvie, and Fuller, "Aftermath: The Summaries and Reception

of the Payne Fund Studies," in Jowett, Jarvie, and Fuller, *Children and the Movies*, 92–125.

28. Steiner, *People Look at Television*, 81, 90.

29. Interestingly, the image of the "Telebugeye" is infused with a negativity of regression that stands in contrast with Rogers's assessment of the mesmerizing power of television in the metaphor of the suckling baby at the mother's breast. While Rogers recognizes in the power of the medium to mesmerize the potential for an ethical and emotional area of growth and positive development, the depiction of the Telebugeye communicates an image of regression, disarray, and sloth that results from the absorption of the viewer into an alienated and dehumanized subject. Instead of the child becoming emotionally and ethically intelligent, the television has made the Telebugeye stupid-looking; it has even deformed him physically, for it has made his eyes deform to look like those of an insect. It has made the Telebugeye a real prisoner, for it never goes into "the fresh air." It has lost its gender identity. Its physical and mental growth has become retarded. Thus, the Telebugeye embodies all of the fears expressed by those wary of television's alienating and dehumanizing force.

30. See Simon, *Double-Edged Sword*, 19. David E. Nye also sees Miller as the root in his *American Technological Sublime*, xv.

31. See Marx, *Machine in the Garden*.

32. See Ong, *Orality and Literacy*; Horton and Wohl, "Mass Communication and Para-social Interaction."

33. Michael S. Mahoney, "Technology and the Democratic Ideal: The Search for a Middle Landscape," Princeton University, https://www.princeton.edu/~hos/h398/midland.html.

34. Rogers, "Senate Statement on PBS Funding," May 1, 1969, American Rhetoric Online Speech Bank, accessed April 29, 2019, http://www.americanrhetoric.com/speeches/fredrogerssenatetestimonypbs.htm.

35. Hedda Sharapan, telephone interview with the author, June 12, 2015.

36. Latrobe Area Historical Society, "Latrobe Area History, 1800–1899," http://www.greaterlatrobe.net/history/1800.htm.

37. Martinson, *American Dreamscape*, 18, 19.

38. Martinson, *American Dreamscape*, 22, 22–23, 24.

39. Sanders, *Writing from the Center*, 49.

40. Martinson, *American Dreamscape*, 23, 24.

41. Kimmel and Collins, *Wonder of It All*, 6.

42. Joanne Rogers, personal communication with the author.

43. Sharapan, telephone interview with the author, June 12, 2015. It is important to note that this dynamic could also be read as an underhanded union-busting approach. That is to say, one could read Rogers's sense of paternalism strictly as an antiunion strategy. Viewed this way, Rogers's actions seem further removed

from an ethos of benevolence and closer to acts of self-interest and power maintenance.

44. Kimmel and Collins, *Wonder of It All*, 6.

45. Nowicki, interview with the author, March 21, 2013. According to Nowicki, Nancy was very active in community outreach through the Presbyterian church. The family, Nowicki said, "always had a very good relationship with the Catholic monks" at Saint Vincent. Nowicki noted that from the proceeds from their Die Casting Company, which was an economic foundation of the city, the Rogers "would set aside a certain amount for charitable distributions." Initially, these charitable donations were small, but as they brought in more money they were later able to give, according to Nowicki, "One million dollars a year. . . . Quite a lot for a local foundation."

46. To add further meaning to these handmade sweaters, it is notable that Nancy made these articles of clothing not only for her family but also for American troops during World War II.

47. Grandfather McFeely was very dear to Rogers, providing him with unconditional love, emotional support, and a sense of freedom. Rogers recalled his grandfather saying, in contrast with his mother's worry, that it would be "a good thing" for Fred to walk along a stone wall. "I climbed that wall," Rogers recounted, "And then I ran on it. I will never forget that day many years later." Woo, "It's a Sad Day in This Neighborhood." Rogers's ritual assertions on *Neighborhood*, which are now considered a hallmark of his program, that "You are special" and "You made this day a special day just for being you," illustrate McFeely's influence on him during his formative years. Rogers recalls his grandfather saying to him during his childhood, "Freddie, you make my day very special." Kimmel and Collins, *Wonder of It All*, 7. As Elaine Woo notes, Rogers's "signature line—'I like you just the way you are'—was taken nearly verbatim from Grandfather McFeely."

48. Christopher Lasch famously called the home space of the family "a haven in a heartless world" in his book by the same name published in 1977.

49. Marx, *Machine in the Garden*, 4, 4, 5.

50. Danbom, "Romantic Agrarianism in Twentieth-Century America," 2.

51. Rogers's work was informed by the work of the philosopher Jean Piaget. According to Margaret A. Boden, Piaget's study of children's development resulted in his advocacy of "school revision and classroom organization toward greater reliance on the child's spontaneous learning by way of concrete activities and self-regulation." Boden, *Jean Piaget*, 2. "Self-regulation" became one of the central tenets of the child development school of thought that McFarland is associated with.

52. Gitlin, *Sixties*, 13.

53. Lewis-Kraus, "Yelp and the Wisdom of 'The Lonely Crowd."

54. Gitlin, *Sixties*, 19.

55. Rytina, "Youthful Vision, Youthful Promise," 563.

56. See *Kirkus Reviews*, unsigned review of *The Insolent Chariots*, by John Keats, September 17, 1958, https://www.kirkusreviews.com/book-reviews/john-keats-2/the-insolent-chariots/.

57. In his 1972 Yale speech, Rogers writes, "Our communication is designed to keep anxiety within manageable limits and then to deal with it. We attempt to provide models of coping—in simple ways." Rogers, "Yale," 2.

58. See Stuckey and Nobel, "Connection between Art, Healing, and Public Health," 254–63.

59. Leo Marx notes an array of visual representation in film and television during the postwar period. Noting the prevalence of pastoral narratives in postwar advertising and films (e.g., TV westerns, Norman Rockwell magazine covers, the use of rustic settings to sell beer and tobacco), Marx writes that "each does express something of the yearning for a simpler, more harmonious style of life, an existence 'closer to nature,' that is the psychic root of all pastoralism—genuine and spurious. . . . The soft veil of nostalgia that hangs over our urbanized landscape is largely a vestige of the once dominant image of an undefiled, green republic, a quiet land of forests, villages, and farms dedicated to the pursuit of happiness." Marx, *Machine in the Garden*, 6.

60. See Wiebe, *Search for Order*; Rodgers, *Atlantic Crossings*; and McGerr, *Fierce Discontent*.

61. Ehrenrich and English, *For Her Own Good*, 5.

62. Hall, *Three Acres and Liberty*, 4.

63. Danbom, "Romantic Agrarianism in Twentieth-Century America," 3.

64. Danbom, "Romantic Agrarianism in Twentieth-Century America," 3.

65. Danbom, "Romantic Agrarianism in Twentieth-Century America," 4.

66. Spigel, "Seducing the Innocent," 112.

67. Ehrenrich and English, *For Her Own Good*, 186, 206–7, 210.

68. See Nasaw, *Children of the City*; and Rosenzweig, *Eight Hours for What We Will*.

69. Spigel, "Seducing the Innocent," 113.

70. Ehrenrich and English, *For Her Own Good*, 210.

71. Ehrenrich and English, *For Her Own Good*, 4, 183.

72. Ehrenrich and English, *For Her Own Good*, 4.

73. Ehrenreich and English, *For Her Own Good*, 5.

74. Romanowski, *Pop Culture Wars*, 19.

75. Vaudeville became the dominant and most popular form of entertainment in the United States during the late nineteenth century and its forms carried over into twentieth-century popular entertainment mediums. Douglas Gilbert identifies "the backbone of vaudeville" as "low comedy," and notes that "dialect, eccentric, and nut comedians in exaggerated costumes and facial makeups predominated." Gilbert, *American Vaudeville*, 393.

76. Romanowski, *Pop Culture Wars*, 19.

77. See Levine, *Highbrow/Lowbrow*; Gans, *Popular Culture and High Culture*; Rubin, *Making of Middlebrow Culture*.

78. Levine, *Highbrow/Lowbrow*, 200.

79. Romanowski, *Pop Culture Wars*, 24. Note also that American evangelicals were at the forefront of utilizing the new mass media to promote conversion and engage in other persuasion efforts that sought to influence the public mind. See Nord, *Evangelical Origins*, and Nord, *Faith in Reading*.

80. Henry James, qtd. in Levine, *Highbrow/Lowbrow*, 172.

81. Levine, *Highbrow/Lowbrow*, 172–73.

82. Romanowski, *Reforming Hollywood*, 4–5, 5.

83. Romanowski, *Reforming Hollywood*, 5.

84. For a primary source discussion on the increasing recognition of an emerging cultural pluralism in early twentieth century America, see Bourne, "Trans-national America." Bourne notes that the "discovery of diverse nationalistic feelings" has "brought about the unpleasant inconsistencies of our traditional beliefs" (1). Rosenthal notes that this shift is illustrative of the group's gradual loss of cultural power. Interestingly, I came across a typed document by Rogers, titled "Protestant Hour," written on February 2, 1976. This program was never produced but the document lays out the bare bones of a script that begins with the opening *Neighborhood* song, "Won't You Be My Neighbor?" The introductory sentence of the document reads: "It seems to me that one of our most important tasks as parents and Christian educators is to help and encourage both children and adults to discover their own unique ways of expressing love." Fred Rogers, "Protestant Hour" transcript, February 25, 1967, folder "Judson Press," box CW11, Fred Rogers Archive.

85. Romanowski, *Reforming Hollywood*, 6.

86. See Draper, "Controversy Has Probably Destroyed," 187–201. See also Skinner, *Cross and the Cinema*.

87. Romanowski, *Reforming Hollywood*, 6.

88. For a broader account of the travail and declension of the American Protestant establishment's cultural authority during the first half of the twentieth century, see Hutchison, *Between the Times*.

89. Rogers, "Children's TV: What Can the Church Do about It?," 1. This document is not dated. We can tell that it is authored by Rogers because he signs off at the bottom of the document as "Rev. Fred Rogers, Director of the United Oakland Ministry's Center for Creative Work with Children; Visiting Lecturer in Children's Work, Pittsburgh Theological Seminary; Consultant in Creative Media: Arsenal Child Study Center; Department of Psychiatry, University of Pittsburg, and Creator, writer, producer of television series: "MISTEROGERS' NEIGHBORHOOD." We can deduce from the spelling of the show here that the document

probably was written before 1968, when the title was changed to *Mister Rogers' Neighborhood*.

90. Rogers, "Children's TV: What Can the Church Do about It?," 1.

91. Here, Rogers appears to be pointing to animation that entered cinema in the 1920s and later television (e.g., Warner Brothers, Disney). See Perlmutter, *America Toons In*.

92. Trained in music composition at Rollins College, Rogers was acutely aware of the role that music plays in perception and communication. Here, he points to the ways that musical soundtracks in the common television fare add to what he considers an overstimulation of the audience. In contrast, on *Neighborhood*, he provides calming, complementary, and invitational music in order to facilitate the kind of thoughtful conversations he wishes to have with his audience.

93. For more on the relationship between the emergence of childhood and the institutions that fostered this new conception of the young, see Postman, *Disappearance of Childhood*.

94. Rogers, "Protestant Hour."

95. Notably, rhetorical moves like this one are historically rooted in the social gospel tradition as it played into social hygiene movements of the Progressive Era. But the turn begins even earlier, with Theodore Parker, who was probably the first minister to draw extensively upon social science in his sermons advocating social reforms like abolition.

96. Note that this document was most likely created during the mid-1960s, when Rogers was working on the Canadian program *Misterogers*, and thus cannot be read as a retroactive attempt to scrounge up material support for what some will read as a kind of moral crusade project.

97. This final line is a rhetorical example of peroration, seen in many missionary speeches.

98. For another perspective on these developments as related to the feminization of culture through the avenues of the literary and the religious, see Douglas, *Feminization of American Culture*.

99. Margaret McFarland, "To Whom It May Concern," box # EU68, Fred Rogers Archives. Note that McFarland's assertion here is not a novel contention. See Bailyn, *Education in the Forming of American Society*. See also the scholarship of Lawrence A. Cremin, the seventh president of Columbia University's Teachers College.

100. In *Radio's Hidden Voice: The Origins of Public Broadcasting in the United States*, Slotten discusses how early university radio stations employed the technology for public service programming including dissemination of new agricultural methods and programs for rural schools that included music lessons and calisthenics programming. University radio stations were "especially distinctive in helping to establish public-service ideals that would provide a robust alternative to

commercial practices" and were central to "establishing the idea of broadcasting as a noncommercial public service" (41–42).

101. Erikson, *Childhood and Society*, 23.

102. Sharapan, interview with the author, June 19, 2013, Pittsburgh, PA.

103. "Arsenal Family and Children's Center was founded in the Lawrenceville section of Pittsburgh in 1953 by pediatrician Dr. Benjamin Spock. Then on the faculty of the University of Pittsburgh School of Medicine, Dr. Spock designed the Center as a training site for pediatric students to study normal child development in the context of a neighborhood that was highly ethnic (Eastern European) and stable. Dr. Spock believed this would secure longitudinal study of child growth and development across generations." Arsenal Family and Children's Center, "History," accessed May 16, 2019, https://www.arsenalfamily.org/home/about-us/.

104. See Seiter, "Children's Desires/Mother's Dilemmas," 297–317.

105. Caulfield, "'Trust Yourself'," 264. Horace Bushnell, the grandfather of Spock's wife, made similar prescriptions a century earlier in *Christian Nurture* (1861). Spock was an avowed atheist. John B. Watson famously wrote: "Never hug and kiss [your children]. Never let them sit in your lap. If you must, kiss them once on the forehead when they say goodnight. Shake hands with them in the morning. Give them a pat on the head if they have made an extraordinary good job of a difficult task." Watson, "Against the Threat of Mother Love," 474.

106. Caulfield, "'Trust Yourself,'" 264.

107. Spock, *Baby and Childcare*, Kindle location 7824.

108. Caulfield, "'Trust Yourself,'" 264.

109. In 1972, Spock noted that "John Dewey and Freud said that kids don't have to be disciplined into adulthood but can direct themselves toward adulthood by following their own will." Quoted in Eric Pace, "Benjamin Spock, World's Pediatrician, Dies at 94," *New York Times*, March 17, 1998.

110. Maier, *Dr. Spock*, 214. "Nothing less than the fate of America's children seemed to rest in Dr. Spock's hands, or so it appeared from the hundreds of parents asking advice, reporters and television commentators seeking words of wisdom, and even politicians, who implied that the nation, by some silent and unanimous plebiscite, had given him this awesome responsibility."

111. Spigel, "Seducing the Innocent," 115.

112. Spigel, "Seducing the Innocent," 115.

113. It is also important to note that over time, Spock acquired many critics who spoke out against what they identified as his "permissive" child-rearing style. In the 1960s Spock began protesting the Vietnam War and the development of nuclear arms often in solidarity with members of the generation of babies he had helped raise. In the early 1970s he became a presidential candidate of the far-left People's Party and ran on a platform of free medical care, the legalization of abortion and marijuana, a guaranteed minimum wage, and the withdrawal of

American troops from all foreign nations. The Rev. Dr. Norman Vincent Peale noted the ways Spock's politics aligned with the platforms of radical youth movements of the time, stating that the doctor had entered the streets "with these babies raised according to his books, demonstrating with them for things they claim we should not deny them." Peale reduced Spock's child care messages to the phrase, "Feed 'em whenever they want, never let them cry, satisfy their every desire." Spock refuted these kinds of critiques, stating that he did not wish to "encourage permissiveness" but rather to "relax rigidity" (quoted in Pace, "Benjamin Spock"). Similar critiques have also been mounted against the messaging of *Mister Rogers' Neighborhood.* After his death in 1993, Rogers became the target of criticism from anchors at Fox News who pointed to his pedagogy as the "root cause" of youth entitlement among the millennial generation. See Prachi Gupta, "The 10 Worst Fox News Interviews of the Decade," *Salon,* July 20, 2013, http://www.salon.com/2013/07/30/10_worst_fox_news_interviews_of_the_decade/.

CHAPTER 2. CREATING THE DIALOGIC

1. Margaret McFarland to Margaret Rasmussen, December 1, 1966, folder "Prof. Early Endorse," box EU68, Fred Rogers Archive, Latrobe, PA.

2. Rogers, untitled notes, 19 Sept. 1984, folder "Save Inspirational/Spiritual," box EU36, Fred Rogers Archive.

3. See Eichsteller and Holthoff, "Social Pedagogy as an Ethical Orientation," 176–86.

4. McKim, *Ever a Vision,* 59.

5. Rogers, untitled notes, 19 Sept. 1984, folder "Save Inspirational/Spiritual," box EU36, Fred Rogers Archive.

6. See Archive of American Television website, "Children's Corner, The," http://emmytvlegends.org/interviews/shows/childrens-corner-the. The program was described in some print media as a "calm" alternative to the "frantic antics" of "the usual" television programming for children. "In Review," *Broadcasting, Television* 50, no. 1 (Jan. 2, 1956): 14.

7. Rubin, *Lessons from* Mister Rogers' Neighborhood.

8. The innovation and efficacy of the observational method was first developed by Jean Piaget in the 1920s and later expanded and refined by Erikson.

9. Calvin Schrag discusses this phenomenon at length in his 1986 *Communicative Praxis and the Space of Subjectivity.* See Arnett, *Dialogic Education,* 18, for a discussion of Schrag.

10. Freire, *Pedagogy of the Oppressed,* 119.

11. Watson and his contemporaries who espoused similar authoritarian methods of parenting have since been characterized by Harvard Medical School's T. Berry Brazelton, a contemporary pediatrician-author, as employing a didactic style of advice giving. In the *New York Times* obituary (March 17, 1998) of Benjamin

Spock, Brazelton notes that Spock changed the arena of parenting and family dynamics by empowering mothers and fathers, offering them choices and "encouraging them to think things out for themselves."

12. Arnett, *Dialogic Education*, 18.

13. Arnett, *Dialogic Education*, 18.

14. Arnett, Fritz, and Bell, *Communication Ethics Literacy*, 55.

15. Arnett, Fritz, and Bell, *Communication Ethics Literacy*, 55.

16. See Rogers, "The Weekend Song," *Neighborhood Archive*, http://www.neighborhoodarchive.com/music/songs/weekend_song.html. Note here the power of Rogers's use of the interpellative "you," as exemplified in the famous military recruitment poster "Uncle Sam Wants You!," even though he uses mass media that would seem to employ a plural "you" (or in Pittsburghese, "yinz").

17. Rogers, interview by Karen Herman, Archive of American Television and Film, July 22, 1999, https://interviews.televisionacademy.com/interviews/fred-rogers.

18. See Hall, "Encoding/Decoding," 128–38.

19. In her observational study of Australian children watching television in their homes, Patricia Palmer has mapped the variety of children's behavioral patterns for viewing. She found that children had a propensity for engaging with television programming in an active way, such as performing, reenacting, and reinterpreting the content usually as a bonding interaction with other family members and friends. See Palmer, *Lively Audience*.

20. Fiske, "Commodities and Culture," 23–47.

21. Fiske, "Commodities and Culture."

22. In their famous article "Beyond Persuasion," Sonja Foss and Cindy L. Griffin propose an alternative rhetoric to the traditional "patriarchal" understanding of persuasion, which favors changing and thus dominating others. In this regard, they posit the notion of an "invitational rhetoric" rooted in "feminist principles of equality, immanent value, and self-determination," interested not in changing the opinion of another but in achieving mutual understanding (2). In offering an invitation to understanding, the primary communication modes entail the contribution of perspectives and the creation of "conditions of safety, value, and freedom" (2).

23. Horton and Wohl, "Mass Communication and Para-social Interaction," 216.

24. Horton and Wohl, "Mass Communication and Para-social Interaction," 216.

25. Dooe, "How Mister Rogers Shaped."

26. Margaret McFarland, "To Whom It May Concern," box # EU68, Fred Rogers Archives, Latrobe, PA. Fred Rogers Center archivist Emily Uhrin posits the mid- to late 1960s as a rough estimate date for the letter from which these quotations are taken. The letter reads like a grant proposal. Uhrin posits that this letter was likely an appeal for funding so that the program could go national and thus likely written in 1967. In 1968, the program did go national. Note that

McFarland's assertion here is not a novel contention. See Bailyn, *Education in the Forming of American Society*. See also the scholarship of Lawrence A. Cremin, the seventh president of Columbia University's Teachers College.

27. Margaret McFarland, "To Whom It May Concern."

28. McFarland writes during a time in which groups within the adult culture are voicing sharp alarms regarding the vulnerability of youth to antisocial and destructive behaviors and messages textualized and discursively embedded in mass media products. The potential for exposure to such messages during this time of electronic media development and marketing threatened a post-Enlightenment Western society within which adults had ritualized and institutionalized the filtering of knowledge to the young. See Postman, *Disappearance of Childhood*, 53–64. Postman argues that "Locke's tabula rasa created a sense of guilt in parents about their children's development, and provided the psychological and epistemological founds for making the careful nurturing of children a national priority, at least among the merchant classes" (57). Prior to the emergence of mass communication, the church and school struggled to bring about a social situation in which what obtained was a gradual revealing of adult knowledges or "secrets" to the young in "proper" intervals according to age. Postman calls this a "sequence of revealed secrets" (quoted in Steyer, *Other Parent*, 15). This kind of pedagogical wisdom and control, however, was clearly being usurped and disturbed by the power of mass communication technologies.

29. McFarland, "To Whom it May Concern."

30. See Morrow, *Sesame Street*.

31. While *Neighborhood* and *Sesame Street* were produced during the same time period and aired on educational/public television, as children's television shows, they had different missions and were directed toward different audiences. *Sesame Street* aimed to help minority children living in urban settings gain a "head start" on school learning before they entered preschool and kindergarten. Its setting and characters reflected that of a diverse, urban city block. Rogers program did not specifically target such a minority audience, although his program incorporated racially diverse characters during the 1970s and 1980s as multicultural, progressive values became more prominent within the culture at large.

32. The decline of intergenerational living and the rise of the nuclear family during the postwar period contributed to the success of the reliance on "experts" in childcare as the older generation no longer was around, living in the family house, to pass on wisdom and advice to young parents.

33. Caulfield, "'Trust Yourself,'" 264.

34. McFarland, "To Whom It May Concern."

35. McFarland, "To Whom it May Concern."

36. Rogers, "Yale," 2.

37. Horton and Wohl, "Mass Communication and Para-social Interaction," 215.

38. Bowlby, *Attachment and Loss.*

39. Jack P. Shonkoff and Deborah Phillips, quoted in Davies, *Child Development*, 6.

40. Davies, *Child Development*, 10.

41. Davies, *Child Development*, 9.

42. As noted in David Davies's primer *Child Development*, secure attachment provides the child with a base for exploration of his worldly surroundings. That is to say, when a child feels secure in his/her attachment with the parent or primary caregiver, she exudes confidence when engaging in worldly, exploratory actions. If the child feels insecure in the primary relationship, she, consumed by the anxiety produced by the insecurity of the attachment, is less confident in her exploration of the world (9–10). L. Alan Scroufe notes that "the dyadic infant-caregiver organization precedes and gives rise to the organization that is the self . . . the self-organization, in turn, has significance for ongoing adaptation and experience, including late social behavior . . . each personality, whether healthy or disordered, is the product of the history of vital relationships" (quoted in Davies, *Child Development*, 2nd ed., 21). While this details one school of interpretation, it is important to note that this understanding has become the predominant view of child development in the United States and best coincides with Rogers's views and approach to the social-emotional on *Neighborhood.*

43. Caulfield, "'Trust Yourself,'" 265.

44. Kline, "Making of Children's Culture," 101.

45. Fred Rogers, "Invisible Essentials," speech, Memphis Theological Seminary, May 10, 1997, folder "1997," box EU74, Fred Rogers Archive.

46. Hollingsworth, *Simple Faith of Mister Rogers*, 79.

47. Rogers, "Invisible Essentials."

48. Rogers, "Invisible Essentials."

49. Rogers, "Invisible Essentials."

50. Quoted in Hollingsworth, *Simple Faith of Mister Rogers*, 21.

51. Hollingsworth, *Simple Faith of Mister Rogers*, 34-35.

52. Fred Rogers Company Website, "About Us," accessed July 1, 2013, http://www.fci.org/FRC/about-us.html.

53. Saint-Exupéry, *Little Prince*, trans. Woods, 70.

54. Nouwen, *Wounded Healer*, 83.

55. Rogers, "More Than We Know," principal address at the opening ceremonies of the sesquicentennial of Saint Vincent, Saint Vincent Archabbey Basilica, Latrobe, PA, April 25, 1995, "Spirituality Files," speech box 1, Fred Rogers Archive.

56. See Crusalis, "Wounded Healer."

57. For an interesting exploration of the concept of *caritas* from a critical theory perspective, see Coles, *Rethinking Generosity.*

58. Belcher-Hamilton, "Gospel According to Fred," 382.

59. Rogers, "Invisible Essentials," 5–6.

60. Hollingsworth, *Simple Faith of Mister Rogers*, 20–21.

61. Rogers, notes dated September 19, 1984, folder "Save/Inspirational/Spiritual," box EU36, Fred Rogers Archive.

62. Rogers, "We're Not to Be Afraid," *Neighborhood Archive*, accessed June 30, 2015, http://www.neighborhoodarchive.com/music/songs/were_not_to_be_afraid.html.

63. Gundry-Volf, "To such as these belongs the Reign of God'," 469.

64. Rogers, interview by Herman.

65. Rogers, interview by Herman.

66. See Myers, "Remembering Fred Rogers," 1.

67. Buber, quoted in Cooper, Chak, Cornish, and Gillespie, "Dialogue," 3.

68. Buber, quoted in Cooper, Chak, Cornish, and Gillespie, "Dialogue," 3.

69. Cooper, Chak, Cornish, and Gillespie, "Dialogue," 73. See also Bergman, *Dialogical Philosophy from Kierkegaard to Buber*.

70. Cooper, Chak, Cornish, and Gillespie, "Dialogue," 73.

71. Cooper, Chak, Cornish, and Gillespie, "Dialogue," 73.

72. See Cooper, Chak, Cornish, and Gillespie, "Dialogue," 73.

73. Rubin, *Lessons from* Mister Rogers' Neighborhood.

74. Rubin, *Lessons from* Mister Rogers' Neighborhood.

75. Kimmel and Collins, *Wonder of It All*, i.

76. "Erik Erikson, 91, Psychoanalyst Who Reshaped Views of Human Growth, Dies," *New York Times*, May 13, 1994.

77. For more on Erikson's place in the child development theory, see Burston, *Erik Erikson and the American Psyche*.

78. Erikson, *Childhood and Society*, 247.

79. Erikson, *Childhood and Society*, 247.

80. Erikson, *Childhood and Society*, 252.

81. Erikson, *Childhood and Society*, 252–53.

82. "It's No Use" first appeared on *Mister Rogers' Neighborhood*, episode 1608 (1989). Provided courtesy of the Fred Rogers Company.

83. Davies, *Child Development*, 2nd ed., 262.

84. Rogers, "Encouraging Creativity," p. 2, box EU3, Fred Rogers Archive.

85. Rogers, "Encouraging Creativity," 2.

86. The modern school movement of the early twentieth century advocated many of these changes, which, considering the standard practices in the public schools that Rogers identifies in the 1960s, were still at the time considered radical.

87. Rogers, "Encouraging Creativity," 1.

88. Rogers, "Encouraging Creativity," 1.

89. Rogers, "Senate Statement on PBS Funding," May 1, 1969, American Rhetoric

Online Speech Bank, accessed April 29, 2019, http://www.americanrhetoric .com/speeches/fredrogerssenatetestimonypbs.htm.

90. Rogers, "Encouraging Creativity," 2.

91. Kimpton, "Dewey and Progressive Education," 125.

92. Kimpton, "Dewey and Progressive Education," 125.

93. Rogers, "Encouraging Creativity," 2.

94. Kimpton, "Dewey and Progressive Education," 126.

95. Rogers, "Encouraging Creativity," 3.

96. Rogers, "Encouraging Creativity," 3.

97. See "AMERICANS TO VIE IN MUSIC CONTEST; Will Face Russia's Best in 2d Tchaikovsky Event," *New York Times*, March 14, 1962.

98. Rogers, "Encouraging Creativity," 3.

99. As told by Rogers, in Rubin, *Lessons from* Mister Rogers' Neighborhood.

100. Rubin, *Lessons from* Mister Rogers' Neighborhood.

101. Horton and Wohl, "Mass Communication and Para-social Interaction," 223.

102. Horton and Wohl, "Mass Communication and Para-social Interaction," 223.

103. Rubin, *Lessons from* Mister Rogers' Neighborhood.

104. Rubin, *Lessons from* Mister Rogers' Neighborhood.

105. Unfortunately, most of these recorded sessions between McFarland and Rogers are currently unavailable to the public. In March 2015, the Fred Rogers Center announced that Hedda Sharapan, a former producer on *Neighborhood*, would begin to work on a special initiative "to analyze audio recordings of conversations between Fred Rogers and the late Dr. Margaret McFarland." According to the news release, "Sharapan will evaluate a number of episodes of *Mister Rogers' Neighborhood* and reverse engineer them back to the original recorded conversations to illustrate how complex early childhood theory evolved into deep and thoughtful programming for young children." "Fred Rogers Center Names Sharapan PNC Grow Up Great Senior Fellow," press release, March 19, 2015, http://www.fredrogerscenter.org/2015/03/19/ fred-rogers-center-names-sharapan-pnc-grow-up-great-senior-fellow/.

106. Margaret McFarland, "To Whom It May Concern."

107. National Educational Television was founded in 1952. It operated from 1954 to 1970, when it was renamed Public Broadcasting System (PBS).

108. McCarthy, *Citizen Machine*, 249.

109. Rogers, "Senate Statement on PBS Funding."

110. Bill Isler, Hedda Sharapan, David Newell, Joanne Rogers, and Carl Kurlander, "The Making of *Mister Rogers' Neighborhood*," featuring University of Pittsburgh panel event, September 16, 2011. See "Pitt to Host Panel on the Making of *Mister Rogers' Neighborhood* Sept. 16," University of Pittsburgh News Services, September 15, 2011, http://www.news.pitt.edu/news/ pitt-host-panel-making-mister-rogers-neighborhood-sept-16.

111. See Giroux, *Mouse That Roared*, Critics and scholars alike have posited the notion that *Neighborhood* has elements of a countercultural project, especially in regards to the emerging consumer and commercial postwar culture. Patricia Pace argues that "Rogers' TV aesthetic provides an antidote to those slicker television productions intent on the manufacture of kid-size consumers with adult appetites for commodified pleasures of all sorts." See Pace, review, 384. Scholar Michael Long has recently argued that the fundamental ethos of Rogers's program is a radical religious and political pacifism operating against the dominant forces of violence and war in postwar American society. Long, *Peaceful Neighbor.*

112. Rogers, "Philosophy," folder "Videodiscs," box EU88, Fred Rogers Archives.

113. Rogers, "Philosophy," 3.

114. This phrase, that "feelings are mentionable and therefore manageable," is used by Rogers is several interviews. He credits the idea to McFarland. See Rogers, interview by Herman.

115. Grossman, *Saturday Morning TV*, 123.

116. Quoted in Roderick Townley, "Fred's Shoes," 70.

117. See Gary H. Grossman, "Uncle Hosts and Other Video Relations," in *Saturday Morning TV*, 105. Another example of a children's television program character who maintains the personality and orientation of a responsible, nurturing, adult figure is Shari Lewis (*The Shari Lewis Show*, 1960–1963), who illustrates well the similarities between her educational philosophy of children's television and that of Rogers in saying, "Self esteem comes from doing something and accomplishing something. It doesn't come from watching TV. I try to do activities, I try to turn TV into an activity." See "'Lamb Chop' Creator Shari Lewis Dead at 65," CNN.com, August 3, 1998, http://www.cnn.com/SHOWBIZ/TV/9808/03/shari.lewis.obit/.

118. Rubin, *Lessons from* Mister Rogers' Neighborhood.

119. Rogers, "Philosophy," 7–8.

120. Rogers, "Philosophy," 7.

121. In the field of child development, then and now, "fantasy play" is understood to be used by children to compensate for difficult feelings of inadequacy and fear. "The 4-year-old, for example, may be anxious about the fact that she is smaller and less competent than adults but compensates by playing adult roles or becoming idealized characters who represent power in her dramatic play. By becoming the powerful queen or heroine, she temporarily diminishes and masters feelings of inadequacy." Davies, *Child Development*, 289.

122. Davies, *Child Development*, 260.

123. See Piaget, *Play, Dreams, and Imitation in Childhood.*

124. Rogers, "Philosophy," 7.

125. While the presentation of puppets and humans in dialogue was present

on his former show, *The Children's Corner*, as well as on WBKB's *Kukla, Fran and Ollie* and the *Soupy Sales Show*, the integration of puppets and actors in the same dramatic situation is new and unique to *Neighborhood*. For example, on both *Kukla, Fran and Ollie* and *The Shari Lewis Show*, puppets had sometimes silly, sometimes serious conversations with the female human leads with whom they conversed. On *The Howdy Doody Show*, the boy-like puppet character Howdy Doody interacted with the adult, cowboy character Buffalo Bob within a dramatic situation often characterized by confusion, chaos, excitement and anxiety. In *Neighborhood*, the puppets and actors engage only in the "fantasy" segment of the program, the Neighborhood of Make-Believe—an environment contrasted with that of "reality" and characterized by Rogers as "the playground of the imagination from which creative ideas and fine distinctions can be drawn and understood."

126. Townley, "Fred's Shoes," 68.

127. Rogers quoted in Townley, "Fred's Shoes," 68.

128. Rogers wrote over two hundred songs for *Neighborhood*. See "Songs and Lyrics," *Neighborhood Archive*, accessed July 3, 2013, http://www.neighborhoodarchive.com/music/songs/.

129. Rogers, "Philosophy," 9.

130. Rogers quoted in Townley, "Fred's Shoes," 70.

131. Rogers quoted in Townley, "Fred's Shoes," 71.

132. Rogers quoted in Townley, "Fred's Shoes," 70.

133. Rogers quoted in Townley, "Fred's Shoes," 71.

134. This line is a quotation by William Ralph Inge, a prominent religious and ecclesiastic English thinker in the early twentieth century. Inge argued that a secure society was one rooted on the invisible and eternal values of truth, beauty, and goodness that ultimately are derived from God. See "Inge, William Ralph," in Borchert, ed., *Encyclopedia of Philosophy*, 685–86.

135. Rogers, untitled notes, September 19, 1984, folder "Save Inspirational/ Spiritual," box EU36, Fred Rogers Archive.

136. Also notable in this dynamic is a relational setup in which the teacher structures the space of the dialogue and employs an invitational rhetoric to elicit dialogue.

137. *Pedagogy of the Oppressed*, 72.

138. Kimmel and Collins, *Wonder of It All*, 25.

139. McKim, *Ever a Vision*, 59.

140. See Eichsteller and Holthoff, "Social Pedagogy as an Ethical Orientation," 176–86.

141. McKim, *Ever a Vision*, 26.

142. Guy, "Theology of *Mister Rogers' Neighborhood*," 116.

143. Fred Rogers, "The Beginning of Faith," in "Faith Through the Eyes of a Child," May 2, 1983, folder "These Days, 1983," box EU88, Fred Rogers Archive.

144. Guy, "Theology of *Mister Rogers' Neighborhood*," 116. See Foucault's essays on care of the soul (*epimeleia*), in *Technologies of the Self.*

145. See Miell, MacDonald, and Hargreaves, *Music Communication.*

146. Pope John Paul II decried the normalizing of what he termed a "culture of death" in his 1995 Papal Encyclical, "Evangelium Vitae," translated as "The Gospel of Life." See Paul Galloway, "John Paul Condemns 'Culture of Death,'" *Chicago Tribune*, March 31, 1995. He cited examples of abortion on demand, the increased use of euthanasia, and capital punishment as illustrative of a postmodern society in which such "moral crimes" are justified by a misguided understanding of individual rights. Rich, *Of Women Born*, 285.

147. Guy, "Theology of *Mister Rogers' Neighborhood*," 110–11.

148. McKim, *Ever a Vision*, 92.

149. McKim, *Ever a Vision*, 93.

150. McKim, *Ever a Vision*, 94.

151. Slater, *Pursuit of Loneliness*, 1.

CHAPTER 3. INSIDE *MISTER ROGERS' NEIGHBORHOOD*

1. Provided courtesy of the Fred Rogers Company.

2. One of the most prominent and widely viewed children's television programs of the 1950s was *Howdy Doody*. This program begins with a shot of a cuckoo clock, its hands spinning out of control around the clock face while the clock shakes violently against a black screen and a bell dings rapidly. A fireball emerges from the clock's door and spins as it comes closer and closer toward the viewer, and then explodes. Cymbals crash as the fireball fades out and the face of a freckled, white, cartoon-like boy appears in the center of the screen. His mouth opens, revealing his status as a puppet, and he says, "Say, kids, what time is it?" What sounds like a crowd of at least a dozen kids then screams, "It's Howdy Doody Time!" as the puppet's face is overcast by large carnival font that reads HOWDY DOODY in all capital letters. The program then opens on the freckle-faced puppet, Howdy Doody, his full puppet body "standing" in on a stage in front of a curtain. He greets the in-house child audience with a loud, "Well, How-dee-doody, kids," and then turns to greet the human host of the show, Buffalo Bob Smith. Bob is a gruff, loud, large man in a kiddie cowboy costume, who says a voluminous hello to Howdy Doody and then says assertively, looking into the camera, "Say, boys and girls at home, and kids here in the gallery, stay right where you are, kids, because you're going to see Howdy Doody stop Mr. X's fedoozler with our sensational new invention, the switcheroo." He then raises his voice and shouts to the group of children sitting next to him in the gallery, "But first, come on, gang let's go!" The prompt is met by the gallery children who begin to sing, "It's Howdy Doody Time," the kind of "catch-song" of the show. The camera pans their faces, some blank, some excited, others visibly confused as they all sing in unison the *Howdy Doody* theme song. At the end, Bob

proceeds immediately into a theatrical scene that ensues in the theater just off the gallery.

The opening scenes of *Howdy Doody* create a sense of disorder and chaos, with the one grownup in the shot behaving like an overgrown child, shouting at the gallery children to burst out in song. Its message, from the beginning explosive clock scene on, seems to be: "This is a time to let off steam in an unstructured, nonsensical, and carnivalesque kind of way." The gallery children, who act like a kind of Greek chorus directed by man-child Bob, sit and sing in all different body poses, some looking at the camera, others at each other, and still others at Bob to their right and Howdy Doody to their left. The producers attempt to grant some power to the gallery children and home audience by having them sing the opening song. But any real sense that the children occupy a place of shared power on the program is lost by the air of disorder and neglect revealed by their undisciplined bodies, their lack of energy, and the song's lyrics, which introduce the main players of the show and work to cement their power and agency.

The invitation to enter *Howdy Doody* time is directed to a group—the dozen or so children in the show's gallery and the viewers at home. The message to the viewer is that you are one of many, and like the distracted and disorderly children in the gallery, you are one face in an audience of many. Your job is to assume the role of theatrical spectator.

3. The opening song lyrics also hint at Louis Althusser's concept of interpellation in the sense that Rogers's rhetoric calls at a willing subject and the subject has no alternative but to recognize and respond to the interpellating agent. Althusser, "Ideology and Ideological State Apparatuses," 309.

4. See Csikszentmihalyi and Halton, *Meaning of Things*; Douglas and Isherwood, *World of Goods*.

5. In the accompanying music, the celeste and the piano begin to play a duet. The celeste, an instrument often featured in children's music, plays lighter, delicate tones in the middle and upper registers. In contrast, the piano, which would seem to represent the adult figure of Rogers, has a fuller and grander presence, its lower-register bass notes representing perhaps the deeper voice of an adult male creating a feeling of holding, stability, reliability, and protection. The two instruments, celeste and piano, coming together in a duet symbolize the meeting and dialogical intertwining of Rogers and the viewer, inviting a sense of mutuality and togetherness.

6. "Episode 0004," *Mister Rogers' Neighborhood*, February 22, 1968.

7. Lydia Stout is the author of a 1958 *Atlantic Monthly* article titled "What Strangles American Teaching—The Certification Racket," a topic that would likely appeal to Rogers.

8. Provided courtesy of the Fred Rogers Company.

9. Punch clocks hit at the heart of labor management relations, as pointed out in Hareven, *Family Time and Industrial Time*, 147.

10. The king does not voice a word in this first (invisible) appearance. The piano is intended to represent the king's speech, which Rogers understands but the audience is not explicitly privy to. We only are able to guess the gist of what the king is communicating to Rogers by listening to Rogers's responses.

11. The human characters listed here are those who appeared in episodes from the first season. Over one hundred appeared over the course of the thirty-three-year run of the program. Some became fixtures and some did not. It should also be noted that, like Rogers, all of these human characters use their real-life names.

12. This music is used in every episode as an audio cue signaling to the viewer that an environmental transition is about to occur.

13. I have made Trolley a "he" because Rogers has anthropomorphized the object and it does not feel right to call Trolley an "it."

14. A political system of absolute power reigns in the Neighborhood of Make-Believe. King Friday is the sovereign power and all other human and puppet characters are subjects in his polis. They address him as the supreme authority. However, the characters in the neighborhood are portrayed as more likable than Friday, and more often than not, their ideas are wiser than his. They are often shown negotiating with a stubborn but amenable Friday to help him see their perspective on a matter. Indeed, when Friday listens to his subjects, which he almost always does, he quite often changes his mind on a subject and alters his approach to accommodate the concerns of "his people." In this way, he could be read as an authoritative, yet approachable, father figure, who exerts power and management but who also is amenable to conversation, arbitration, and compromise.

15. Notably, there are no French subtitles, nor is there an oral translation for the viewer.

16. Provided courtesy of the Fred Rogers Company.

17. The following account of the various details of *Neighborhood* film production are from a phone conversation between the author and longtime lead *Neighborhood* producer Hedda Sharapan, March 20, 2016.

18. Tuber, *Attachment, Play, and Authenticity*, 119.

19. It also hints at a position of anticommodity fetishism.

20. DeNora, *Making Sense of Reality*, xx.

21. And Rogers sees himself in dialogue not just with the very young, who are the primary audience for his program. Rather, he understands that because his communication channel is in the home space, the program addresses the family at large and thus an intergenerational audience.

22. DeNora, *Making Sense of Reality*, xxiiii.

23. See Casto, "Concept of Hand Production," 321–25.

24. Provided courtesy of the Fred Rogers Company.

25. Paraphrased in Abram, "Transitional Phenomena," in *Language of Winnicott*, 313.

26. Abram, "Transitional Phenomena," 313.

27. Abram, "Transitional Objects," 233.

28. Abram, "Transitional Objects," 232.

29. Tuber, *Attachment, Play, and Authenticity*, 153.

30. Rogers Silverstone would later explore the idea of television as transitional object. "I want to suggest," he writes, "that our media, television perhaps preeminently, occupy the potential space released by blankets, teddy bears and breasts (Young, 1986), and function cathectically and culturally as transitional objects." Silverstone, "Television, Ontology, and the Transitional Object," in *Television and Everyday Life*, 23.

31. Abram, "Transitional Objects," 233.

32. Abram, "Transitional Objects," 317.

33. Tuber, *Attachment, Play, and Authenticity*, 156.

34. Tuber, *Attachment, Play, and Authenticity*, 157.

35. Tuber, *Attachment, Play, and Authenticity*, 157.

36. Tuber, *Attachment, Play, and Authenticity*, 157.

37. Tuber, *Attachment, Play, and Authenticity*, 158.

38. Winnicott, *Playing and Reality*, 47.

39. Winnicott, *Playing and Reality*, 48.

40. As quoted by Carolyn Robertson, "Mister Rogers' Sweet Message to Grownups Is All You Need to Hear," *Baby Center Blog*, February 2, 2016, http://blogs.babycenter.com/mom_stories/mr-rogers-message-to-02032016grown-up-fans-is-all-you-needs-to-hear/.

41. Rogers, "Philosophy," folder "Videodiscs," box EU88, Fred Rogers Archives.

42. Rogers, "Philosophy."

43. Many mothers worked during this period. In 1970, between 20 and 25 percent worked during their childbearing years. By 1976, 40 percent of women with children aged three to six worked and other cared for the child. See "Facts Over Time: Women in the Labor Force," United States Department of Labor, http://www.dol.gov/wb/stats/facts_over_time.htm.

44. Winnicott, *Playing and Reality*, 51.

45. This episode aired on March 11, 1968. For a summary of the episode, see "Episode 0016," in *Neighborhood Archive*, http://www.neighborhoodarchive.com/mrn/episodes/0016/index.html.

46. Winnicott, *Playing and Reality*, 51–52.

47. See Gary Rotstein, "Virgil D. Cantini / Acclaimed Artist, Longtime Pitt

Professor," *Pittsburgh Post-Gazette*, May 5, 2009, http://www.post-gazette.com/news/obituaries/2009/05/05/Virgil-D-Cantini-Acclaimed-artist-longtime-Pitt-professor/stories/200905050171.

48. "Episode 0016," *Mister Rogers' Neighborhood*, March 11, 1968.

49. Note that this episode occurred a little over a year before the July 21, 1969, moon walk. US space exploration was glorified by Kennedy and was an exciting topic of the national public discourse.

50. Rogers does, however, imagine a symbolic creation during this process when he ascribes each nail a role as a family member.

51. Winnicott, *Playing and Reality*, 51.

52. Note how Cantini, reifying gender norms of the time, assigns his own interests in manipulating everyday objects as characteristically and exclusively male. His statement effectively teaches that only boys are to be interested in this kind of play. It is most unwelcoming to female viewers in general and in particular to those who find his craft of interest.

53. Winnicott, *Playing and Reality*, 52.

54. Many viewers express the same feeling in their letters to Mister Rogers (see chapter 4).

55. For an in-depth, groundbreaking examination and analysis of the sensations I describe here see Csikszentmihalyi, *Flow*.

56. Rogers summered with his family on Martha's Vineyard in a small house on the ocean. The named the house "The Crooked House."

57. For further discussion on the cultural relationship to the antique in the United States, see Kammen, *Mystic Chords of Memory*.

58. Noble, *Children in Front of the Small Screen*, 17.

59. Noble, *Children in Front of the Small Screen*, 11.

60. Bloom, "Why We Like What We Like."

61. Bloom, "Why We Like What We Like."

62. Bloom, "Why Do We Like What We Like?"

63. Baudrillard, *System of Objects*, 76.

64. Saint-Exupéry, *Little Prince*, trans. Woods, 66.

65. Saint-Exupéry, *Little Prince*, trans. Woods, 67.

66. Just as he decries the consumer culture of buying premade products, the fox mourns the loss of rites and rituals in modern society, stating that rites "are actions that are often neglected. They are what make one day different from the other, one hour from the other hours. . . . If the hunters danced at just anytime, every day would be like every other day, and I should never have any vacation at all." Notably, Rogers sticks to a very clear order of rites and rituals on his television program. Indeed, rites are arguably one of those other invisible essentials—hidden phenomena that bring pleasure.

67. Saint-Exupéry, *Little Prince*, trans. Woods, 68.

68. Saint-Exupéry, *Little Prince*, trans. Woods, 68.

69. Saint-Exupéry, *Little Prince*, trans. Woods, 70.

70. Saint-Exupéry, *Little Prince*, trans. Woods, 70.

71. Saint-Exupéry, *Little Prince*, trans. Woods, 71.

72. Sara Saturday is Friday's female friend who in later seasons becomes his wife.

73. For a discussion on the phenomenon of hobbies in American life and its relationship to work, see Gelber, *Hobbies*.

74. Provided courtesy of the Fred Rogers Company.

75. "Mime Walker" is the famous mime Jewel Walker. For more on Walker, see Lust, *From the Greek Mimes*, 171.

76. See *Mister Rogers and Me*, dir. Wagner and Wagner.

77. Provided courtesy of the Fred Rogers Company.

78. Abrams, "Transitional Phenomena," 111.

79. "Episode 0111," *Mister Rogers' Neighborhood*, July 22, 1968.

80. Ong, *Orality and Literacy*, 133–34.

CHAPTER 4. "WON'T YOU BE MY NEIGHBOR?"

1. See Bakhtin, "Discourse in the Novel," 672; and Murray, "Bakhtinian Answerability and Levinasian Responsibility," 133–50.

2. Holquist, *Dialogism*, 30.

3. Holquist, *Dialogism*, 30.

4. Burggraeve, "Holistic Values Education," 7.

5. Holquist, *Dialogism*, 30.

6. Paulo Freire, *Pedagogy of the Oppressed* (New York: Continuum, 1993), 69.

7. Gareis and Cohn, *Communication as Culture*, 15.

8. Carey, *Communication as Culture*, 18.

9. Anderson, Baxter, and Cissna, "Texts and Contexts of Dialogue," 6.

10. Grant Noble, *Children in Front of the Small Screen* (Beverly Hills, CA: Sage Publications, 1975), 19.

11. Hanson, *Mass Communication*, 236.

12. This document, "Children's TV: What the Church Can Do about It," is not dated. Rogers signs off at the bottom of the document as "Rev. Fred Rogers, Director of the United Oakland Ministry's Center For Creative Work With Children; Visiting Lecturer In Children's Work, Pittsburgh Theological Seminary; Consultant In Creative Media: Arsenal Child Study Center; Department of Psychiatry, University of Pittsburgh, and Creator, writer, producer of television series: "MISTEROGERS' NEIGHBORHOOD." We can deduce from the spelling of the show here that the document probably was written before 1968, when the title was changed to *Mister Rogers' Neighborhood*.

13. Fred Rogers, "Yale," Television Professionals Look at Children's Programs, New Haven, CT, Oct. 16, 1972, box EU3, Fred Rogers Archive, Latrobe, PA.

14. Family Communications Inc., founded by Fred Rogers in 1971, became the Fred Rogers Company seven years after Rogers's death, in 2010.

15. Singer and Singer, eds. *Handbook of Children and the Media*, 1.

16. Rogers, "Senate Statement on PBS Funding," May 1, 1969, http://www.americanrhetoric.com/speeches/fredrogerssenatetestimonypbs.htm.

17. Horton and Wohl, "Mass Communication and Para-social Interaction," 215–29.

18. Arnett, Fritz, and Bell, *Communication Ethics Literacy*, 11.

19. Arnett, Fritz, and Bell, *Communication Ethics Literacy*, 13.

20. Slater, *Pursuit of Loneliness*, 17.

21. See Gabriela Nunez, "Reading Jose Maria Arguedas' Letter: Building Communication Bridges in Mid-twentieth Century Peruvian Society" (PhD diss., University of Pittsburgh, 2015).

22. Glenn Greenwald to Rogers, Feb. 11 1982, folder 5, box EUFan4, Fred Rogers Archive.

23. Judy Rubin, trailer for "Lessons from *Mister Rogers' Neighborhood*," see Expressive Media Inc. website, February 3, 2015, http://www.expressivemedia.org/f15.html#.

24. Greg Williams to Rogers, May 8, 1981, folder 14, box EUFan4, Fred Rogers Archive.

25. Greg's concern for his peers illustrates the points that both Martin Buber and Emmanuel Levinas make in respect to the responsive construction of the "I," which "moves from individualism to responsible attentiveness of the Other and to the historical situation." Arnett, "Dialogic Ethic 'Between' Buber and Levinas," 76.

26. Newcomb, "On the Dialogic Aspects," 39.

27. Newcomb, "On the Dialogic Aspects," 39.

28. Newcomb, "On the Dialogic Aspects," 40.

29. Newcomb, "On the Dialogic Aspects," 40.

30. Bahktin, *Dialogic Imagination*, 277.

31. Adelman, Parks, and Albrecht, "Nature of Friendship," 306.

32. Adelman, Parks, and Albrecht, "Nature of Friendship," 307.

33. Noble, *Children in Front of the Small Screen*, 36–37.

34. Noble, *Children in Front of the Small Screen*, 37.

35. Adelman, Parks, and Albrecht, "Nature of Friendship," 308.

36. Noble, *Children in Front of the Small Screen*, 21.

37. Adelman, Parks, and Albrecht, "Nature of Friendship," 308.

38. Julie Cruise to Fred Rogers, March 4, 1975, folder 3, box EUFan4, Fred Rogers Archive.

39. The absence of Julie's nephew is notable here, as Julie's second round of viewing takes place in a setting where only she and Rogers are the only two (read: dialogic) present in her space.

40. Freire, *Pedagogy of the Oppressed*, 69.

41. Freire, *Pedagogy of the Oppressed*, 69.

42. "Fox News Spends 6 Minutes Describing Why Mr. Rogers Was an Evil, Evil Man," Upworthy.com, accessed September 21, 2015, http://www.upworthy .com/fox-news-spends-6-minutes-describing-why-mr-rogers-was-an-evil-evil -man-5.

43. Burggraeve, "Holistic Values Education," 1, 17.

44. Burggraeve, "Holistic Values Education," 17.

45. Burggraeve, "Holistic Values Education," 1.

46. Burggraeve, "Holistic Values Education," 2.

47. Rogers to Julie Cruise, April 2, 1975, folder 3, box EUFan4, Fred Rogers Archive.

48. Rogers, "Yale."

49. Rogers to Cruise, April 2, 1975.

50. Freire, *Pedagogy of the Oppressed*, 52.

51. Freire, *Pedagogy of the Oppressed*, 60.

52. Freire, *Pedagogy of the Oppressed*, 60.

53. Freire, *Pedagogy of the Oppressed*, 61.

54. Fred Rogers, "Invisible to the Eye," draft of speech to Pittsburgh Theological Seminary, April 26, 1994, folder "1997," box EU74, Fred Rogers Archives.

55. Sally Rector to Rogers, October 23, 1974, folder 4, box EUFan4, Fred Rogers Archive.

56. Freire, *Pedagogy of the Oppressed*, 70.

57. Freire, *Pedagogy of the Oppressed*, 71.

58. Freire, *Pedagogy of the Oppressed*, 72.

59. Sally Rector to Fred Rogers, October 23, 1974, folder 4, box EUFan4, Fred Rogers Archive.

60. Nouwen, *Wounded Healer*, back cover.

61. Freire, *Pedagogy of the Oppressed*, 53.

62. Alan G. Headbloom to Rogers, 1983, folder "Grateful Parents," box EUFan5, Fred Rogers Archive.

63. Johannesen, "Emerging Concept of Communication," 377.

64. On this program, Rogers and Hamilton sit down in Rogers's home to discuss his questions on Hamilton's role as the Wicked Witch. He prompts discussions on Halloween and costume play, in which Hamilton talks about how she liked to dress up as a witch for the holiday when she was a young girl.

65. Thomlison, *Toward Interpersonal Dialogue*, 86.

66. Thomlison, *Toward Interpersonal Dialogue*, 87.

67. Thomlison, *Toward Interpersonal Dialogue*, 87.

68. Thomlison, *Toward Interpersonal Dialogue*, 23.

69. Thomlison, *Toward Interpersonal Dialogue*, 38.

70. Thomlison, *Toward Interpersonal Dialogue*, 38.

71. Kathy Glaser to Fred Rogers, December 18, 1981, EU Fan5, Fred Rogers Archive.

72. Stewart and D'Angelo, *Together*, 6.

73. Kaufmann, "Karl Jaspers and a Philosophy of Communication," 230–31.

74. Thomlison, *Toward Interpersonal Dialogue*, 48.

75. Thomlison, *Toward Interpersonal Dialogue*, 48.

76. Gary P. Gormin to Fred Rogers, December 1, 1981, folder 14, box EUFan4, Fred Rogers Archive.

77. Anne P. Copeland to Fred Rogers. November 1981, folder 14, box EUFan4, Fred Rogers Archive.

78. Mary Beth Hagaman to Fred Rogers, undated, folder 2, box EUFan4, Fred Rogers Archive.

79. Wilma Caldwell to Fred Rogers, November 24, 1981, folder 14, box EUFan4, Fred Rogers Archive.

80. Dottie Jeffries to Fred Rogers, February 27, 1975, folder 2, box EUFan4, Fred Rogers Archive.

81. Linda Levgnino to Fred Rogers, June 23, 1975, folder 4, box EUFan4, Fred Rogers Archive.

82. Sharapan to Levgnino, July 24, 1975, folder 4, box EUFan4, Fred Rogers Archive.

83. Arnett, Fritz, and Bell, *Communication Ethics Literacy*, 9.

84. Rogers, "Opportunity for Creative Work Needed in Our Educational System," Cong. Rec. July 29, 1969: E6404–E6405.

85. Rogers, "Opportunity for Creative Work."

86. Rogers, "Opportunity for Creative Work."

87. Arnett, "Toward a Phenomenological Dialogue," 203.

88. Arnett, "Toward a Phenomenological Dialogue," 203.

89. Arnett, "Toward a Phenomenological Dialogue," 204.

90. Arnett, "Toward a Phenomenological Dialogue," 206–7.

91. Arnett, "Dialogic Ethic 'Between' Buber and Levinas," 81.

92. See Lasch, *Culture of Narcissism*.

93. See Morgenlander, "Adult-Child Co-viewing of Educational Television."

CONCLUSION

1. See Coan's "Creating Connections" website, http://www.creatingconnec-tions.nl/social-baseline-theory-and-the-social-regulation-of-emotion1.html.

2. See Arnett, Bell, and Fritz, "Dialogic Learning as First Principle," 111–26.

3. See "Stephen Porges, Clinical Applications of the Polyvogal Theory: The Transformative Power of Feeling Safe, June 14–18, 2014," *Cape Cod Institute*, http://www.cape.org/2014/stephen_porges.html.

4. Rogers, "Encouraging Creativity," p. 2, box EU3, Fred Rogers Archive.

5. Buber, *I and Thou*, 11. Todorov, *Mikhail Bakhtin*, 97.

6. See Flecker, "When Fred Met Margaret," 26.

7. Hollingsworth, *Simple Faith of Mister Rogers*, 38.

8. Rogers, "Senate Statement on PBS Funding," May 1, 1969, http://www.americanrhetoric.com/speeches/fredrogerssenatetestimonypbs.htm.

Bibliography

Abram, Jan. *The Language of Winnicott: A Dictionary of Winnicott's Use of Words.* London: Karnac Books, 1996.

Adelman, Mara B., Malcolm R. Parks, and Terrance L. Albrecht. "The Nature of Friendship and Its Development." In *Bridges Not Walls: A Book about Interpersonal Communication*, edited by John Stewart, 303–11. New York: McGraw-Hill, 1995.

Alasuutari, Pertti. "Three Phases of Reception Studies." Introduction to *Rethinking the Media Audience: The New Agenda*, edited by Pertti Alasuutari, 7–28. London: Sage, 1999.

Althusser, Louis. "Ideology and Ideological State Apparatuses." In *Cultural Theory and Popular Culture: A Reader*, edited by John Storey, 302–12. Edinburgh: Pearson, 2009.

Anderson, Rob, Leslie A. Baxter, and Kenneth A. Cissna. "Texts and Contexts of Dialogue." In *Dialogue: Theorizing Difference in Communication Studies*, edited by Anderson, Baxter, and Cissna, 1–18. Thousand Oaks, CA: Sage, 2004.

Aquinas, Thomas. *Summa Theologiae: A Concise Translation.* Translated by Timothy McDermott. Allen, TX: Christian Classics, 1989.

Ariès, Philippe. *Centuries of Childhood: A Social History of Family Life.* Translated by Robert Baldick. New York: Vintage, 1962.

Arnett, Ronald C. *Dialogic Education: Conversation about Ideas and between Persons.* Carbondale: Southern Illinois University Press, 1993.

Arnett, Ronald C. "A Dialogic Ethic 'Between' Buber and Levinas." In *Dialogue: Theorizing Difference in Communication Studies,* edited by Rob Anderson, Leslie A. Baxter, and Kenneth N. Cissna, 75–90. Thousand Oaks, CA: Sage, 2004.

Arnett, Ronald C. "Toward a Phenomenological Dialogue." *Western Journal of Speech Communication* 45, no. 3 (1981): 201–12.

Arnett, Ronald C., Leeanne Bell, and Janie M. Harden Fritz. "Dialogic Learning as First Principle in Communication Ethics." *Atlantic Journal of Communication* 18, no. 3 (2010): 111–26.

Arnett, Ronald C., Janie M. Harden Fritz, and Leeanne M. Bell. *Communication Ethics Literacy: Dialogue and Difference.* Thousand Oaks, CA: Sage, 2009.

Aubry, Timothy, and Trysh Travis. *Rethinking Therapeutic Culture.* Chicago: University of Chicago Press, 1975.

Auter, Philip J., and Donald M. Davis. "When Characters Speak Directly to Viewers: Breaking the Fourth Wall in Television." *Journalism and Mass Communication Quarterly* 68, no. 1–2 (1991): 165–71.

Bailey, Liberty Hyde. *The Outlook to Nature.* Rev. ed. New York: Macmillan, 1911.

Bailyn, Bernard. *Education in the Forming of American Society.* New York: Vintage Books, 1960.

Bakhtin, Mikhail M. *The Dialogic Imagination.* Edited by Michael Holquist. Translated by Caryl Emerson and Holquist. Austin: University of Texas Press, 1981.

Bakhtin, Mikhail M. "Discourse in the Novel." Translated by Caryl Emerson and Michael Holquist. In *Critical Theory Since 1965,* edited by Hazard Adams and Leroy Searle, 668–70. Gainesville: University Presses of Florida, 1986.

Barnouw, Erik. *The Image Empire: A History of Broadcasting in the United States from 1953.* Oxford: Oxford University Press, 1970.

Barnouw, Erik. *Tube of Plenty: The Evolution of American Television.* New York: Oxford University Press, 1975.

Barton, David, and Nigel Hall, eds. *Letter Writing as a Social Practice.* Philadelphia: John Benjamins, 2000.

Baudrillard, Jean. *The System of Objects.* Translated by James Benedict. New York: Verso, 1996.

Belcher-Hamilton, Lisa. "The Gospel According to Fred: A Visit with Mr. Rogers." *Christian Century* 111, no. 12 (1994): 382–84.

Bell, Daniel. *The Cultural Contradictions of Capitalism.* New York: Basic Books, 1976.

Bellah, Robert, Richard Madsen, William M. Sullivan, Ann Swidler, and Steven M. Tipton. *Habits of the Heart: Individualism and Commitment in American Life*. Berkeley: University of California Press, 1985.

Bender, Thomas. *Community and Social Change in America*. Baltimore: Johns Hopkins University Press, 1978.

Berger, Peter. *The Sacred Canopy: Elements of a Sociological Theory of Religion*. New York: Anchor, 1967.

Bergman, Samuel Hugo. *Dialogical Philosophy from Kierkegaard to Buber*. Albany: State University of New York Press, 1991.

Berry, Wendell. "Health is Membership." In *The Art of the Commonplace: The Agrarian Essays of Wendell Berry*. Edited by Norman Wirzba. Washington, DC: Counterpoint, 2002.

Bianculli, David. "The Myth, the Man, the Legend." In *Mister Rogers' Neighborhood: Children, Television, and Fred Rogers*, edited by Mark Collins and Margaret Mary Kimmel, 37–50. Pittsburgh: University of Pittsburgh Press, 1996.

Billig, Michael. "Commodity Fetishism and Repression: Reflections on Marx, Freud and the Psychology of Consumer Capitalism." *Theory and Psychology* 9, no. 3 (1999): 313–29.

Bloom, Paul. "Why Do We Like What We Like?" Part 2 of episode "Brand over Brain." *TED Radio Hour*, May 9, 2014. NPR. https://www.npr.org/2014/05/09/308755710/why-do-we-like-what-we-like.

Bloom, Paul. "Why We Like What We Like." *Observer*, October 2010. http://www.psychologicalscience.org/index.php/publications/observer/2010/october-10/why-we-like-what-we-like.html.

Blum, Lawrence A. *Friendship, Altruism, and Morality*. New York: Routledge, 1980.

Boden, Margaret A. *Jean Piaget*. Kingsport, TN: Kingsport Press, 1975.

Borchert, Donald M., ed. *Encyclopedia of Philosophy*. 2nd ed. Detroit: Macmillan Reference USA, 2006.

Borsodi, Ralph. *This Ugly Civilization*. New York: Simon and Schuster, 1929.

Bourne, Randolph S. "Trans-national America." *Atlantic Monthly*, July 1916. http://www.theatlantic.com/past/issues/16jul/bourne.htm.

Bowlby, John. *Attachment and Loss*. Vol. 2, *Separation*. New York: Basic Books, 1973.

Boyer, Paul. *Purity in Print: The Vice-Society Movement and Book Censorship in America*. New York: Scribner, 1968.

Braithwaite, Dawn O., Kathleen M. Galvin, Benjamin Chiles, and Esther Liu. "Family Communication." In *Oxford Bibliographies in Communication*. Edited by Patricia Moy. Oxford: Oxford University Press, 2013. Last modified February 27, 2013. https://doi.org/10.1093/obo/9780199756841-0104.

Buber, Martin. _I and Thou_. Translated by Ronald Gregor Smith. Edinburgh: T. & T. Clark, 1950.

Burggraeve, Roger. "A Holistic Values Education: Emotionality, Rationality and Meaning." EFTRE European Conference, Järvenpää, 2004.

Burston, Daniel. _Erik Erikson and the American Psyche: Ego, Ethics, and Evolution_. Lanham, MD: Jason Aronson, 2006.

Butsch, Richard. _The Making of American Audiences: From Stage to Television, 1750–1990_. New York: Cambridge University Press, 2000.

Caffin, Caroline. _Dancing and Dancers of Today_. New York: Dodd, Mead, 1912.

Caldwell, Lesley, and Angela Joyce. Editors' introduction to "Playing: A Theoretical Statement," by Donald Winnicott. In _Reading Winnicott_, edited by Caldwell and Joyce, 231–34. New York: Routledge, 2011.

The Cambridge Dictionary of Philosophy. 2nd ed. Cambridge: Cambridge University Press, 1999.

Carey, James W. _Communication as Culture: Essays on Media and Culture_. New York: Routledge, 1989.

Casto, Marilyn. "The Concept of Hand Production in Colonial Revival Interiors." In _Re-creating the American Past: Essays on the Colonial Revival_, edited by Richard Guy Wilson, Shaun Eyring, and Kenny Marotta, 321–35. Charlottesville: University of Virginia Press, 2006.

Caulfield, Rick. "'Trust Yourself': Revisiting Benjamin Spock." _Early Childhood Education Journal_ 26, no. 4 (1999): 263–65.

Cohen, Jonathan. "Defining Identification: A Theoretical Look at the Identification of Audiences with Media Characters." _Mass Communication and Society_ 4, no. 3 (2001): 245–64.

Cohen, Lizabeth. _A Consumers' Republic: The Politics of Mass Consumption in America_. New York: Knopf, 2003.

Coles, Romand. _Rethinking Generosity: Critical Theory and the Politics of Caritas_. Ithaca, NY: Cornell University Press, 1997.

Collins, Claudia. "Viewer Letters as Audience Research: The Case of Murphy Brown." _Journal of Broadcasting & Electronic Media_ 41, no. 1 (1997): 109–31.

Condit, Celeste Michelle. "The Rhetorical Limits of Polysemy." _Critical Studies in Mass Communication_ 6, no. 2 (1989): 103–22.

Conkin, Paul Keith. _Tomorrow a New World: The New Deal Community Program_. Ithaca, NY: American Historical Association, 1995.

Connell, R. W. _Gender and Power: Society, the Person, and Sexual Politics_. Stanford, CA: Stanford University Press, 1987.

Cooper, Mick, Amy Chak, Flora Cornish, and Alex Gillespie. "Dialogue: Bridging Personal, Community, and Social Transformation." _Journal of Humanistic Psychology_ 53, no. 1 (2012): 72–78.

Costello, Denis. "Selflessness as a Virtue in Social Work Practice." *Social Work and Christianity* 40, no. 3 (2013): 271–86.

Cott, Nancy F. *The Grounding of Modern Feminism.* New Haven, CT: Yale University Press, 1987.

Cowan, Ruth Schwartz. *More Work for Mother: The Ironies of Household Technology from the Open Hearth to the Microwave.* New York: Basic Books, 1983.

Cremin, Lawrence A. *The Transformation of the School: Progressivism in American Education, 1876–1957.* New York: Knopf, 1961.

Crusalis, Bonnie Smith. "Wounded Healer." In *Encyclopedia of Psychology and Religion,* edited by David Adams Leeming. New York: Springer, 2014.

Csikszentmihalyi, Mihaly. *Flow: The Psychology of Optimal Experience.* New York: Harper Perennial, 1990.

Csikszentmihalyi, Mihaly, and Eugene Rochberg-Halton. *The Meaning of Things: Domestic Symbols and the Self.* Cambridge: Cambridge University Press, 1981.

Cuddy, Amy. *Presence: Bringing Your Boldest Self to Your Biggest Challenges.* Boston: Little, Brown, 2015.

Cuddy, Amy. "Your Body Language May Shape Who You Are." TED Talk, June 2012. https://www.ted.com/talks/amy_cuddy_your_body_language_shapes_who_you_are?language=en.

Danbom, David B. "Romantic Agrarianism in Twentieth-Century America." *Agricultural History* 65, no. 4 (1991): 1–12.

Davies, Douglas. *Child Development: A Practitioner's Guide.* 2nd ed. New York: Guilford, 2004.

Day, James. *The Vanishing Vision: The Inside Story of Public Television.* Berkeley: University of California Press, 1996.

Decker, William Merrill. *Epistolary Practices: Letter Writing in America before Telecommunications.* Chapel Hill: University of North Carolina Press, 1998.

DeNora, Tia. *Making Sense of Reality: Culture and Perception in Everyday Life.* London: Sage, 2014.

Dhoest, Alexander. "'If You Asked Me . . . ': Exploring Autoethnography as Means to Critically Assess and Advance Audience Research." In *Revitalising Audience Research: Innovations in European Audience Research,* edited by Frauke Zeller, Cristina Ponte, and Brian O'Neill, 29–43. New York: Routledge, 2005.

Dooe, Mary. "How Mister Rogers Shaped What It Means to Grow Up—and Live in Pittsburgh," *Public Radio International.* September 25, 2015. http://www.pri.org/stories/2015-09-25/how-mr-rogers-shaped-what-it-means-grow-and-live-pittsburgh.

Douglas, Ann. *The Feminization of American Culture.* New York: Knopf, 1977.

Douglas, Mary, and Baron Isherwood. *The World of Goods: Towards an Anthropology of Consumption.* New York: Routledge, 1999.

Douglas, Susan J. *Listening In: Radio and the American Imagination*. Minneapolis: University of Minnesota Press, 2004.

Draper, Ellen. "'Controversy Has Probably Destroyed Forever the Context': *The Miracle* and Movie Censorship in America in the 1950s." In *Controlling Hollywood: Censorship and Regulation in the Studio Era*. Edited by Matthew Bernstein. New Brunswick, NJ: Rutgers University Press, 1999.

Durkheim, Emile. *The Elementary Forms of Religious Life*. Translated by Karen E. Fields. New York: Simon & Schuster, 1995.

Ehrenrich, Barbara, and Deirdre English. *For Her Own Good: 150 Years of The Experts' Advice to Women*. New York: Anchor Books, 1978.

Eichsteller, Gabriel, and Sylvia Holthoff. "Social Pedagogy as an Ethical Orientation towards Working with People–Historical Perspectives." *Children Australia* 36, no. 4 (2011): 176–86.

Engelman, Ralph. *Public Radio and Television in America: A Political History*. Thousand Oaks, CA: Sage, 1996.

Erikson, Erik. *Childhood and Society*. New York: Norton, 1963.

Fiske, John. "Commodities and Culture: Formations of the People." In *Popular Culture*, 23–47. New York: Routledge, 1989.

Fitzgerald, Maureen. "National Congress of Mothers." In *The Reader's Companion to U.S. Women's History*, edited by Wilma Mankiller, Gwendolyn Mink, Marysa Navarro, Barbara Smith, and Gloria Steinem, 394. New York: Houghton Mifflin, 1998.

Flecker, Sally Ann. "When Fred Met Margaret." *Pitt Med*, Winter 2014. http://www.pittmed.health.pitt.edu/story/when-fred-met-margaret.

Foss, Sonja, and Cindy L. Griffin. "Beyond Persuasion: A Proposal for an Invitational Rhetoric." *Communication Monographs* 62, no. 1 (1995): 2–18.

Foucault, Michel. *Technologies of the Self: A Seminar with Michel Foucault*. Edited by Luther H. Martin, Huck Gutman, and Patrick H. Hutton. Amherst: University of Massachusetts Press, 1988.

Foucault, Michel. "What is an Author?" Translated by Donald F. Bouchard and Sherry Simon. In *Language, Counter-memory, Practice: Selected Essays and Interviews*, by Foucault, edited by Bouchard, 124–27. Ithaca, NY: Cornell University Press, 1977.

Fred Rogers Archives. Fred Rogers Center. Latrobe, PA.

Freire, Paulo. *Pedagogy of the Oppressed*. Translated by Myra Bergman Ramos. New York: Continuum, 1970.

Gans, Herbert J. *Popular Culture and High Culture: An Analysis and Evaluation of Taste*. New York: Basic Books, 1999.

Gareis, Jack, and Ellen Cohn. *Communication as Culture: An Introduction to the Communication Process*. Dubuque City, IA: Kendall/Hunt, 2008.

Geertz, Clifford. *The Interpretation of Cultures: Selected Essays.* New York: Basic Books, 1973.

Gelber, Stephen M. *Hobbies: Leisure and the Culture of Work in America.* New York: Columbia University Press, 2013.

Geraghty, Lincoln. "Help When Times Are Hard: Bereavement and *Star Trek* Fan Letters." In *The* Star Trek *Universe: Franchising the Final Frontier,* edited by Douglas Brode and Shea T. Brode, 175–84. Lanham, MD: Rowman & Littlefield, 2015.

Gilbert, Douglas. *American Vaudeville: Its Life and Times.* New York: Dover, 1968.

Gilbert, James. *A Cycle of Outrage: America's Reaction to the Juvenile Delinquent in the 1950s.* New York: Oxford, 1986.

Giroux, Henry A. "Paulo Freire and the Politics of Postcolonialism." http://www .henryagiroux.com/online_articles/Paulo_friere.htm.

Giroux, Henry A. "Theories of Reproduction and Resistance in the New Sociology of Education: Toward a Critical Theory of Schooling and Pedagogy for the Opposition." In *The Giroux Reader,* 3–46. Boulder, CO: Paradigm, 2006.

Giroux, Henry A., and Grace Pollock. *The Mouse that Roared: Disney and the End of Innocence.* New York: Rowman & Littlefield, 2010.

Gitlin, Todd. *The Sixties: Years of Hope, Days of Rage.* New York: Bantam Books, 1993.

Gould, Jack. "Elvis Presley: Lack of Responsibility Is Shown by TV in Exploiting Teenagers, September 16, 1956." In *Watching Television Come of Age:* The New York Times *Reviews by Jack Gould,* edited by Lewis L. Gould, 131–32. Austin: University of Texas Press, 2002.

Gray, Jonathan, and Amanda D. Lotz. *Television Studies.* Malden, MA: Polity Press, 2012.

Green, Lucy. *Music, Informal Learning and the School: A New Classroom Pedagogy.* Farnham, England: Ashgate, 2012.

Greenfield, Patricia M. "Technology and Informal Education: What Is Taught, What Is Learned." *Science* 323, no. 5910 (2009): 69–71.

Grossman, Gary H. *Saturday Morning TV.* New York: Popular Science Publishing Co., 1981.

Gundry-Volf, Judith. "'To such as these belongs the Reign of God': Jesus and Children." *Theology Today* 56, no. 4 (2000): 469–80.

Guy, William. "The Theology of *Mister Rogers' Neighborhood.*" In *Mister Rogers' Neighborhood: Children, Television, and Fred Rogers,* edited by Mark Collins and Margaret Mary Kimmel, 101–21. Pittsburgh: University of Pittsburgh Press, 1996.

Hall, Bolton. *Three Acres and Liberty.* New York: Grosset & Dunlap, 1907.

Hall, Edward T. *The Hidden Dimension.* Garden City, NY: Doubleday, 1966.

Hall, Stuart. "Encoding/Decoding." In *Culture, Media, Language,* edited by Stuart

Hall, Dorothy Hobson, Andrew Lowe, and Paul Willis, 128–38. London: Routledge, 1991.

Hanson, Ralph E. *Mass Communication: Living in a Media World*. 5th ed. Thousand Oaks, CA: Sage, 2016.

Hareven, Tamara K. *Family Time and Industrial Time: The Relationship between the Family and Work in a New England Industrial Community*. Cambridge: Cambridge University Press, 1983.

Hartmann, Tilo, and Charlotte Goldhorn. "Horton and Wohl Revisited: Exploring Viewers' Experience of Parasocial Interaction." *Journal of Communication* 61, no. 6 (2011): 1104–21.

Hollingsworth, Amy. *The Simple Faith of Mister Rogers: Spiritual Insights from the World's Most Beloved Neighbor*. Nashville: Thomas Nelson, 2005.

Holquist, Michael. *Dialogism: Bakhtin and His World*. New York: Routledge, 1990.

Holt, L. Emmett. *The Care and Feeding of Children: A Catechism for the Use of Mothers and Children's Nurses*. New York: D. Appleton, 1894.

Horton, Donald, and Richard Wohl. "Mass Communication and Para-social Interaction: Observations on Intimacy at a Distance." *Psychiatry* 19, no. 3 (1956): 215–29.

Huizinga, Johan. *Homo Ludens: A Study of the Play-Element in Culture*. New York: Roy, 1950.

Hutchison, William R., ed. *Between the Times: The Travail of the Protestant Establishment in America, 1900–1960*. Cambridge: Cambridge University Press, 1989.

Isler, Bill, Hedda Sharapan, David Newell, Joanne Rogers, and Carl Kurlander. "The Making of *Mister Rogers' Neighborhood*." Panel, University of Pittsburgh, September 16, 2011.

Ivaniushina, V. A., and D. A. Aleksandrov. "Socialization through Informal Education: The Extracurricular Activities of Russian Schoolchildren." *Russian Education and Society* 57, no. 4 (2015): 189–213.

Jacobson, Lisa. *Raising Consumers: Children and the American Mass Market in the Early Twentieth Century*. New York: Columbia University Press, 2004.

Jaspers, Karl. *Existentialism and Humanism: Three Essays*. Edited by Hanns E. Fischer. New York: Russell R. Moore, 1952.

Johannesen, Richard. "The Emerging Concept of Communication as Dialogue." *Quarterly Journal of Speech* 57, no. 4 (1971): 373–82.

Jowett, Garth S., Ian C. Jarvie, and Kathryn H. Fuller. *Children and the Movies: Media Influence and the Payne Fund Controversy*. New York: Cambridge University Press, 1996.

Kammen, Michael. *Mystic Chords of Memory: The Transformation of Tradition in American History*. New York: Vintage Books, 1993.

Kates, James. "Liberty Hyde Bailey, Agricultural Journalism, and the Making of the Moral Landscape." *Journalism History* 36, no. 4 (2011): 207–17.

Kaufmann, Fritz. "Karl Jaspers and a Philosophy of Communication." In *The Philosophy of Karl Jaspers*, edited by Paul Arthur Schilpp, 211–95. New York: Tudor, 1957.

Kimmel, Margaret Mary, and Mark Collins. *The Wonder of It All: Fred Rogers and the Story of an Icon*. Latrobe, PA: Fred Rogers Center, 2008.

Kimpton, Lawrence A. "Dewey and Progressive Education." *School Review* 67, no. 2 (1959): 125–27.

Kirkus Reviews. Unsigned review of *The Insolent Chariots*, by John Keats, September 17, 1958. https://www.kirkusreviews.com/book-reviews/john-keats-2/the-insolent-chariots/.

Kline, Stephen. "The Making of Children's Culture." In *The Children's Culture Reader*, edited by Henry Jenkins, 95–109. New York: New York University Press, 1998.

Knaak, Stephanie. "Benjamin Spock." In *Oxford Bibliographies Online: Childhood Studies*. Edited by Heather Montgomery. Oxford: Oxford University Press, 2013. https://doi.org/ 10.1093/obo/9780199791231-0096.

Lasch, Christopher. *The Culture of Narcissism: American Life in an Age of Diminishing Expectations*. New York: W. W. Norton, 1991.

Lasch, Christopher. *Haven in a Heartless World: The Family Besieged*. New York: Basic Books, 1977.

Lears, T. J. Jackson. *No Place of Grace: Antimodernism and the Transformation of American Culture, 1880–1920*. Chicago: University of Chicago Press, 1981.

Lehman, Christopher P. *American Animated Cartoons of the Vietnam Era: A Study of Social Commentary in Films and Television Programs, 1961–1973*. Jefferson, NC: McFarland, 2006.

Levine, Lawrence W. *Highbrow/Lowbrow: The Emergence of Cultural Hierarchy in America*. Cambridge, MA: Harvard University Press, 1988.

Lewis, Robert M., ed. *From Traveling Show to Vaudeville: Theatrical Spectacle in America, 1830–1910*. Baltimore: Johns Hopkins University Press, 2003.

Lewis-Kraus, Gideon. "Yelp and the Wisdom of 'The Lonely Crowd.'" *New Yorker*, May 7, 2013. http://www.newyorker.com/tech/elements/yelp-and-the-wisdom-of-the-lonely-crowd.

Linn, Susan. *Consuming Kids: The Hostile Takeover of Childhood*. New York: New Press, 2004.

Lippmann, Walter. *Public Opinion*. New Brunswick, NJ: Transaction, 1998.

Long, Michael. *Peaceful Neighbor: Discovering the Countercultural Mister Rogers*. Louisville, KY: Westminster John Knox, 2015.

Lull, James. "Family Communication Patterns and the Social Uses of Television." *Communication Research* 7, no. 3 (1980): 319–33.

Lust, Annette. *From the Greek Mimes to Marcel Marceau and Beyond: Mimes, Actors, Pierrots, and Clowns: A Chronicle of the Many Visages of Mime in the Theatre.* Lanham, MD: Scarecrow, 2003.

Maier, Thomas. *Dr. Spock: An American Life.* New York: Harcourt Brace, 1998.

Malin, Brenton J. *Feeling Mediated: A History of Media Technology and Emotion in America.* New York: New York University Press, 2014.

Marchand, Roland. *Advertising the American Dream: Making Way for Modernity, 1920–1940.* Berkeley: University of California Press, 1986.

Martinson, Tom. *American Dreamscape: The Pursuit of Happiness in Postwar Suburbia.* New York: Carroll & Graf, 2000.

Martocci, Laura. *Bullying: The Social Destruction of the Self.* Philadelphia: Temple University Press, 2015.

Marx, Karl, and Friedrich Engels. "Manifesto of the Communist Party." In *The Marx-Engels Reader,* edited by Robert C. Tucker, 469–500. New York: Norton, 1978.

Marx, Leo. *The Machine in the Garden: Technology and the Pastoral Ideal in America.* New York: Oxford University Press, 1964.

McCarthy, Anna. *The Citizen Machine: Governing by Television in 1950s America.* New York: New Press, 2010.

McChesney, Robert W. "Conflict, Not Consensus: The Debate over Broadcast Communication Policy, 1930–1935." In *Ruthless Criticism: New Perspectives in U.S. Communication History,* edited by William S. Solomon and McChesney, 222–58. Minneapolis: University of Minnesota Press, 1993.

McChesney, Robert W. *The Political Economy of Media: Enduring Issues, Emerging Dilemmas.* New York: Monthly Review, 2008.

McChesney, Robert W. *Rich Media, Poor Democracy: Communication Politics in Dubious Times.* Urbana: University of Illinois Press, 1999.

McElvaine, Robert S., ed. *Down and Out in the Great Depression: Letters from the Forgotten Man.* Chapel Hill: University of North Carolina Press, 2008.

McGerr, Michael. *A Fierce Discontent: The Rise and Fall of the Progressive Movement in America, 1870–1920.* New York: Oxford University Press, 2005.

McKim, Donald K. *Ever a Vision: A Brief History of Pittsburgh Theological Seminary, 1959–2009.* Grand Rapids, MI: William B. Eerdmans, 2009.

Meyrowitz, Joshua. *No Sense of Place: The Impact of Electronic Media on Social Behavior.* New York: Oxford University Press, 1995.

Miell, Dorothy, Raymond MacDonald, and David J. Hargreaves. *Music Communication.* Oxford: Oxford University Press, 2005.

Milne, Esther. *Letters, Postcards, Email: Technologies of Presence.* New York: Routledge, 2010.

Mister Rogers and Me. Directed by Benjamin Wagner and Christofer Wagner. Arlington, VA: PBS, 2010.

Morgenlander, Melissa. "Adult-Child Co-viewing of Educational Television: Enhancing Preschoolers' Understanding of Mathematics Shown on *Sesame Street*." PhD diss., Columbia University, 2010.

Morrow, Robert W. *Sesame Street and the Reform of Children's Television*. Baltimore: Johns Hopkins University Press, 2006.

Murray, Jeffrey. "Bakhtinian Answerability and Levinasian Responsibility: Forging a Fuller Dialogical Communicative Ethics." *Southern Communication Journal* 65, no. 2 (2009): 133–50.

Myers, E. Kay. "Remembering Fred Rogers." *Loyalhanna Review*, 2009, 1–2. https://docs.wixstatic.com/ugd/2f9987_fc5d944b4756400b938f490d-b152ced8.pdf.

Nasaw, David. *Children of the City: At Work and at Play*. New York: Anchor, 1985.

Neill, A. S. *Summerhill: A Radical Approach to Child Rearing*. New York: Hart, 1961.

Newcomb, Horace N. "On the Dialogic Aspects of Mass Communication." *Critical Studies in Mass Communication* 1, no. 1 (1984): 34–50.

Noble, Grant. *Children in Front of the Small Screen*. London: Constable, 1975.

Nord, David. *The Evangelical Origins of the Mass Media in America, 1815–1835*. Columbia, SC: Association for Education in Journalism, 1984.

Nord, David. *Faith in Reading*. New York: Oxford University Press, 2004.

Nouwen, Henri J. M. *The Wounded Healer: Ministry in Contemporary Society*. New York: Image, 1972.

Nunez, Gabriela. "Reading Jose Maria Arguedas' Letters: Building Communication Bridges in Mid-twentieth Century Peruvian Society." PhD diss., University of Pittsburgh, 2015.

Nye, David E. *American Technological Sublime*. Cambridge, MA: MIT Press, 1994.

Ong, Walter. *Orality and Literacy: The Technologizing of the Word*. New York: Methuen, 1983.

Pace, Patricia. Review of *Mister Rogers' Neighborhood: Children, Television and Fred Rogers*, edited by Mark Collins and Margaret Mary Kimmel. *Lion and the Unicorn* 22, no. 3 (1998): 383–87.

Packard, Vance. *The Hidden Persuaders*. New York: McKay, 1957.

Palmer, Patricia. *Lively Audience: A Study of Children around the TV Set*. Sydney: Allen and Unwin, 1986.

Pecora, Norma Odom. *The Business of Children's Entertainment*. New York: Guilford, 1998.

Perlmutter, David. *America Toons In: A History of Television Animation*. Jefferson, NC: McFarland, 2014.

Piaget, Jean. *Play, Dreams, and Imitation in Childhood*. New York: Norton, 1962.

Pollock, Linda A. *Parent-Child Relations from 1500 to 1900*. Cambridge: Cambridge University Press, 1984.

Ponterotto, Joseph. "Brief Note on the Origins, Evolution, and Meaning of the Qualitative Research Concept 'Thick Description.'" *Qualitative Report* 11, no. 3 (2006): 538–49.

Post, Stephen. "Disinterested Benevolence: An American Debate over the Nature of Christian Love." *Journal of Religious Ethics* 14, no. 2 (1986): 356–68.

Postman, Neil. *The Disappearance of Childhood.* New York: Vintage, 1994.

Putnam, Robert. *Bowling Alone: The Collapse and Revival of American Community.* New York: Simon and Schuster, 2000.

Rich, Adrienne. *Of Women Born: Motherhood as Experience and Institution.* New York: W. W. Norton, 1976.

Riesman, David. *The Lonely Crowd.* New Haven, CT: Yale University Press, 1962.

Rodgers, Daniel T. *Atlantic Crossings: Social Politics in a Progressive Age.* Cambridge, MA: Belknap Press of Harvard University Press, 1998.

Rogers, Fred, and Linda Philbrick. "Television and the Viewing Child." *Pittsburgh Area Preschool Association Publication,* October 1969, 1–23.

Rogers, Fred, and Linda Philbrick. "Opportunity for Creative Work Needed in Our Educational System," Cong. Rec. July 29, 1969: E6404–E6405.

Romanowski, William D. *Pop Culture Wars: Religion and the Role of Entertainment in American Life.* Downers Grove, IL: InterVarsity, 1996.

Romanowski, William D. *Reforming Hollywood: How American Protestants Fought for Freedom at the Movies.* New York: Oxford University Press, 2012.

Rosenthal, Michele. *American Protestants and TV in the 1950s: Responses to a New Medium.* New York: Palgrave, 2007.

Rosenzwieg, Roy. *Eight Hours for What We Will: Workers and Leisure in an Industrial City, 1870–1920.* Cambridge: Cambridge University Press, 1978.

Rubin, Joan Shelley. *The Making of Middlebrow Culture.* Chapel Hill, NC: University of North Carolina Press, 1992.

Rubin, Judith, dir. *Lessons from* Mister Rogers' Neighborhood. DVD. Pittsburgh: Expressive Media, 2015.

Ryan, Mary. *Cradle of the Middle Class: The Family in Oneida County, New York, 1790–1865.* Cambridge: Cambridge University Press, 1981.

Rytina, Steven. "Youthful Vision, Youthful Promise, Through Midlife Bifocals: C. Wright Mills' *White Collar* Turns 50." *Sociological Forum* 16, no. 3 (2001): 563–74.

Saint-Exupéry, Antoine de. *The Little Prince.* Translated by Richard Howard. New York: Harcourt, 2000.

Saint-Exupéry, Antoine de. *The Little Prince.* Translated by Katherine Woods. New York: Harcourt Brace, 1971.

Sanders, Scott Russell. *Writing from the Center.* Bloomington: Indiana University Press, 1997.

Scharfstein, Ben-Ami. *Ineffability: The Failure of Words in Philosophy and Religion*. Albany: State University of New York Press, 1993.

Schor, Juliet B. *Born to Buy: The Commercialized Child and the New Consumer Culture*. New York: Scribner, 2004.

Schrag, Calvin O. *Communicative Praxis and the Space of Subjectivity*. Bloomington: Indiana University Press, 1986.

Seiter, Ellen. "Children's Desires/Mothers' Dilemmas: The Social Contexts of Consumption." In *The Children's Culture Reader*, edited by Henry Jenkins, 297–317. New York: New York University Press, 1998.

Seiter, Ellen. *Sold Separately: Children and Parents in Consumer Culture*. New Brunswick, NJ: Rutgers University Press, 1993.

Sennett, Richard. *Families against the City: Middle Class Homes of Industrial Chicago, 1872–1890*. Cambridge, MA: Harvard University Press, 1979.

Shahar, Shulamith. *Childhood in the Middle Ages*. London: Routledge, 1992.

Sheridan, Kimberly, Kevin Clark, and Asia Williams. "Designing Games, Designing Roles: A Student of Youth Agency in an Urban Informal Education Program." *Urban Education Program* 48, no. 5 (2013): 734–58.

Silverstone, Roger. *Television and Everyday Life*. New York: Routledge, 1994.

Simon, Zoltán. *The Double-Edged Sword: The Technological Sublime in American Novels Between 1900 and 1940*. Budapest: Akadémiai Kiadó, 2003.

Singer, Dorothy G., and Jerome L. Singer, eds. *Handbook of Children and the Media*. Thousand Oaks, CA: Sage, 2001.

Singer, Mark I., Karen Slovak, Tracey Frierson, and Peter York. "Viewing Preferences, Symptoms of Psychological Trauma, and Violent Behaviors among Children Who Watch Television." *Journal of the American Academy of Child and Adolescent Psychiatry* 37, no. 10 (1998): 1041–48.

Skinner, James M. *The Cross and the Cinema: The Legion of Decency and the National Catholic Office for Motion Pictures, 1933–1970*. Westport, CT: Praeger, 1993.

Slater, Philip Elliot. *The Pursuit of Loneliness*. Boston: Beacon, 1970.

Slotten, Hugh Richard. *Radio's Hidden Voice: The Origins of Public Broadcasting in the United States*. Urbana: University of Illinois Press, 2009.

Snow White and the Seven Dwarfs. Directed by David Hand, William Cottrell, Wilfred Jackson, Larry Morey, Perce Pearce, and Ben Sharpsteen. Burbank, CA: Walt Disney Video, 2001.

Sood, Suruchi, and Everett M. Rogers. "Dimensions of Parasocial Interaction by Letter-Writers to a Popular Entertainment-Education Soap Opera in India." *Journal of Broadcasting & Electronic Media* 44, no. 3 (2000): 386–414.

Spigel, Lynn. *Make Room for TV: Television and the Family Ideal in Postwar America*. Chicago: University of Chicago, 1992.

Spigel, Lynn. "Seducing the Innocent: Childhood and Television in Postwar America." In *The Children's Culture Reader*, edited by Henry Jenkins, 110–35. New York: New York University Press, 1998.

Spock, Benjamin. *Dr. Spock's Baby and Child Care*. 9th ed. Updated and revised by Robert Needlman. Kindle Edition. Mary Morgan Trust, 2017.

Stanley, Liz. "The Epistolarium: On Theorizing Letters and Correspondences." *Auto/Biography* 12, no. 3 (2004): 216–35.

Steiner, Gary A. *The People Look at Television: A Study of Audience Attitudes*. New York: Knopf, 1963.

Stewart, John, and Gary D'Angelo. *Together: Communicating Interpersonally*. 2nd ed. Reading, MA: Addison-Wesley, 1980.

Stewart, John, and Milt Thomas. "Dialogic Listening: Sculpting Mutual Meanings." In *Bridges Not Walls: A Book about Interpersonal Communication*, edited by Stewart, 184–201. New York: McGraw-Hill, 1995.

Steyer, James. *The Other Parent: The Inside Story of Media's Effect on Our Children*. New York: Atria Books, 2002.

Stout, Lydia. "What Strangles American Teaching—The Certification Racket." *Atlantic Monthly*, April 1958, 59–63.

Strasser, Susan. *Never Done: A History of American Housework*. New York: Pantheon, 1982.

Stuckey, Heather L., and Jeremy Nobel. "The Connection between Art, Healing, and Public Health: A Review of Current Literature." *American Journal of Public Health* 100, no. 2 (2010): 254–63.

Telleen, Maurice. "The Mind-Set of Agrarianism . . . New and Old." In *The Essential Agrarian Reader: The Future of Culture, Community, and the Land*, edited by Norman Wirzba, 52–61. Lexington: University Press of Kentucky, 2003.

Thomlison, Terry Dean. *Toward Interpersonal Dialogue*. New York: Longman, 1982.

Tindall, George Brown, and David Emory Shi. *America: A Narrative History*. 8th ed. New York: W. W. Norton, 2010.

Tobin, Joseph Jay. *Good Guys Don't Wear Hats: Children's Talk about the Media*. New York: Teachers College Press, 2000.

Todorov, Tzvetan. *Mikhail Bakhtin: The Dialogical Principle*. Translated by Wlad Godzich. Minneapolis: University of Minnesota Press, 1984.

Tönnies, Ferdinand. *Community and Society*. Edited and translated by Charles P. Loomis. Mineola, NY: Dover, 2002.

Toqueville, Alexis de. *Democracy in America*. Translated by Gerald Bevan. 1835. New York: Penguin Classics, 2003.

Townley, Roderick. "Fred's Shoes: The Meaning of Transitions in *Mister Rogers'*

Neighborhood." In *Mister Rogers' Neighborhood: Children, Television, and Fred Rogers*, edited by Mark Collins and Margaret Mary Kimmel, 67–76. Pittsburgh: University of Pittsburgh Press,

Tuber, Steven. *Attachment, Play, and Authenticity: A Winnicott Primer.* Lanham, MD: Jason Aronson, 2008.

Tulloch, John. "The Implied Audience in Soap Opera Production: Everyday Rhetorical Strategies among Television Professionals." In *Rethinking the Media Audience: The New Agenda*, edited by Pertti Alasuutari, 151–78. London: Sage, 1999.

Vande Berg, Leah R., Lawrence A. Wenner, and Bruce E. Gronbeck, eds. *Critical Approaches to Television.* Boston: Allyn and Bacon, 2003.

Vande Berg, Leah R., Lawrence A. Wenner, and Bruce E. Gronbeck, eds. *Critical Approaches to Television*, 2nd ed. Boston: Houghton Mifflin, 2004.

Waller, Willard W. "Courtship as a Social Process." *On the Family, Education, and War: Selected Writings.* Edited by William J. Goode, Frank F. Furstenberg Jr., and Larry R. Mitchell, 193–199. Chicago: University of Chicago Press, 1970.

Watson, John B. "Against the Threat of Mother Love." In *The Children's Culture Reader*, edited by Henry Jenkins, 470–475. New York: New York University Press, 1998.

Watson, John B., and Rosalie Alberta Rayner Watson. *Psychological Care of Infant and Child.* New York: W. W. Norton, 1928.

Weiner, Lynn. "Maternalism as a Paradigm: Defining the Issues." *Journal of Women's History* 5, no. 2 (1993): 96–98.

Wiebe, Robert H. *The Search for Order, 1877–1920.* New York: Hill and Wang, 1967.

Wilson, Barbara J., Cynthia Hoffner, and Joanne Cantor. "Children's Perceptions of the Effectiveness of Techniques to Reduce Fear from Mass Media." *Journal of Applied Developmental Psychology* 8, no. 1 (1987): 32–52.

Wimsatt, William K. *The Verbal Icon: Studies in the Meaning of Poetry.* Lexington: University of Kentucky Press, 1954.

Winnicott, D. W. *Playing and Reality.* New York: Tavistock, 1971.

Wirzba, Norman. "Placing the Soul: An Agrarian Philosophical Principle." In *The Essential Agrarian Reader: The Future of Culture, Community, and the Land*, edited by Norman Wirzba, 80–97. Lexington: University Press of Kentucky, 2003.

Wivestad, Stein M. "The Educational Challenges of *Agape* and *Phronesis*." *Journal of Philosophy of Education* 42, no. 2 (2008): 307–24.

Woo, Elaine. "It's a Sad Day in This Neighborhood." *Los Angeles Times*, February 28, 2003, http://www.latimes.com/local/obituaries/la-me-fred-rogers-20030228-story.html.

Zboray, Ronald J. *A Fictive People: Antebellum Economic Development and the American Reading Public.* Cambridge: Oxford University Press, 1993.

Zboray, Ronald J., and Mary Saracino Zboray. "Books, Reading, and the World of Goods in Antebellum New England." *American Quarterly* 48, no. 4 (1996): 587–622.

Zboray, Ronald J., and Mary Saracino Zboray. *Everyday Ideas: Socioliterary Experience among Everyday New Englanders.* Knoxville: University of Tennessee Press, 2006.

Zelizer, Viviana. *Pricing the Priceless Child: The Changing Social Value of Children.* Princeton, NJ: Princeton University Press, 1985.

Index